DESERTS TO MOUNTAINTOPS

AN ANTHOLOGY

DESERTS TO MOUNTAINTOPS

OUR COLLECTIVE JOURNEY TO (re)CLAIMING OUR VOICE

BY JESSICA BUCHANAN

New York Times Bestselling Author of *Impossible Odds*
and Other Contributing Authors

Published and distributed by Soul Speak Press.
Photography by Shanen Bussey

Library of Congress Control Number: 2022918712
Deserts to Mountaintops: Our Collective Journey to (re)Claiming Our Voice

ISBN 978-1-958472-00-2

Dedicated to every woman who has been
silenced by self-doubt, fear, abuse and shame.

May you continue to journey
out of the desert toward your healing.

Keep going.

We'll meet you at the mountaintop.

CONTENTS

INTRODUCTION

To My Sister Traveler,

When I first set out on this journey, writing about the lessons I had learned in the aftermath of my kidnapping and rescue, I spent many hours in contemplation and reflection: what truths had I held on to, in order to move out of the metaphorical desert of self-abandonment, to the mountaintop of self-love? I spent time outlining chapters and researching facts to back up all the tools I was hoping to share with women on how to reclaim their voices. I was halfway through writing the first draft of the manuscript when a truth I couldn't ignore illuminated a different path than the one I had mapped out. The world didn't need another memoir from me, it needed me to use what I had learned over the last decade and help other women share their stories. While my circumstances are wildly specific, the actual events leading up to my kidnapping and subsequent ninety-three days as a hostage, sadly, are not. My departure from myself that day in October 2011 was an act of self-abandonment, something I, as a woman, had been conditioned to do by my culture since I drew my first breath.

In my years as a professional speaker, I have shared my story of *Impossible Odds* many times. Often, as I wrap up my talk and prepare to leave the venue, a line of women will form. Some are waiting to hug me, and many wrap their arms around me, shaking and sobbing as they relax into the safety of another woman who gets it. They too have ignored their intuition and made themselves small and silent. Many have paid a steep price for abandoning themselves: they have lost their voice.

It was after one such speaking event, a woman held on to me and as she pulled away, wiping away tears of embarrassment and shame, she shared her own story of survival, and that she was still looking for a way to overcome and find her voice. Back at home, as I sat at my computer, watching snow fall to the ground, I moved myself a little closer to the fire. The knowing was running through me, shooting from my head down to my toes, and I shivered with clarity:

Deserts to Mountaintops is not meant to be just my voice, but it is supposed to include many other women's voices and stories of journeying from self-abandonment to self-love. This was not to be a singular memoir, but an anthology. It would be a melody composed of many harmonies, a place where our stories of courage, tenacity, and fear could be told in community so that we could heal ourselves with our words, and each other with our stories.

As I sat there having the full-body experience of knowing what was next, I had no idea how I was going to do it but I knew it had to be done. I committed to simply following my heart, sending out a song from my soul, and sure enough, the women you will meet in these pages found me.

Deserts to Mountaintops is born of the deepest part of myself. It is the fruition of a commitment I made to myself and the universe when I was wasting away in a goat pen out in the middle of the desert, waiting for something to change. I promised my heart that if I lived through the experience, I would follow her. This anthology is the culmination of that promise. But more than that, it is a declaration of creativity and recovery, of joy and deep sorrow. Together, we honored our grief and then chose to learn from it—not only for ourselves but for you.

In the next twenty-two chapters, you will meet women from all walks of life: different ages, professional backgrounds, races, and experiences. While they are as different from each other as their stories, the thread that weaves them all together is their incredible ability to finally choose themselves, and in this act of bravery, they show us how to do the same. They are mothers, daughters, sisters, friends. Lovers, survivors, dreamers, divine. They are you.

Our hope, as you travel with each woman through the pages of this book, is that you will connect with at least one story, and find whatever you need to carry you along your way. If you have grown weary and doubtful that self-love is available for you, please know you are not alone. That we, too, have struggled to find our voice and ask for what we want: to be loved and accepted, heard and respected, and valued for just continuing to stick around. We have not given up, however hard it has been, and we have found strength and inspiration within each other. We have healed ourselves, at least part of the way, and we invite you to join us in the healing because life is not meant to be lived alone. There is always more room on the trail up to the mountaintop for whoever wants to come along.

Of all the things I know to be true, there are a few I come back to, every single day:

We were given our voices for a reason.

Our desires were placed in us so that they could be fulfilled.

Our truths are worthy of being expressed.

Our lives have sacred meaning, regardless of where we have been or where we are going.

Our voices matter. Full stop.

And more than anything, we are not alone.

You will see a variation of all these themes as you move from one story to the next, and we hope you accept our invitation to not only survive but continue to climb to the top of your own mountain. Take as long as you need to get there, we don't believe in time limits or expiration dates. We only believe in love. And when you get there, when you finally reach the top, we'll be there, waiting, arms open wide, ready to receive you. And together, we will use our voices to sing a song of survival, hope, and sacred love for one another, but mostly, for ourselves.

With light and gratitude,
Jess Buchanan

JESSICA BUCHANAN

In that moment, I know the whole world has gone still to make space for me to hear my internal voice; like a vacuum, empty, devoid of anything but the pounding of my life inside my own heart. But the warning, that quickening in my soul telling me something is absolutely not right here, is pushed into a bottomless sea of ambiguity because it is so familiar. It takes with it any of my bravery, stealing the air that could turn into words that might just save my life. The words of others, their silent threats and subsequent implications, are worth more to me, I think, than my own safety and security.

Their opinions outweigh the value of my own life. They know what's best for me because they said so. In a matter of a few seconds, I'm back in that church, or the classroom, or my parents' living room, dark shadows of authority standing over me, telling me what I should and shouldn't do. It is clear that I don't know how to question what others have declared as my truth, outside of my own beliefs about myself. No one ever taught me how.

THE GREAT
ABANDONMENT

GALKAYO, SOMALIA—GUEST HOUSE

Kicking off the dust from my sandals, I plunk my travel bag down onto the cracked tile floor of the guest house and survey my surroundings. My colleague, Poul, points in the direction of the second-floor veranda and warns me not to sit out there for too long. Random bullets have been whizzing by lately. I can see he is not pulling my leg when, on closer inspection of the space, I count seven bullet holes pocking the cement railing.

"Pirates," he whispers conspiratorially. It sounds so melodramatic. I mean, come on, it's 2011. I look around for the likes of Johnny Depp, gangplanks, and wooden legs. These "pirates" live in a house a stone's throw from the office where we will be conducting our trainings. The hair on the back of my neck stands up as sweat droplets bead on the fine blonde whiskers of my upper lip. "The bullets are celebratory," he assures me. When they get the cash, they shoot their guns. Pirates. Ransoms. Bullets. Life in the field—exotic in the most bizarre ways.

Dinner is delicious. We eat lobster from the coast, a costly luxury, as we are celebrating Poul's sixty trips around the blazing Somali sun. The thirty years between us do not diminish our shared love for music and aid work; it has never gotten in the way of our appreciation for one another. We are friends. And as we spend hours "in the field" strumming guitars, in harmony with the desert, the more boxed wine we drink, the better we sound.

Trailing in the wake of pirate stories, my mind swims from the cheap Pinot Grigio, and I figure it is my hard-earned buzz that ignites the paranoia in my head and sets the panic ablaze in my heart. As I lay down on cool sheets in that space between sober and asleep, I feel something familiar. I search my cobwebbed mind for a frame of reference…there it is: I am afraid. I had been very resistant to the idea of traveling here to this place, but I'd been given a task. Or was it an order? I couldn't figure out the difference between the two, as I lay under an open window, barred for my safekeeping. I had made it to the next level of my job aspirations, and after all, I was just a schoolteacher from Ohio. I grew up in the church. I prayed before bed and asked forgiveness for my sins every night. Nothing was going to happen to me. Bad things don't happen to girls like me.

Shush. Go to sleep now, I whispered to my racing heart.

OCTOBER 25, 2011—DAWN

The hours of darkness fade into the muted sounds of the 5:00 a.m. call to prayer. I wake, weary from nightmares about pirates scaling walls, banging down doors, bullets flying past my head. There is something about my hair—it is always being pulled in my dreams. *Must have something to do with my mom*, I mutter as I wipe sleep away from my eyes. Sweat-soaked, my nightgown clings to me. My aching body limps to the shower. I am exhausted and hungover. My mind has not taken a moment to rest.

Do you really want to do this?

This trip has been the source of much disgruntlement on my part. I have never had a good feeling about it and have canceled the trainings twice before. But here I am, searching for answers within the lines of my face in a small, cracked mirror in the middle of pirate-infested territory of Somalia. The perceived pressure to keep my job has gotten to me. It wasn't said outright, but rather implied: If you want to do this work, you get out there, despite the risks. And if there is a whiff of fear or lack of commitment, you can be replaced in a heartbeat. Plenty of other women, and certainly men, would kill for this job as they work their way up the humanitarian aid ladder. *Shut the hell up and get to work*, I say to myself with a certainty that does not resonate.

Why did I come here anyway?

I'm a young woman trying to make my way in a male-dominated work world. It's the same story many women could tell, just a more exotic locale. I'm constantly trying to prove myself, and I am done with never being taken seriously. The memory of a recent altercation with a supervisor, on a field mission in South Sudan, comes to me: *You can't blame someone for being stupid.* My supervisor said this to me, about me. The rage builds up as I hang onto the edge of the sink. *I am working in another country many women couldn't find on a map, let alone come to*, I tell myself.

I am taut as a rope being tied off at both ends, and a sense of dread begins to uncurl within my belly. The tightness spreads throughout my core, and like a choking fog, it spreads from the soles of my feet to the tips of my fingernails. Silenced by panic and self-doubt, and the fear that everyone else will think I'm stupid—that they already think that—I convince myself that I have no choice. This is the ancient understanding that has been beaten into me mentally, and sometimes physically, by everyone who has ever told me they know more so I should listen less. In this moment, I believe I have no voice. The only words I am hearing are the words I have heard a million times before, and as they bounce from one ear to the other, they snag on dignified reasons, as I continue to harden, deep inside.

You are already here, don't impose on anybody.

Everyone is expecting you.

Your staff is waiting on you to walk in solidarity with them.

You cannot quit.

Do the right thing.

I study my tired yet beautifully young face in the mirror. *Do you want to do this?* I ask my heart, one more time, giving her a last chance to believe in what she knows to be true. But instead of listening to her, I put on my sense of duty, along with a headscarf, and tell my intuition to fuck off. And then I go sit on the edge of my bed.

Nothing is going to happen.

You are just paranoid.

You are tired.

You are being unreasonable.

Just go and get it over with.

It will all be fine.

My ego versus my intuition. Logic versus *that feeling.* Their doubts about me, versus my own belief about myself. This battle—this war. I have been here so many times before. When I critically consider, I have been here for practically my entire life. If you don't learn your lesson the first or fifteenth time, you will keep repeating the same pattern; I know this now. And this pattern, the one of talking myself into something I don't want to do, something I know

I am not supposed to do, is quite clearly ready to be put to rest, gaping at me in exhaustion like the haggard mother who has been up all night with her sick child.

In that moment, I know the whole world has gone still to make space for me to hear my internal voice; like a vacuum, empty, devoid of anything but the pounding of my life inside my own heart. But the warning, that quickening in my soul telling me something is absolutely not right here, is pushed into a bottomless sea of ambiguity because it is so familiar. It takes with it any of my bravery, stealing the air that could turn into words that might just save my life. The words of others, their silent threats and subsequent implications, are worth more to me, I think, than my own safety and security. Their opinions outweigh the value of my own life. They know what's best for me because they said so. In a matter of a few seconds, I'm back in that church, or the classroom, or my parents' living room, dark shadows of authority standing over me, telling me what I should and shouldn't do. It is clear that I don't know how to question what others have declared as my truth, outside of my own beliefs about myself. No one ever taught me how.

I stand slowly and walk away from the battleground of my bed. I am resigned. I have lost the war within myself once again. The window that opened up for me to see that part of me only I can ever know, slams shut, shades dropped with a snap, curtains pulled tight so I can't see. There is no room for light and so I am in darkness. That smiling girl is no longer holding her head up high, proud of who she has become and the work she has come to do. She has been abandoned once again, and knowing she is defeated, she slowly limps away to lick her wounds and take the medicine of excuses, taping up the bruises caused by decades of shame, disappearing in the silence of her own voice.

As I take one last longing look at myself in the mirror, I repeat the words I have always leaned on to move to the next part of my life, even though nothing in me believes them: *What is the worst that can happen anyway?*

The Worst That Can Happen

Goat and rice again. I try to take little nibbles and spit out the food in my napkin when no one is looking. I am surrounded by Somali staff of all ages; there is a lot of shouting and hullabaloo going on around me. I am tired from my night of fitful sleep and now that the training is over and I have fulfilled my duties, I'm ready to get the hell out of here. We've been here all day and I just want to get back to the guest house, put on normal western clothes, and have a glass of wine to celebrate surviving this whole ordeal.

I ask for directions to the restroom. It's a little closet at the back of the compound and of course, the toilet is stopped up, filled with all sorts of filth, and I gag as I back out. I'll hold it. I hear the diesel engines of Land Cruisers roll into the compound and the slam of rusty metal as one of the guards uses his slight body weight to pull the compound gate shut. We are surrounded by walls that are ten feet tall and topped off with barbed wire. I hear a shift in conversation as the Northern Galkayo staff ready themselves to travel through town. We are all ready to go.

Abdi Rizaak, the Somali security advisor hired to keep ex-pats safe for this particular mission, is on the phone. He makes eye contact with me and flashes a big grin. He has a couple of silver teeth to compensate for the black rot that takes over so many Somali mouths as a result of chronic khat chewing and the sweet tea they drink to counteract the bitterness of the plant. He creeps me out. I look away. *God, get me out of here.*

He keeps getting on and off the phone, but I don't really think much about it. This isn't my base. Poul is in charge. He is flitting about, saying final goodbyes to his staff. I pull my phone out and start texting my husband, who is a few hours north in another part of the country doing his own thing. After a few false starts, Abdi Rizaak finally says it's time to move. Poul and I are directed to climb into the middle of three Land Cruisers in the convoy. Poul gets in the front passenger side, which here in Somalia, is on the left. I climb in behind him in the back. Abdi Rizaak takes his place next to me and fastens his seat belt, which in retrospect, I find somewhat odd and out of character. It's Somalia: cars are ancient, and laws are non-existent. No one cares if you wear a seatbelt here. But I follow suit and try to move as far away from him as possible.

The first car in the convoy pulls out slowly through the heavy metal wall that has been opened to allow us through. Then we follow, and the third vehicle, filled with our Northern staff, brings up the rear. We are an ex-pat sandwich surrounded by armed guards who have been hired to protect us as we move from one office to the other. I hear a gunshot but it's off in the distance, and I remember that the main gun market is just down from the compound. We start moving slowly, bumping through the city, people milling about. We drive for a few minutes when suddenly a car roars up on the right side of us and cuts us off abruptly. So jolting is our stop, that my head hits the window and I have to steady myself on the headrest of Poul's seat. Mud covers our windows and windshield. "What a jerk!" I say out loud to no one in particular. "Who drives like that?"

Suddenly, I hear the crack of the butt of an AK-47 on the car hood. I know it's an automatic because of the sound it makes on the metal. I hear shouting. Lots of angry men have surrounded the car, and they are coming closer. Before I can make sense of anything, Abdi Rizaak's door is pulled open, and a Somali man dressed in a police uniform hits him in the temple with his AK and drags him out of the car. I can't even blink before the pock-marked face is inches from mine, his gun even closer.

"Drive!" he screams at the driver in English. The young Somali guy who has been tasked with driving us takes off as if he was waiting for all this to happen. It's as if we have robbed a bank and it is time to make our getaway. At times we are up on two wheels, and as we slam down onto four, Poul begs him to slow down, trying to reason with him that unless he takes it easy, we are all going to die.

I have no idea who this man is. I have no idea what he wants or where he is taking me. And as I am tossed like a rag doll, completely out of control of my own body and breath, I can only think two very basic and fundamental thoughts. The first thought on repeat in my mind is that whatever this is, and I have no words for it, no way to describe it, no frame of reference to compare it to, whatever it is and however one would classify it, this is bad. I know this situation is so bad, I can't even wrap my brain around the depths of how bad it truly is. And as we slam back down onto four wheels, and the metal of the barrel of this man's AK grazes my temple, the second thought that comes to me and loops in my mind: *No matter how this thing pans out, my life has changed forever. From this point on, nothing in my life will ever be the same again.*

We drive for hours, stopping to change vehicles, stopping those vehicles to change personnel, and after some undetermined amount of time, we make our final stop, where we are ordered out of the car and commanded to walk. There is only darkness all around me. It feels like a deep black hole and smells like imminent death. My death. I can't move. I am frozen. A man, head wrapped in a turban, puts the barrel of his long machine gun to my chest and says one word in very clear English: "Walk."

I look down at the tip of metal resting in between my breasts. It's just black everywhere and for some reason, out of the depths of that dark, I find the courage to say simply, "No." Even in that moment, I'm surprisingly direct and resolute. I haven't made a conscious decision not to go down without a fight, but here I am deciding.

"Walk." He says it again. This time, I catch his finger stroking the trigger.

"No." *Go ahead you motherfucker*, I think. This replaces the other loops repeating through my mind. He lifts the barrel a little higher, the cold metal pushes against my throat.

"WALK!" Surprised agitation oozes from his green-stained teeth as he shoves me through the open door of the car. I keep my body pressed up against the side of it because it somehow makes me feel larger, but the reality is that I'm not invincible, and I can feel myself starting to shrink. Poul, who was standing a few feet away watching this all unfold, comes over with his own set of orders, in an awkward attempt to save me from myself. He gently takes my hand, which I notice off-handedly is shaking as much as his voice, and in seven words, he succinctly sums up the truth and gravity of our circumstances: "Jessica, you know we have to walk."

God dammit. He's right. I know we have to walk. I know we have to do what they say. I know that this is my only chance to survive. And as I warily register the clink of ammunition doubling as jewelry around my kidnappers' scrawny necks, I can only think of one thing to say: "Help." I call out to all the heavenly forces that I have been raised to believe in. I scream inside the safety of my own mind, and I call out to my mother who had already crossed to the other side. *Help me be strong*, I whisper. *Help me be brave. O God, O God, O GOD! Help me be dignified.*

Hand in hand, Poul and I begin our march. We trip over thorn bushes and small rocks. We fall and pick each other back up. I cannot see them as much as I can hear them, these men that have taken me away from my life, and it feels as if, with every step I take, more of them come out of the shadows, their guns pointed right at my blonde head.

I feel blood stream down my leg. It pools in between my toes, sticky and warm. Somewhere, amid my terror, I vaguely realize that I've sliced my leg open on something and while the wound throbs, I am grateful for the pain, because this pain means I must be still alive. I can feel something in my body. And even though it also feels like I am floating outside myself, hovering above the nightmare of whatever this is, I must still be *inside* myself and that must mean my heart has not stopped beating.

Always one for closure, as each step gets me closer to what lies ahead, I say goodbye to my husband. We've only had a little over a year together as husband and wife, and no baby. I'm only thirty-two years old. I didn't get the chance to do what I had always felt called to do: become a mother. I say goodbye to that child that will never be. Silent tears stream down my face. I say goodbye to my father and my sister and brother. I briefly worry about how they will manage life now with my mother and me gone. I hope my sister, now the only girl left in the family, can carry on the softer side of what I hope will endure.

As I grow lost in what their lives will look like without me in them, I am jarred to a stop with an abrupt shove and an order to get down onto my knees. I consider, in these final moments, all the times I wondered how my life was going to play out in the end. It had never crossed my mind that I would be put to rest so violently and that I would not even know the reason why. I connect with my mother in these final moments and wonder if she was as terrified as I am now. I picture her confused, my father by her side at a hospital bed, and her last words reverberate over and over in my mind:

Why am I here?

Why am I here?

Why am I here?

Why am I here?

And then I hear one of them speak. The desert goes as still as my breathing, and I give my head a little shake. Surely, I didn't hear that right.

"Sleep," they say. I look up from the ground. I can barely see, but I think I see someone motion to me to lie down. *Could they really want me to just lie down in the dirt and go to sleep?* As the tidal wave of survival swallows me up, I collapse into a heap on the ground. My mind takes this as a positive sign as it searches for relief and my body begins to shut down. I get to live. For now.

My eyelids grow heavy and within minutes I pass out from the deluge of adrenaline and fear. As the world starts to go black behind my eyes, I briefly recall the question I asked myself just a few hours before. I see a girl cloaked in self-doubt, confusion, and pride looking at herself that morning, in the mirror. And suddenly, I know exactly why I'm here.

DAY 60 SOMETHING—DECEMBER 2011

Somewhere in the Somali desert

It's a few weeks before Christmas by my calculations. We have given up believing that we will receive a Christmas miracle: our freedom. Negotiations have stalled. It has been weeks since we have made contact with our organization, and we aren't sure if anyone knows we are still alive. We've been on the move, which means we are often awoken in the middle of the night, forced into vehicles, and driven around for hours in all directions that lead to nowhere. I'm still the only woman living amongst dozens of Somali men, and that living has been done completely outdoors. I spend the daylight hours hunched under bushes or small acacia trees and then sleep out in open fields at night.

We have returned to land that actually has a building on it, but for reasons I am not privy to, it seems no one is actually allowed inside the house. We have been relegated to a goat pen constructed of twigs and thorny branches. It's the closest thing we have been given to shelter, and so I try to find a strand of gratitude for it. I have nothing to do, other than to spend my days searching for small miracles in this strange and unpredictable existence that has become my life.

I woke up today.

I was brought a bottle of water and it's sort of clean.

I can stretch my legs out under this tree.

I haven't been raped yet.

Gratitude takes on new meaning when you are a hostage.

For some reason the pirates on duty this particular day seemed to be feeling empathetic toward their poor female hostage. I must have looked pretty down because one of them went the extra mile to dig around in the back of his vehicle to produce my work bag. He proudly brought it over to me and let me empty the contents onto my mat. I held up each item as if it were a precious commodity that I could use to buy my freedom. Most of the items were work materials that I had zero interest in at that point but, nestled in between my computer bag and a stack of worksheets, were pieces of my life. As I flipped through a workbook I had designed, something small and black fell out from between the pages. I looked down to see it was the Kindle that I usually traveled with on long flights. Anxiously, I flipped the cover off and tried the power button-my heart skips several beats when I see that the battery is fully charged! Maybe I am getting a Christmas miracle after all.

I chuckle as I flip through to the library to see what books are stored there, but my excitement is short-lived as I see quickly that I have all of two options of downloaded material to read: *Freakonomics* by Steven D. Levitt and Stephen J. Dubner, a comprehensive economics study of "the hidden side of everything"—interesting for sure, but not exactly relevant to my current situation. And then there's the King James version of the Holy Bible. Given my past of a good Midwestern upbringing infused with Bible studies and prayer circles, and my present, literally navigating death on a daily basis, I figure reading the Bible might do me a little more good. And as it was almost Christmas time, from what I could tell (it really *is* hard to keep track of time out there in the desert) it seemed fitting to keep with the spirit and begin with the Nativity story from the perspective of all the Gospels.

I moved through the first chapter of Matthew quickly. It had been years since I had cracked open the Bible, but if there was one thing in my life that hadn't changed, The Bible would be it. It had stood the test of time and was as familiar to me as the smell of my mother's fried chicken. It felt like home. I glanced up to make sure none of the pirates were paying attention to what I was doing. They were doing what they always did, lying under a scrubby desert tree in hopes of shade, laughing while chewing khat. I had been forgotten—for the moment. As I read through the second chapter of Matthew, it was not lost on me that Mary and Joseph too were wandering through the desert in search of rest. I was literally lying on the dirt floor of a goat pen—if ever there was a stable, I was in it—and rest was just as elusive for me. I was exiled, lost, running from something, afraid. I nearly jumped out of my skin when I read the next part in Matthew, chapter two, verse twelve: "And being warned of God in a dream that they should not return to Herod, they departed into their own country another way.

[13] And when they were departed, behold, the angel of the Lord appeareth to Joseph in a dream, saying, Arise, and take the young child and his mother, and flee into Egypt, and be thou there until I bring thee word: for Herod will seek the young child to destroy him.

[14] When he arose, he took the young child and his mother by night, and departed into Egypt…"

All of a sudden, it felt like a freight train of *knowing* had barreled into that goat pen, and hit me, smack in the middle of the face. Joseph had had a dream. It was a warning. He had been visited by an angel in order to save their lives. And he listened. Joseph listened.

Suddenly, there I was, back on my bed in the guest house in Galkayo on the morning of October 25, some fifty or sixty days earlier, drenched in sweat, pondering whether I wanted to go on this training, aware of what my gut was saying but ignoring it anyway. A dream started coming back to me. Visions and rememberings of pirates, scaling walls, gunshots, hair pulled, my door knocked down, and…a kidnapping.

It was me. My intuition, my knower. She *knew* something bad was about to happen all along. And she knew it so clearly, she gave it to me in a dream, play-by-fucking-play before it was going to happen. And I didn't listen. I just didn't God damn listen.

I could see her again, the girl staring at herself in the mirror, and in my mind's eye, I watched in quiet horror as she considered herself and weighed all that she was against the consequences of what they said would be.

Sweat dripping down my sunburnt body, hands shaking from understanding, I turned the kindle off and hid it beneath my mat. Burning tears carved rivers of regret into my dirt-caked face as shame began to choke me while I studied my filthy feet. I picked up a decaying piece of straw that was meant to be bedding for the goats but was now a bed for me. I ripped the straw into tiny pieces, bitterly sobbing as I contemplated the mess that was left of my life.

Clarity. Understanding. Mistakes revealed. In a goat pen. But why? *Why?* At thirty-two years old, after having managed to survive a traumatic childhood fraught with mental illness, having escaped an abusive marriage in my early years, and deconstructed the brainwashing dogma of an institution called church, had I gotten it so completely and absurdly wrong? I had traveled to Africa on my own, I had gotten a job, started a new life, and yet, I had still managed to screw myself so completely, so fundamentally. I thought I *knew* myself: what I wanted and what I would put up with. I was strong, Miss Independent, vibrant and carefree! *How the hell had I gotten myself here?*

As I considered the likeness to where I was sitting to where baby Jesus had laid, I had a revelation: I was also being born. As I laid my head down on tufts of straw and stared out at the expansiveness of the desert sky, I felt the vastness of realization, lost in the emptiness of my own making.

And I prayed.

Show me how to fix this. I whispered into the Universe. *If you get me out of this thing alive, I promise, I won't ever abandon myself again.*

It took another month and a few days, but God did show up again. Only this time, it was in the form of dozens of Navy SEALs who parachuted into the desert in the middle of the night, several miles in, just so they could carry me out of hell.

While I wish I could report that once I was delivered out of the desert, it was easy for me to commit to my inner knowing and I never once felt myself, or anyone else, silence my voice, no, it would take years for me to figure out how to get out of that space of self-abandonment and hike to the mountaintop of self-love. And while there were moments when I didn't think I was going to make it, I did. Again and again and again.

My inner knowing has shown up in little and big ways in my life. Ending a friendship that made me feel ashamed of being myself or choosing to speak up in relationships even if it was going to rock the boat, were seemingly small, but such incredibly significant events when it came to the practice of taking my power back. On a larger scale, I have spent the last decade really getting to know myself, devoting myself to the journey of self-exploration, fueled by curiosity and a commitment to figure some tough shit out. It takes practice, this reclaiming our voice stuff. Even though I get up in the morning intending to live out my truth and show up as authentically as I possibly can in every interaction, I can still get off course, even when I can see exactly where it is I want to go.

It's been a long time, and a lot of survival since I studied that girl in the mirror and chose to leave her behind. In some ways, I have mourned her, the life that she could have had, the work she could have done. But as I continue to hike my way to the top of my particular mountain, I also rejoice. Yes, that girl died that day, and there are moments when I deeply miss her. But in her place, a woman was born—and this woman is not only a survivor who was able to stand up to Somali pirates for ninety-three days, but she was also able to reconstruct a life built on a firm foundation of love for herself, a trust in her wants and desires, and a commitment to explore.

I've always joked with people that I have taken the scenic route in life. I have meandered, gotten lost, and collapsed on the side of the trail in despair. But I have also gotten back up every single time and continued to put one foot in front of the other, determined to get to the top of the mountain to see what is waiting for me up there. As it turns out, it is more than just the view I have found, it is more than just a mountain I have climbed. Because I am the mountain. And I have been there, waiting for myself to find myself, all along.

ABOUT THE AUTHOR

On October 25, 2011, while on a routine field mission in Somalia, working as the Education Advisor for her non-governmental organization, Jessica was abducted at gunpoint and held for ransom by a group of Somali pirates for ninety-three days. Forced to live outdoors in deplorable conditions, starved, and terrorized by more than two dozen gangsters, Jessica's health steadily deteriorated until, by order of President Obama, she was rescued by the elite SEAL Team VI on January 25, 2012.

Jessica's ordeal is detailed in her *New York Times* bestselling book, *Impossible Odds: The Kidnapping of Jessica Buchanan and Her Dramatic Rescue by SEAL Team Six*.

Jessica has been named one of the "150 Women Who Shake the World" by *Newsweek* and her story was the most highly viewed *60 Minutes* episode to air, to date. Jessica is a highly sought-after inspirational speaker and her TEDx Pearl Street talk, *Change is Your Proof of Life* has been the foundation for which she travels the world, inspiring audiences to access their resilience by identifying their own autonomy and choice in the middle of their own life-changing event.

Jessica is the founder of Soul Speak Press, an imprint of Merack Publishing, where she supports women who are ready to share their stories through Memoir Manifestos—books that are one part memoir, one part self-help, and one part inspiration. Jessica is the co-host of the TOP 1% ranking podcast worldwide, *We Should Talk About That,* where she and her co-host Jessica Kidwell attempt to unpack the uncomfortable topics that nobody is talking about, but definitely should.

And in her free time, Jessica can be found hiking mountains all over the world with her husband and two kids.

To learn more about Jessica go to www.jessbuchanan.com and follow her on Instagram @jessicacbuchanan.

RULA ABIRAFEH

No one prepares us for the emotional unraveling of parenthood. I somehow thought our traumas resolved themselves casually with adulthood. Instead, they just fester. The grandest exhaustion I have shouldered as a mother has been for my child to belong. Academics take a backseat. The guttural desire for my daughter to be seen, to feel seen, and to know acceptance marks all my success as a parent.

HYPHENATED

I could feel how amplified my heartbeat was. It was all-consuming. Just exploding and radiating louder—and hotter—as his words continued. Generational trauma, he said. How it's passed on through the family, subconsciously or consciously. He discussed minority groups, relationship dynamics, and oppression. And empathy. He was interested and engaging. I was not prepared.

I dread intimate settings, especially when we're all configured in a circle, just so painfully visible. I was already sitting in my anxious sweat before he spoke, trying to breathe through everyone's individual introductions. I wanted to hear them. My anxiety is just always louder.

I silently, obsessively, rehearsed but kept my ear on their stories. My presence became clouded by discomfort and regret. And to think I showed up voluntarily. I would have loved to be truly present without unwelcome emotional weight. Not today. But I was there for my daughter: a second grader growing up in Los Angeles, in a world that's trending towards diversity, whatever that even means. The event is a parent panel for our children to discuss what school is really like for minority children. Every single parent brought childhood wounds to the table. Unhealed.

Distant me, from six weeks before, was so ready and open, without trepidation. Current me just wanted to bail, even before arrival. Current me is, and always has been, childhood me. Fragmented. Uprooted. Alien. The Only. Constantly looking left and right, all for the sake of belonging. And still at 42, at my wounded childhood core, I have no idea if I will ever belong.

On cue, I repeated the magnetism I felt towards this environment from my very first introduction: the dropdown box declaring your child's ethnicity. I scrolled through the list of choices I never had growing up. It scrolled with visibility, presence, and acknowledgment. And right there, for every applicant to browse, was a choice that made me catch my breath. A choice I had never witnessed but longed to read. The identity that described me, described her, and validated our belonging: Middle Eastern-American.

Yet, I slouched in a cheap foldable plastic chair, shifting every which way. There was no way I was ever going to be comfortable enough to get through an introduction after what he said. How did he just see all the weight I've carried in my lifetime and name it? And declare it interesting?

All that empathy. I was not prepared. Anxiety can be so painful in your body and can surround you, suffocatingly, yet at the same, remove you for survival. I have no idea how I blurted out my name, not in my usual rehearsed and coherent way. I gave no one a chance to understand it. I was rushing past my name, my background, and the reason I was there, just to get it done. But I failed.

My voice cracked, my eyes pooled, my gaze down. It wasn't going to let me go quietly, that generational trauma. I put my hand to my mouth and with permission took my minute. Caught my breath. Sat in the messy shit I have held onto for so long. Sat in that suppression that no longer wanted to be silenced. Sat in that anger that was tired of fighting. Sat in the space that was quietly held just for me.

The twisty scenic roads of rural Virginia were my parents' favorite. Or perhaps they feared American highways. I never felt like I got the true story. But those backroads bought us green views and extra time. In the backseat of a cushy classic Benz, my childhood friend and I sat gazing out our respective windows. My parents in the front, clicking through the dial for a radio station without static. They landed on the news and took pause. There was talk of heightened issues of the eighties—a buzz around terrorism, airplane hijackings, the PLO, Palestinians, violence, American hostages. I couldn't piece it all together, partly because I was young, but memorably, as quickly as it was announced, it vanished. My mom scrambled to change the dial, clicking through anything, just to land anywhere else. And at that moment, there was nothing else spoken. The discomfort was tangible. She wore it every day. She wore it loudly, but it was inaudible.

It was that day she told me, pulling me aside privately from my American friend, that I would not say I was Palestinian. I would only say Lebanese if asked. It was that day I was taught to stay silent for safety and belonging. It was that day I immediately knew that even if I lied and suppressed, I would never belong.

I'll never know in detail my parents' experience of war. They're short, no-nonsense communicators. The sharing of emotions and struggles was so tightly controlled. But I knew they were fighters. They rebelled against the law of the land in Lebanon, eloping to Cyprus to marry. Cross-religion communion was forbidden and still has lingering judgment.

They lived in the heart of Beirut during periods of civil unrest, food rationing, bombs, days-long electricity outages, and incredible violence. I was never given the chance to grasp the details of those experiences, but the guttural pain of being forced to leave your home, your land, was, and will always be, a palpable sadness that has no words. Because they never truly went back.

My parents came to the States, as the immigrant story goes, for a better opportunity for their children and themselves. And so many of those dreams were fulfilled. They found entrepreneurial business potential, renowned education, more freedom for women, and Domino's pizza. Inside our suburban brick building in Northern Virginia, we were Arab. Outside, amidst the greenery and fair skin, we were American. I was always the brownest girl in class.

My eyebrows were thick, my hair dark and unruly, my arms hairy, and my eyes big, brown, and lost. I always stood out in a sea of blondes. Some call it exotic or unique, but I just felt foreign and strange. No one knew where Lebanon was. I was ignorantly clumped in with the few Indian classmates. It was my closest social connection even though it couldn't be any further geographically.

Distance and disconnect start with my name: Rula. My name is not so unheard of in my mother country, but I've always been the only one, for all my existence. The Only. I've never had to differentiate by a last initial in America. I'm on automatic recall: when I say it, I spell it. It goes hand in hand. And even when I articulate the four single letters, it still mystifies people. Forget rolled r's and proper pronunciation; the effort feels beyond the reward. My favorite reaction to my name is always awe and flattery. Not necessarily because I believe a word, but because it is so clearly prompted from discomfort—as if any foreign name needs questioning or has meaning. My name alone built a wall, immediately separating me from fitting in. My name isolated me in America. It was an audible feeling of not belonging. I was always an Only.

That feeling bubbled and festered inside me, creating insecurity and anxiety. I spent my youth staring down at floors, never looking up, never accepting. I found safety at home: inside the walls of our house, then even more enclosed, locked in my room, and even further retreated under my bed covers. I hid. It didn't hold me back at the time, but it would heavily hinder me after college.

At home, we culturally combined America with our heritage, away from inquiring critical eyes. Our Thanksgivings and Christmases were culinary fusions. Spinach pies, sweet potatoes, Lebanese meat and rice, hummus, and a turkey. My parents spoke to me in Arabic; I answered in English. They insisted. In the early years, their English was broken at best, their accents heavy. They wanted me to master English. But I understood everything in Arabic.

Once a week I had an Arabic tutor. I didn't even try. Every Monday was pure dread. I never did any homework, conversationally refused to speak, and loathed that I even had to mention it to friends. I didn't want to preserve any of my identity. While we all laughed at my parents' language mishaps, most of my sentiment was venomous frustration. I just wanted to be "normal", with parents who didn't need translation. I had no patience when they asked for help or tried to explain anything to me in English. I was cruel. I took all my foreign anger out on them and covered them in constant blame.

In public together they would speak to me in Arabic, and I would answer in English. We were a spectacle to many. Simple grocery conversations would invite onlookers and bold commentators asking us what language it was or fascinated that I knew English. It was exhausting, feeling like a museum exhibit in the produce aisle. Where are you from? Oh, that's so interesting that you can speak English without an accent! What language is that? All the inquiries would be uninvited. I didn't realize at the time that even an innocent, inquisitive approach would wear me down inside. While my parents' accent dissipated over the years, it never fully went away.

My childish frustrations subsided as I grew into my identity. After decades of slow assimilation—fusing cultures and finding niches—I almost felt as if I had settled.

Immigrant parents universally have the same philosophies. They demand your success be based on their sacrifice. The pressure is funneled into education and traditional careers. The pressure is unnamable; the guilt of not wanting it, enormous.

All my pre-college years were mapped out. They would scribble down classes, which extracurriculars, what colleges, who to connect with, whose child succeeded. There were infinite lectures about the importance of education, how it can never be taken from you, how it is the only way to make money, how it brings esteem and societal recognition.

My academics were never up to par. As the youngest, I swayed. My older sister was definitive and direct. Her focus was and still is uninterrupted. While she didn't follow our parents' wishes (which could truly be called demands), she was unwavering in her direction and is now an expert in her field. It was impossible to argue with her commitment.

I felt clueless. I had no idea about anything at all. There wasn't a school or profession that pulled. I just wanted to enjoy myself. I was, and am, a creative person at heart: not linear and easily distracted. I love the challenge of new learning, but I easily fall off course when it becomes monotonous. That made it so easy for my parents to impose their plans of security. If the older daughter didn't do it, then the younger one most certainly would. I didn't argue. I followed suit for the sake of conflict avoidance. Just quietly channeling that anxiety inward.

In high school, within the confines of their dictation, I found ways to have fun. It didn't weigh on me at the time because I had temporarily—superficially—grown out of that "foreign child" feeling.

I had global friends with cultural empathy who taught me about new identities and embraced mine. We fused together in relationships that were irreplaceable. I thought I had internally started to settle. It felt welcomed and on course.

College applications and standardized tests took over. It was a blur of number 2 pencils and filling in guessed circles. I know my parents could sense my lack of grounded academics, but as long as I showed up, there was no fuel to argue. They were intimately involved in the process.

The only authority I had, that I felt conviction for, was my checked ethnicity. They always checked Caucasian, believing the definition included Middle Eastern. I never argued ethnic technicalities, I was choosing by emotion. I never identified as Caucasian; it didn't feel right. Without any historical knowledge (and before Google), I always checked Other. That was the only other option.

My parents feared this choice would hinder my applications and admittance. Just as they counseled me to deny half of my Palestinian identity, they disputed my checkbox choice. I was quiet and obedient as a child, but at seventeen I hadn't lived what I deemed a Caucasian existence—only Other. On my list of priorities, it wasn't worth discussing with them. But for me, it was the beginning of my journey toward belonging. I had been othered. I was Other. It wasn't a celebratory option, but it was where I belonged. Every application reflected that vague, expansive choice. And I was proud of that.

Immigrant parents also look to other immigrant family success stories as examples. There's always someone else's daughter or son who scored an Ivy League education and is now a doctor. Or excelled in dual degrees in a powerhouse trajectory toward law. Every lecture, some new rumored recent millionaire would set the standard. And they would study the methodology.

What did the parents do, where did they study, how did they get in, and who did they know? How could we become them? My parents had a top-tier school in mind for me. It was a calculated choice based on education and what they deemed "fit." I don't think I even toured the school. I just shrugged and went. It was such a stretch it didn't merit thought.

Following examples of immigrant kids before me, I would apply to this school declaring a major in languages. At the time I had studied and embraced Spanish; It seemed like the logical choice. Yet, Arabic was an option and it intrigued me. It felt fun. Somehow the thought enticed me. I felt recognized and excited. After decades of avoidance, frustration, embarrassment, and denial, I would now embrace and possibly enjoy diving into my native language. I checked Arabic, and I got accepted. And the fun turned into fear.

My parents were elated. Elated. It was such a memorable, celebratory occasion. It was a marker of their success. It validated all their struggles in America. It made it all worthwhile.

I vividly remember being in bed when my mother rushed in with a small envelope to open. It used to be that big manila envelopes indicated acceptance, with welcome packets and paperwork, and small, single letters indicated rejection. I sat up to tear it open without much care, only to read welcoming words. I didn't even finish the letter before she snatched it out of my hand to verify and scream, calling in Arabic for my dad, "She got in!"

I was still in bed. That bed that had enveloped me as a child. That bed that had welcomed me without judgment. That bed that knew me. And I stayed in that bed and cried. It has always felt entitled, selfish, and unappreciative to be upset about a top-tier college acceptance. But I didn't want it. I did not want to go. I didn't know where I wanted to go, but I just knew I did not want to go there. It's possible that I didn't want to attend any of my options because I was a passive passenger in the process. But this school had been a reach, and it wasn't supposed to happen.

I felt so disconnected from such an achievement that I didn't even allow myself to celebrate. All my other classmates were bragging with excitement for themselves. I shrank in defeat. The celebratory dust clouded my choice of major: Arabic. I had to remind myself that I had authority in my future. I chose to embrace my identity, even study it. I checked that box, and it was mine. It was hard to see or touch a future at the time, but I would try with hope and optimism.

College quickly turned into a typical experience. Sleepless partying nights, skipped classes, weekends away, late-night library cramming, and Domino's pizza. I eventually adjusted, navigating campus my way. Studying Arabic demanded my time. It was a challenge to master its formality, grammar, and literature. But listening to it felt like home.

It was the fall of my senior year in D.C., which still felt like summer. Clear blue skies and warm air. Arabic was every day, Monday through Friday, first thing in the morning, every single year. It challenged my will to attend, but it became routine. I was always up early; campus was always quiet when my day started.

But that day it was exceptionally quiet, almost eerie. The only other student walking past me was on his cell phone, sounding alarmed, asking for information: What is going on, are you okay? Just as we brushed shoulders and I checked out of his confusing conversation, my sister called me, asking the same. She was trying to reach me, the rest of our family, and everyone between New York and D.C.. It was September 11, 2001.

That day became a distinct marker in my life that would unearth every single uncomfortable foreign memory I thought I had diffused. It would cement my childhood insecurities about belonging. It would take me straight to the backseat of that cushy eighties Benz, to the fear and panic my mother felt, and to the denial I carried for so long.

As the news unfolded, so did my fear. I quickly started carrying the guilt of being Arab. It was immediate. I felt association, culpability, and even responsibility for something horrifying. The initial shock was enormous, but the aftermath was even bigger.

It wasn't long before I started receiving phone calls advising my family on safety, asking me to be low-key and aware of my surroundings. Anger was awakening but without clarity. Understandably. I looked too much like them, I was from the same region, and the time was ripe for racism and disinformation.

Photos of the terrorists looked eerily like an uncle. Carrying Arabic literature books felt unsafe. Any ease felt speaking Arabic on airplanes was rapidly erased. Buying one-way tickets invited extra scrutiny and security, and being born in Beirut, brought additional speculation. I had special safety screenings at every airport countless times. My parents' accents haunted us with unwelcome heckling: Go back to your country. Simply: it sucked being Arab in America.

Navigating the aftermath was an unexpected interruption. Lost was the serene sensation of being settled. I got so heavily knocked off track that I emotionally shut down. I abruptly changed majors. I wanted nothing to do with fluency or translation or association. I scraped by the following semester, lost. And as soon as I could, I crawled into bed. Depression swallowed me whole after college. I became completely isolated.

I questioned everything. I found myself not only lost in my ethnic identity but lost in all my other identities. I wasn't a corporate climber, a passionate advocate, an artist, a wife, or a mother. I wasn't anything. I sat on the fringe of every group, peering in wondering what it would be like to feel that longed-for settled self-contentment. The pressure of performance made me crumble. The pressure of finding myself was daunting.

Those years were fragmented as I tried all avenues to find what fit. Trying on everyone else's direction with envy. There were a few truths I held onto quietly. I knew, and know, that connection to culture fulfilled me. And my desire to regain authority over my future angrily pushed me.

Authority meant autonomy and autonomy meant managing myself, my work, my income, and my choices. I could feel entrepreneurial rumblings alongside insecure discouragement. It took me many tries to mute the lure of being in bed. With each try, the distance grew further and the fear smaller. Opportunities began to present themselves and I would take those challenges. Setbacks came along for the ride. And while I certainly can't claim to cut ties with depressive retreats, I can say with authority that I have mastered persevering through the restart.

After a decade of fragmented soul searching, I still could not package myself into a sensical box. I felt like I was stretched out, straddling all directions, emotions, identities, and beings. There was relentless frustration. I never made sense, I couldn't make sense, and I was forever conflicted. There was always an itch, an insecurity, and a sense of being foreign.

No one prepares us for the emotional unraveling of parenthood. I somehow thought our traumas resolved themselves casually with adulthood. Instead, they just fester. The grandest exhaustion I have shouldered as a mother has been for my child to belong. Academics take a backseat. The guttural desire for my daughter to be seen, to feel seen, and to know acceptance marks all my success as a parent.

Until my daughter is old enough, I have inherited the duty of checking her ethnic box. It isn't without weight. She is fully Lebanese-Palestinian, born in America, and too young to declare for herself. As I navigate the never-ending number of applications, forms, and files I need to submit for her, I always take pause at her ethnicity.

And so, I sat. In that space. My eyes pooling, thinking of my daughter's big brown eyes looking up at me. I sat in that space raw and real with resolve for her future. And I remembered why I was there. Middle Eastern-American. It was all in that hyphen.

When I mustered up enough composure to speak, the words inaudibly tumbled out. When my eyes averted from the floor and I could look at the circle surrounding me, I made out slight nods of understanding and empathy. When my voice finally overcame the hiccups of sadness, I shared a truth that resonated with everyone, crossing all identity lines. I released an unscripted, unanticipated, mumbling monologue that said nothing with certainty. I had no idea where I belonged, what I was doing, or what I even wanted.

I had searched for belonging, from the outside in, for decades. I longed for external acceptance to validate my identity, my culture, and myself, not realizing that belonging starts within. Belonging is the self-acceptance of the in-between, the conflicting, the confusing, the fringe, and the hurt. Belonging is the hyphen that fuses the many facets of me.

ABOUT THE AUTHOR

Born in Beirut, raised in the suburbs of Washington, D.C., now living in Los Angeles—Rula has straddled words, seeking belonging and balance. As an immigrant, she struggled placing herself in the right check box. Her varied identity, once a puzzle, now provides her with purpose. Rula has an undergraduate degree from Georgetown University, a Personal Coaching certification from New York University, and is ICF ACC credentialed. She has worked as a copy editor, content developer, Pilates instructor, and former cookie company founder. She's a mother, a partner, a dog lover, and a murder mystery lover. Her path was never linear, each creative direction ultimately leading her to her own successful business as a Professional Life Coach. Rula brings understanding, compassion, and her story to each individualized session. Find her at www.rulaabi.com or @rula.abi.

SUSIE DENT

I refused to acknowledge the answers and chose to abandon myself out in the middle of an emotional desert night after night after night. No, none of those things matter, I'd convince myself. Follow the formula. Check the boxes. Get the prize. But it was an empty battle because there is no prize. Life is not an academic course.

What did I think the prize was anyway? My parents reading my resume aloud at dinner parties? As if my career or personal life choices reflected upon them favorably and made me matter more to them? Was I really going to live my life as a shadow of my authentic self, just on the off chance that a stranger would give my choices the stamp of approval over a martini with my mother?

RUNNING AWAY FROM THE ALTAR... AND BACK TO MYSELF

My pile of shoes jostled around inside a brown U-Haul box as I walked out the door, like those goldfish you see in twist-tied plastic bags at the pet store. The sound provided a steady rhythm as my mind raced with every thought and every feeling imaginable. I felt torn between freedom and fear as I struggled to wrap my head around how the world was going to react to what had just happened. What will everyone think? How will I tell them to return the gifts? Should I have just gone through with it and claimed "just kidding" the next day? How typical of me. Even in my first moment of freedom, I was still living in fear of judgment and invalidation from outsiders. But this had nothing to do with anyone but me.

A few nights before, I'd driven up to Los Angeles so I could practice how I was going to do the thing I was dreading most with one of my closest friends. I had carefully worded each justification: "He isn't good with money," "We just don't understand each other," and "He has no passions." Clearly, these justifications were my attempt to put a neat bow on a very messy decision. I could have come up with a thousand reasons why I shouldn't get married, but only one of those reasons mattered: I didn't want to.

I intended on staying overnight at my sister's house just a few blocks from dinner, but I couldn't stand to be in my own skin, so I went home to San Diego in the middle of the night. I put my talking points next to my pillow—safely stowed in my iPhone—and fell asleep. I knew I had to jump off the emotional cliff looming just steps in front of me. I had to end it; I had to stop the wedding.

I couldn't meet my fiancé, or any other man, at the altar if I wanted to live a life true to myself. I knew in my heart that I should never have been in this position—with a man. I was absolutely head over heels and inescapably in love with women. With one woman in particular. There was only one person who had run marathons through my mind since the day we met ten years before. Her name was Emily. I am, was born as, and will always be a lesbian. It was time to come out to myself, for myself.

I had waited on having the conversation, taking it down to the wire, because I was too afraid of how my decision was going to impact other people. I knew the decision to call off the wedding would seem like it came out of left field. To make matters worse, the next morning was the deadline for every single wedding vendor to receive their full balances and final headcounts.

As it turned out, my decision was not as surprising as I thought. In fact, it must have been radiating out of me. I woke up abruptly the next morning to my iPhone being hurled at my head. My fiancé, Stephen, had found my phone on the bedside table. He found my entire breakup thesis and read it before I could even open my mouth and say the words. He finally knew the truth.

"So you're saying you don't want to get married? What the fuck?"

At that moment, I felt like I was having an out-of-body experience. Like I was a marionette and something (or someone, a greater power, perhaps) was pulling my strings. I was watching the motions take place without any resistance or control of my own. It has happened three times in my life, and all three times had to do with Emily. This time was the third.

I sat up, staring at the bedroom door behind Stephen. A larger-than-life spirit seemed to fortify my voice with the calmest assurance I've ever felt in my life.

"No."

"Are you fucking serious?!"

"Yes."

"Is there anything I can do to change your mind?"

"No."

"Then get out of my house."

And with the help of that larger-than-life spirit holding my hand and pulling me along, I walked in a silent haze towards my closet and threw several pairs of shoes into a still-halfway unpacked moving box. (I don't know why shoes were my Noah's ark item—perhaps the spirit knew I'd need a few pairs of shoes to walk away.) I walked out of the apartment and towards the rest of my life.

I was so stunned that I started laughing, perhaps out of shock, perhaps out of relief. It felt like my house, the one I had spent a lifetime working so hard to build, was falling apart, and I was dancing on top of the rubble as it was coming down. I was free for only a moment before the panic set in. And then, I called my mom.

"I can't do it. I just can't. There are a thousand reasons why I should, but I just can't."

There was a pause on the other end, and then, a matter-of-fact response: "I know." She had seen something in my eyes that I couldn't. Maybe it had been my feet dragging at every matrimonial decision, or my complete aversion to discussing the wedding at all. Or perhaps she had seen the light slowly leaving my eyes as I drifted deeper into the desert. At that moment, she knew I was searching for my mountaintop: a truer, freer life. She offered to call a handful of my family members and let them know to cancel their plans. It was just nineteen days before the wedding.

As my phone was flooded with calls, texts, and emails, I drove straight to my best friend's door and started crying. "I don't have anywhere to go," I sputtered, "It's over. I'm not doing it."

What followed were tearful hours that turned into emotional days that turned into blurry weeks. I had jumped off the edge of the cliff and the freefall just kept going. At first, I felt like I needed to defend a thesis as to why I'd made my decision. I even practiced what I'd say to people, but to my surprise, no one asked why. Maybe they could see before I could that I didn't owe anyone an explanation. I didn't owe anyone a talking point. This was my story, and I held the pen and paper in my own hands. I had been waiting for ten years to write it down.

I was not a believer in love at first sight. Nor was I a believer in marriage, and because I worked in family law, my family and friends joked that I worked at a "divorce hotline." I would often get out in front of it and make the joke at my own expense. My parents had been married at least seven different times between the two of them. The phrase "marriage is a contract" was thrown around my childhood as a regular reminder (warning?) to never let matrimony overtake your emotions—or your life.

As a result, I was never one to dream of an elaborate wedding for myself, or even the process leading up to the actual event. And I had only been to a handful of weddings as a child (including my parents' respective ceremonies). However, my attention was never on the couple or the ceremony, but on the videographers who would hand off the mic for a recorded congratulations to the "happy" couple. On more than one occasion, I took the opportunity to sing Britney Spears ballads for the cameras (sorry, Aunt Gencie and Uncle Jerry!). The takeaway for me was that if you want to have a wedding, it's simply a party. Nothing more.

That all changed for me on a particularly hot Tuesday in August. I was attending an LGBTQ Law event at Santa Clara University's "officially unofficial" dive bar, The Hut. (Ironically, this would also be where I met my future ex-fiancé almost a year later). I walked in the door and scanned the room for my cousin, who was hosting the mixer. She was standing in the corner by a back patio door, excitedly talking to the most beautiful woman I had ever seen. As soon as I saw her, I felt my entire world stop, like a record scratch moment in time.

I said out loud to no one in particular: "I have to know you—I have to know this person" as I bumped past buzzed college graduates at the bar, I made my way directly to her, hand outstretched, and with my biggest Southern California smile, I chirped:

"Hi, I'm Susie!"

She took off her aviators and smiled back at me "Hi, I'm Emily." Her handshake was firm but intentionally lingering, and her eyes looked beyond the depths of mine, unlocking the most wonderful warmth I'd ever felt.

That would be the first and last time I would see her. I spent the entire next year desperately trying to track Emily down again. As one of the few (wise) people who had remained off social media, she was nowhere to be found. I scoured the internet for any sign of her presence, and finally, I found her a year later at a speaker panel sponsored by our law school. I excitedly waited in the wings for her to finish her presentation and greeted her in the student lounge with an even bigger smile than the first.

"You're hard to find, I never see you on campus!" I exclaimed, still in disbelief that after a year of searching I had actually tracked her down.

"I know! I'm never here, my class schedule is crazy. I haven't even had time to eat...I'm starving."

Wracking my brain for any bid for connection, and afraid she'd disappear into the ether again, I offered to bring her a snack pack before her next set of classes.

"Here, take down my number," I told her, "I'll bring you something a little sweet, a little salty. Whatever you like. I'll take care of you."

The next few weeks were like the montage scene in a romantic comedy. We were constantly in contact, via text, phone, and the ubiquitous gChat. I had never met anyone with whom I wanted to share all the facets of myself. There was no one I felt comfortable enough with before I met Emily. From my deepest thoughts on Stephen Sondheim to the ugliest skeletons in my closet, I felt compelled to lay out every piece that was me. I put it all on the table for her to hold in her hands.

Our early emotional flurries reached a crescendo about three months in—I had spent an evening at a local wine bar with classmates, brushing up the courage to ask Emily to spend time together, in person, alone. On brand, I overestimated the amount of liquid courage I'd need, and showed up at her door later that evening, not so subtly asking her to let me in. Eventually, she let me in.

"No, you don't really want to do that. You don't really feel that way about me," she said. I had finally opened up, telling her that I'd been waiting for years in crowded rooms just for a moment to be alone with her, away from the noise and eyes of others. After an hour of unsuccessful persuasive efforts, I left, dejected, and, in my petty emotional state, I was ready to let her know just how wrong she was about me.

And then the very next night, I met Stephen. Out of spite, I decided to give this nice boy from the Midwest a chance. Our short courtship turned into a relationship within a few weeks, which turned into months, and then into years. It's easy to let the time slip by when nothing is rocking the boat, good, bad, or otherwise. Our relationship lasted through my final year of law school without fanfare or memorable flashpoints, and before I knew it, we were living together with two cats, passing the time by watching comedy shows on Netflix and scrolling through our phones next to one another in silence.

Two years after we met at the Hut, and six months into my relationship with Stephen, Emily asked me to marry her. And I didn't say no...but I didn't say yes. We had spent the previous five months continuing our unparalleled, emotionally-on-fire friendship, despite my newly formed relationship with Stephen and Emily's ongoing long-distance relationship with her high school girlfriend, to whom she was engaged.

Finally, Emily's graduation day came. My cousin, who was Emily's year in school, threw a graduation party in my aunt and uncle's backyard to celebrate her own graduation, and Emily and I were both invited, along with our respective plus-ones. Mine had opted out, and hers made herself scarce, and we found ourselves alone near the barbeque pit next to the pool.

"I'm so afraid this is the last time I'm going to see you," she said to me, downtrodden, under her breath. "I just don't know what to do."

"I promise that you'll see me again, even if things have to be… the way they are," I responded. "I'm so happy for your new life to begin." Indeed, Emily was on track to get married that fall, a wedding to which I had been invited. I started to turn away and head back to the gazebo where my family was sitting, but Emily grabbed my hand.

"Marry me? Please. Don't leave this party without saying you'll be with me."

I looked at her in disbelief. How could she have waited months to tell me this, after I'd bared myself to her on the steps of her front porch in a drunken rant? How could she have waited this long to tell me how she felt?

"You can't ask me that," was all I could muster. I said it again and again, until there were clearly people waiting in the pathways to walk past us.

"You can't."

I left the party and started the four-hour drive south to Santa Barbara, where I was to spend the week with Stephen and his family for a summer vacation. I spent the first four days of the trip largely alone, isolating myself next to the Meyer lemon trees, thinking about what would have happened if I'd just said yes. *She wouldn't have really married me,* I kept telling myself. *She's already engaged. But I told her no. All the pain I'm feeling I brought upon myself because I wouldn't answer her question.* On the fifth day, Emily called. It was the longest we'd gone without speaking in nine months.

"It's me," she said on the other end of the line. I could hear she'd been crying, and I could hear the sadness in her voice. "I'm going to ask you again. There is a difference between old love and new love. But my new love with you feels like it's old love. It feels like nothing I've ever experienced. Please marry me, please say yes."

I was on the edge of the canyon staring into the valley of everything I'd ever wanted, but I was too scared to jump.

"It will make so many people upset," I said again, quietly, "You just can't ask me that."

APRIL 6, 2015—KYOTO, JAPAN

"Oh. Okay... Thank you?"

I had practiced what I was going to say for days, because of course Stephen had not kept the engagement a secret. Every detail previously passed amongst my friends, with the hope that they'd all tune in on Snapchat for the grand fairytale moment, under the cherry blossoms framing a bridge in Kyoto.

This is the moment every woman waits for, I kept telling myself. *Act more excited, make yourself cry, do something to make it feel like it's supposed to–* yet there I was, humiliated and hot-faced—convinced everyone around us was staring and could see right through me. I could tell Stephen was waiting for a more reassuring answer.

"Well...sure!" I said, grabbing the ring and haphazardly putting it on what turned out to be the wrong finger. In my mind, I'd thought that this moment would be like the part in Wizard of Oz where everything turns to color from black and white, and I'd suddenly become a quintessential bride-to-be, excited to pick out every detail for the impending fête. None of that happened.

As it sunk in that I'd contractually obligated myself to be with this person, I began to panic. The lump which had formed in my throat, perhaps a cue to cry, had slid south to my stomach, landing like a boulder at the bottom of a quarry. I've always been a naturally anxious person (or so I had convinced myself) but this engagement had sent those feelings of angst into overdrive. The rest of the trip was just a blur, and the flight home a week later from Japan to San Francisco felt like an eternity.

I hoped I would become a wellspring of emotion as I described the proposal to my friends and family—I wanted so badly to have excitement buoy my voice—but instead, I found the same hot-faced feeling when describing the proposal. It was nice, I'd say. "Nice." A neutral word that did not invite further inquiries. In my mind, "nice" was the end goal that people boast about in their life highlight reels. Non-offensive, non-volatile, non-threatening. A beige, one-dimensional feeling. Not a feeling that would bring life into your veins, or your heart, or your spirit. But one that I could just float along on in perpetuity, without really feeling anything.

The sleepless nights should have been my first sign that something was off. As with many students who had spent their entire lives parroting a future for themselves (imagine me as a kindergartener telling people I wanted to grow up to be a lawyer, which I said so many times the phrase lost its meaning), I found myself thrown into the shock of a world where there was no rubric. No pre-designed goals to set and no brackets on either edge as to how I did, and did not, spend my time. After twenty-five years of instruction, I was let out into the world armed with ideas of what I was supposed to be in the eyes of others, but not one idea of what I should be, or who I should be.

My childhood messaging was very clear: get as many degrees and academic accolades as possible because that will define your value. With that instruction, I spent decades of my life building an ironclad pile of academic receipts so no one would ever be able to question my intellect, my purpose, or my validity. But not once did I stop along the way and ask myself what I would need to do in life to find out who I was.

On those sleepless nights, I would do whatever I could to get myself to sleep—an entire bottle of wine that I selected solely by the label, various edibles, and at times, prescription sleeping pills—but I always woke up at 2:10 a.m. At the same time, every single night. I'd sit there and stare at the ceiling as the cold feelings of anxiety and dread filled my body and mind. Eventually, I would get up and walk over to the couch and stare outside. "Please help me," I'd whisper to the moon, tears of frustration dripping from my tired eyes. "Please help me figure out what I'm supposed to do. I don't feel peace in my body, and I don't feel peace in my heart." Something very big was missing, and even though I sat alone pleading with a planet to give me the answers, I was too afraid to even ask myself the questions.

Who makes your heart light up? Who makes you feel like you have rediscovered who you were before life took the light from your eyes? Whose face do you feel as you listen to the pining love songs on evening radio?

I refused to acknowledge the answers and chose to abandon myself out in the middle of an emotional desert night after night after night. *No, none of those things matter,* I'd convince myself. Follow the formula. Check the boxes. Get the prize. But it was an empty battle because there is no prize. Life is not an academic course.

What did I think the prize was anyway? My parents reading my resume aloud at dinner parties? As if my career or personal life choices reflected upon them favorably and made me matter more to them? Was I going to live my life as a shadow of my authentic self, just on the off chance that a stranger would give my choices the stamp of approval over a martini with my mother?

I'd go through this same cycle after sitting up staring out the living room window, falling asleep by 5:00 just to wake up a few hours later in an even lower space. The cycle progressed to the point where I, someone who had been in professional therapy weekly since kindergarten, decided I needed to call in greater support. Researching the closest psychiatrist, I grabbed the first available appointment and prepared to unload on this poor soul.

Again, my expectations and my reality were wildly different. Even in the confines of a medical professional's office, I couldn't spit the words out succinctly. All I could utter was "I just feel...*so...bad,*" before crying in frustration. A few sessions in, my doctor prescribed me entry-level SSRI medication to address what would be diagnosed as Generalized Anxiety Disorder. To my surprise, the medicine did make a difference, but not how I'd expected. The newfound chemical balance in my brain did take the place of my less savory coping mechanisms, and then some. I couldn't feel...anything. It was SUCH a relief because it meant I didn't have to address these feelings anymore. The power of brain-altering drugs, I decided, would be my life preserver out of this rough patch. Just a few months, I told myself, and surely, I'd snap right into excitement about the big day.

Unsurprisingly, that didn't happen. While I was able to finally stay asleep, I still felt an impending sense of doom surrounding the entire wedding. I couldn't decide on anything, from florals to appetizers, to seat placement. Afraid that anything coming out of my mouth wouldn't portray enough excitement and people would see right through me, I'd defer to others and back myself out of any actual decisions.

As it turns out, taking a deferential role in planning an event like a wedding is pretty easy. Everyone, and I mean everyone, has an opinion. On how you wear your hair, how you should coordinate a song list, or what forks you should choose from a vendor. Sitting in silence making space for the loudest person in the room to make my decisions had worked out for me my entire life, so why wouldn't it now?

As the day loomed closer, instead of feeling like the Swarovski crystal ball dropping in Times Square, it felt like watching one of those doomsday clocks tick down to utter destruction. As the numbers got lower, the pressure to listen to what I wanted grew even more, but I still couldn't figure out how to use my voice.

The day our first venue deposit came due, I called my mom and asked, in tears, "Is this all there is? You grow up, you get engaged, and it feels like this? Is this all there is to life?"

Her silence on the other end of the line was answer enough, but she punctuated it with "well...sometimes."

MAY 2012—JUNE 2016—SAN JOSE, CA

I'd sit there with a melting iced tea in my hand as if I needed more caffeine to intensify the jolts moving around my body. Looking back now, it's a wonder that I was able to sit still at all.

After thirteen months of silence since the Santa Barbara call, Emily and I resolved to be friends. It was the best solution, we thought, to keep a light alive, even if it didn't ease the hurt. Once a quarter, I would block out two hours on my calendar and tell my assistant that I was meeting for a working lunch. The only thing working, though, was my nervous system, trying to keep my cortisol levels in check. I'd spend the morning with knots in my stomach, trying to keep calm about the impending shock to my emotions.

I'd arrive fifteen minutes early and park around the corner from Roy's, a small, reimagined gas station turned artisan coffee spot in buzzy Japantown. I'd keep my sunglasses on so no one could see the excitement, fear, and heartbreak in my eyes, and I'd wait. I was always so afraid she wouldn't show up, deciding I wasn't worth the drive, the time, and the effort. She'd tell me she was driving down to Nordstrom to pick up a blush from NARS, or to meet her dad for a sandwich at the local Zonotto's market. I couldn't get it through my head that she would be driving seventy-five miles every time just to see me.

But every time, Emily showed up. Rounding the corner in aviators and a smile. Just two hours alone with her felt like a month-long vacation. The waves of anxiety melted off me (sometimes thanks to the Xanax I'd taken right before). The interactions always started the same, with both of us so full of nerves and hurt and excitement that we'd babble on about menial topics: parking, the weather, what types of new teas Roy's had behind the counter. I never really remember the details of that part of the conversation.

After a few minutes, the adrenaline would subside and the peace would sweep back in, and each of us would ask the same, painfully loaded question:

"Are you ok?"

And every time, it would be like someone had peeled back the layers of all my protective emotional gear and could see that I was still sitting in the corner, scared of myself and my own shadow. She could help me see reality; she was that someone who could hold my hand and tell me that the way I was—who I am—was okay. More than okay, actually. That who I am is good. And wanted. And seen. And perfect.

As the armor came down, our conversation flowed like no time had passed. A few minutes in, our hands would grow closer, and we'd hold pinkies, and then fully interlace our fingers. The electricity was always there, it never faded, and it surrounded us both with the most reassuring pink glow, protecting us from the bleak gray or our respective realities. The time would always go by too fast, and after what felt like mere minutes, I'd start getting calls from the office wondering where I was. She would have to start heading back to San Francisco to beat the afternoon traffic.

We would hold hands as she walked me back to my car and give me a lingering hug. "Be safe, please" she would always say, and I'd watch her walk back to her car. I would drink in the smell of lavender, tea tree, and a signature L'Occitane perfume that always followed her.

The rest of those afternoons would always be a blur. I'd autopilot back to my office and close the door, sit at my desk, and stare at the wall to decompress until the end of the workday finally came and I had to head home.

We continued this terrible cycle for nearly five years, straddling the painful line between just friends and wanting something more. We would try to have our Roy's time once a quarter, and in the margins would come up with every creative smoke signal possible to let the other know we were ok.

We'd meet up in hallways at group dinner parties (still commonplace as our friends from law school settled around the Bay Area) on the way to grab another drink from the kitchen or on the way to the bathroom. We'd engage in game after game of Words with Friends or Scrabble, coming up with the most emotionally loaded singular nomenclature to capture the sentiment bubbling behind the silence and separation.

This is fine, we both convinced ourselves. It was "nice." We could go on with our regular lives, minimally medicated to keep floating above the surface. Being friends was better than nothing. Roy's was better than absence. The pain was better than forgetting.

And we did this spin cycle for four years until my wedding was just three months away. I'd pushed off every specific matrimonial decision possible, much to the frustration of Stephen and those around me. "You have to decide!" he'd say, exasperated with my inability to move on anything.

And he was right. I did have to decide.

Three months before we were to say "I do," Stephen found out that he'd been offered a prestigious position at a biotech firm in San Diego, a perfect chance to start anew and perpetuate his career. I'd felt stuck in my own job, and stuck in my own body, which by that time was clearly dripping off me, so I too went along with the exciting news. As timing would have it, we were scheduled to have a pizza-making party with Emily and her partner in San Francisco on the evening we found out the news. "If you could do me a favor," I said to him as I walked numbly to the car, "please let me tell them in my own time?"

We made the trek from San Jose to San Francisco that evening in silence. Not five minutes into our arrival at the party, Stephen blurted out "We've moving! To San Diego! Next week!" My heart sank as I immediately looked over at Emily to check her reaction. Again, the hot face set in. As color crept up my neck and flooded my cheeks, I could see in her eyes that she felt exactly as I did: that our routine, our cycle, our emotional triage that we'd resigned to for propping up our lives, was going to be ripped from beneath us. Our pretense was sputtering its last wheezing breaths.

"Mazel!" she said without skipping a beat. "Let me go get a bottle of champagne to celebrate!" Later she told me that she went down to her basement, stood in front of the fridge, and felt like she'd been hit by a truck. She came back up a few minutes later, but I was so ashamed and hurt that Stephen had blurted out (what only I knew was) such hurtful information against my wishes, that I couldn't even bear to make eye contact with her.

"You sure were in a weird mood the entire evening" he commented, as we weaved through the streets of San Francisco to get back onto the highway. "I'm just going to miss my friends," I said in a monotone, trying to hide the internal avalanches falling inside my heart.

We were set to leave for San Diego a week after the dinner party, and I had packed my car to the limits readying for the solo drive. The days leading up to the move had gone by so quickly that somehow Emily and I couldn't even find a way to have a Roy's moment until the very last day. So, hours before I headed down south with my box of shoes and my two Siamese cats, we agreed to meet for "just a few minutes" before I hit the road.

I pulled up to the same corner we always parked near and saw Emily waiting for me with a smile on her face. "I have something for you," she said, as she pulled out her phone. "It's a playlist...it's for you. I can't explain everything I want to say to you right now, but the music will."

She pulled up the screen and hit share on a thirty-four-song playlist entitled *Inter Nos*. "It means between us," she said, as she tried her very best not to let me hear the cracks in her voice. "Listen to it on your drive down and let me know what you think?"

My second out-of-body, marionette experience happened in the middle of the Grapevine overpass of Interstate 5 as Rihanna's "Love on the Brain" started playing, one hundred fifty miles from San Diego. I had started the playlist about an hour earlier and found myself completely overwhelmed with a hot face, guilt, remorse, fear, and regret.

I pulled over at the top of the Grapevine in the very sad, sun-bleached town of Gorman. "Oh my God," I said out loud, "I'm in love with her." "I'm so in love with her and I cannot spend another second without her." Pulling into a Carl's Jr. parking lot to get my bearings, I texted her back, "I listened to the playlist. It's changed my life." Sitting there, three hours to San Diego, six weeks away from my wedding, I had the breakthrough I'd desperately needed.

I *knew* who I was. I *knew* who I loved. I *knew* why nothing in my life had felt right, until that moment. I knew that I'd spent my entire life waiting to find the person with the key to my core, and she had been there, right in front of me, for years. In that parking spot of a fast-food dive, I decided that I'd rather spend my entire life alone, waiting for her to feel the same way, than lie to myself a moment longer and try to live without her.

In a last-ditch effort to see me, two months before the wedding Emily offered to design Stephen's wedding tuxedo. This meant she would have to fly down to San Diego at least one time before the wedding to accomplish final fittings and adjustments. It wasn't Roy's, but it was the closest opportunity we'd get to be together.

By this time, I was resigned to knowing that while I was absolutely in love with her, there was no way she would have, or could have, the same feelings for me. We were just friends. Nonetheless, I knew this was my one shot to tell her how I felt, even if it was unrequited. I'd yet to find a new job while in San Diego, so I'd been spending my days around the house grappling with this newfound realization of who I was.

My bachelorette party was set for Labor Day Weekend, and the wedding date was set in stone. To build in enough timing, Emily planned to come into town for one afternoon only in the middle of August. Just days before her trip, Emily sent me a bid for connection: "I hope this isn't too uncomfortable for you to hear, but I miss you very much and I want to know what you thought of the playlist."

"I'll tell you when you get here," I replied, as I felt the force of something greater, now for the third time, kicking into gear the plans to reveal my truest, deepest, feelings.

The fitting day arrived, and I spent the morning readying the house for my most coveted guest. I bought bouquets upon bouquets of pink roses to distribute around the house (which of course my cats promptly ate and vomited all over the rug, perhaps channeling my nerves). I stocked the fridge with wine and took myself to Trader Joe's to pick out a greeting card. I felt like I was floating through the store and back to my apartment, like some greater power was my puppet master and I was Pinocchio. I sat down at our table, put the pen to paper, and completely blacked out. It was like a divine being was moving the pen across the paper at feverish speed, spilling onto the cardstock everything I'd kept inside myself for twenty-nine years.

It was you. It has always been you.

I sealed the card, stuffed it in a happy, unassuming yellow envelope, and then headed to the airport to pick Emily up from her 3:35 flight from San Francisco. As I waited in the arrivals line, I knew I had my entire heart written out and it was burning a hole in my pocket. *What would other people think? I'm going to blow up the house and my parents will talk badly about me at dinner parties! How will I explain myself?* At that moment, I didn't care.

My grandmother used to always say never to put anything in writing that you would not want to be read aloud in court. Fitting for my ultimate career choice, but I felt so strongly about my manifesto that at that moment, I wanted to publish it on the front page of the *New York Times*. I'd never, ever felt that strongly or sure in my life about anyone, anything, anywhere. This is what I had always imagined love feeling like, I realized with such relief. I just had to wait for the perfect moment to give it to her.

The fitting was fine, uneventful, and a blur, as I could barely follow the conversation over the beating of my own heart inside my eardrums.

As we readied to go to dinner, in a fraction of a moment alone, I handed her the envelope.

"Here—read this when you're alone."

Emily looked at me with half a smile and a raised eyebrow, but then our moment of privacy quickly ended.

"An early birthday card!" I nervously exclaimed as Stephen came around the corner. We all headed out to dinner. We sat across from one another ("Here, you sit across so we can both look at her," I remember Stephen saying to Emily, in an attempt to be witty), and I triaged my pangs of emotion with cocktails and forced conversation until the clock finally reached 8:30 and it was time to drop Emily off at the airport. I looked at her with the most anticipatory eyes and said, "Happy Birthday." I hugged her at the curb and went home to anxiously wait for the rest of my life to start.

———————

I am sitting alone in the living room when I hear the text message bell sound on my phone. My heart shocks my entire body into consciousness. I'm shaking so much I can barely even enter my passcode to unlock my message inbox.

"Susie...me too."

———————

In April 2021, nearly seven years after running away from the altar, I ran towards it without looking back. Two years prior, on April 6, 2019, Emily asked me to marry her for the third time. It was the same day that, four years earlier, while standing on a bridge in Kyoto Japan, I couldn't even utter an answer. But this time I gave Emily the quickest, most resounding "Yes!"

All my generalized anxiety symptoms completely disappeared. I was able to ramp down from my medications almost immediately, and, after years, I was finally able to sleep soundly through the night. By saying yes to Emily, I said yes to myself, and only to myself. I was able to give my body the break it had been waiting for its entire life.

Emily and I were married under a beautiful rainbow arch in front of our closest family and friends in Montecito, and it was the most certain I'd ever been of any decision I'd ever made in my life. Just like the afternoon I wrote "the card," my vows came pouring out of me and onto the page:

"I always tell you I've been writing these words to you for years. If I were more honest with myself, it would be more accurate to say they have been blossoming inside my mind ever since the first day I met you, over a decade ago on an unseasonably muggy August afternoon. The sunlight streamed in behind you as you walked in the door, casting your smile into spaces of myself I'd buried for years. You never minded the Lateness of the Hour that we came into each other's lives. You embraced it; your acceptance and protection serving as the sweetest Burberry blanket to melt into after what felt like years of standing outside in the rain.

When we are younger, we have such an idyllic picture of how the world will unfold for us, and how we will experience the oft-sought-after moment of peace that love brings, as if it will abruptly appear if we just continue on, check the boxes, do what we "should" do. Yet despite all the wide-eyed optimism (and stubborn grit), we can put into following such a directive, at some point, life begins to show us its splinters, its fractal patterns of grief, pain, unexplainable loss, and uncertainty. And, if we let it, the combination of an inauthentic life and the ink of these darker moments will poison our soul's zest, our heart's hopefulness, and our relentless pursuit of unequivocal love and romance.

There is no clear answer for how to keep going, after so many of these hard moments. And because of them, I often am filled with wonderings, questions, and doubts, but of one thing I am certain. I tell you every chance I get, but today is the most important chance I get. It will always be you that gives flight to the butterflies inside me, calm to the sea I have become, and hope to the darkness all around us. It is you and it has always been you. You who kissed my tired eyes awake, and showed me that true peace lies in finding, living, and loving my true self.

If life is a question mark, then you, Emily, are the proud, bold, period typed with certainty at the end of my answer. And I'd choose you as the answer, in a hundred lifetimes, in a hundred worlds, in any version of reality, I'd find you and I'd choose you.

I will love you through dark winters that simply forget how to end. I will love you through desert heat, through pouring Miami rain, through West Texas dust storms, and San Francisco fog. I promise not to forget how to love you. I promise not to grow weary of it. I won't ever call it a burden or find a way to set it down. I will hold you up and hold you to yourself—I'll save you if you'll save me. I will love you simply, deeply, softly, with a joy that borders on madness, without reservation, and without pre-condition.

Thank you for being alive.

Thank you for finding me.

Thank you for creating a love with me that is the antidote to life's darkest poisons.

Thank you for waiting a decade for my "Yes"—it is yours forever."

It took me three decades to realize I could have—and deserved to have—a credit-roll ending in life. I deserved to embody the feelings that one gets watching the end of a movie, when the camera pulls away over a jet ski speeding through the bay at sunset to a wily saxophone solo.

When I tell this story to new and old friends, strangers, and family alike, I tell them that if they take anything away from my experience, I hope it's that they can always blow up the house and start over. My body was the greatest source of guidance through the process, but only once I allowed myself to listen to what it was saying. I had to learn to make my decisions for myself, saying "yes out loud," for me and only me. It's scary: at times it felt like I was dying but I was actually coming alive.

And in the end, it turns out I did give my parents a very spicy soundbite to tell their friends at cocktail parties.

ABOUT THE AUTHOR

Susie Dent is an out and proud wife, cat mom, and advocate for performing arts and creative writing as integral forms of self-expression, preservation, and authenticity. An attorney by day, she serves as a mentor for younger associates throughout the country, and regularly presents on the intersectionality of Diversity, Equity, and Inclusion issues in leadership, as well as on intergenerational mentorship. When not practicing law, Susie serves as a Parks and Recreation Commissioner for the City of Palm Springs, and spends her mornings mastering aqua aerobics at the local municipal pool. Aside from a PowerPoint slide deck she "authored" entitled "My Life" at the age of nine, this is Susie's first contribution to a published anthology. To learn more about Susie, follow her @susiefmeyer on Instagram.

ANDREA BIRSKOVICH

"I love!" Matt expelled in a small but sure voice, and he turned his head to kiss our mom on the cheek. "I love!" he kept repeating while turning his head from side-to-side kissing each of our cheeks, first one and then the other. In that moment, I experienced the essence of Matt while engulfed by the powerful energy of our soul family connection—how could I not when he'd declared it to me so clearly so as not to be misunderstood? He loved and WAS love. Without thinking, I instinctually opened myself up at the beckoning of my big brother's tender loving energy. Matt and I had always trusted each other implicitly, so I allowed myself to soften and receive every ounce of the love he was giving. In that moment, Matt's love transformed me.

INDISPUTABLE
KNOWING

"What do the nurses say?" I asked my mom as I walked into my brother's room. I'd driven straight to the hospital in East Los Angeles after wrapping up a work trip across town in Beverly Hills. I'd traded one situation where I was leading, and in charge, for another where I had no control. I was trapped in between the polarities of a professional high and a personal low. My choice was either to surrender to a whirlpool of confusion or allow myself to expand to hold both the joy and the pain in equal measure.

It was the summer of 2012 and at thirty-three years old, I had finally hit my professional stride, building a career at a small public relations firm servicing some of Hollywood's premiere film and television studios. Spending long hours slogging away behind a computer screen, I forged relationships with journalists and bloggers. More specifically, mom bloggers were quickly becoming my most valuable partners. They were eager and engaged members of the studios' target audience, and I groomed them to promote my client's latest DVD and Blu-ray releases in exchange for free products. Before they were paid "influencers" or legally contracted "content creators," twenty-five North American mom bloggers of my choosing were flown out to L.A. for an all-expenses-paid three-day trip to promote some of my client's upcoming home entertainment releases, a not-yet-open-to-the-public theme park attraction, and several soon-to-be-released lines of merchandise. The trip had been a huge success, but I wasn't celebrating. My beloved big brother, Matt, had gone to the hospital with an out-of-control pain spike caused by the cancerous tumor lodged in his sinuses.

"The nurses won't touch any real medications without a doctor's orders," my mom replied wearily. She and Matt had arrived via a private ambulance in the early morning hours from Orange County, and no one had expected or prepared to receive them in Los Angeles. With the staff still trying to reach Matt's oncologist, he was admitted, and given a bed in a room on the post-anesthesia floor with patients that had undergone both urgent and elective surgeries. It was a completely inadequate level of care for his leiomyosarcoma and terminal prognosis.

"That's crazy," I said over my shoulder as I turned on my heel and strode out of the room toward the nurses' station. I'd just spent the last three days corralling a bunch of star-struck selfie-shooting moms around an active studio lot, two crowded theme parks, and several busy city streets; I was still in my "get it done" mode.

Even though I was nineteen months his junior, I'd been advocating for Matt our whole lives. Matt lost his sight entirely right after I was born as a result of retinoblastoma, a rare cancer of the eyes. The same tumors were also discovered on my infant eyes, but my sight was spared after a simple surgery when I was only a few months old. In elementary school, Matt's blindness made him an oddity to kids who had never seen any physical disabilities up close, and a target for bullies. Navigating through the corridors to class, kids would sneak up on Matt, waving their hands in his face or standing silently in front of his white cane. Aided by his acute hearing and well-developed proprioception, Matt would slap their hands, stop short, and quickly pivot to maneuver away, but if I was there, I'd retaliate. Using my razor-sharp tongue to administer a good verbal lashing, I was quick to defend my big brother. I would call out the things Matt couldn't see about his bullies—their weight; old, mismatched, or ill-fitting clothes; birthmarks; acne—whatever. Surfacing their vulnerabilities, I'd shame them mercilessly. My attempts to level the playing field for Matt also created distance between myself and others. I built a wall around my tender heart and avoided showing any weakness. I was protective of Matt, and I was indebted to him. After all, I had my vision because Matt had lost his first: the doctors knew to check my eyes when I was born.

While we were growing up, our parents never treated Matt as disabled or fragile; they encouraged his adventurous spirit and his aptitude for music and academics. He'd been living away from home, entirely self-sufficient for fifteen years before his second cancer diagnosis. However, the disease and debilitating side-effects from treatment undermined his autonomy. I knew how hard it was for him to be enfeebled again at thirty-five years old. With our mom enveloped by her own trauma, and his girlfriend frozen with grief, I was one of the most assertive people closest to him, and I didn't hesitate to speak up to demand care for Matt. The summer before his hospitalization, Matt found a private clinic offering personalized treatments for grave diagnoses in Houston, Texas. He had an appointment scheduled, but with his health declining rapidly, I compressed the long drive, got us to the clinic a day early, and insisted that he be seen, and he was. I didn't hesitate to challenge the staff of a private clinic that could easily deny Matt entry, so I wasn't about to let the staff of a public hospital ignore the urgency of my dear brother's need for care.

As I approached the nurses' station, the woman behind the counter did not look up from the computer she was working on. I waited respectfully for her acknowledgment. "Can I help you?" she asked in a monotone voice without diverting her eyes from the monitor.

"Hi, yes," I smiled with tight lips, already annoyed at her detached demeanor. "My brother is in 112B. He's in a lot of pain. I was hoping that you might be able to give him something?" I asked.

Her eyes moved slowly from her monitor to scan the patient roster. "He can have another Tylenol with codeine in an hour," she said. Her eyes still did not meet mine.

"Tylenol?" I asked. "For Matthew Birskovich? He has cancer and prescriptions for morphine, methadone, and gabapentin in his backpack. His pain's a bit beyond what Tylenol with codeine can handle." I tried to chuckle lightly to hide my incredulity.

The nurse slowly lifted her eyes to meet my gaze and exhaled audibly. "We need a doctor's orders to give him anything stronger. Someone will check on him in a few minutes," she said flatly, her eyes returning to the computer monitor.

I could feel the heat creep up my neck and my throat constrict with rage. I wanted to scream, cry, and bang my fist on the counter, but I didn't. I knew better. I had to reign it in, for Matt's sake. These were the only people who could help us now, and we needed them on our side. I couldn't lash out or disrespect them or Matt would pay the hefty price. "Thanks," I grumbled and walked back to Matt's room. The floor was busy with patients and visitors coming and going. The halls were filled with the sounds of phones ringing, monitors beeping, and people chatting. Outside Matt's room, the mood was light as other patients were recovering and going home. Inside, my brother was clinging to life, and "home" felt very far away. We were in the wrong place for so many reasons.

Because I worked full time, I'd been setting aside my grief for eight to ten hours every Monday through Friday. I'd focus on deadlines, status reports, and online banter with my colleagues, until I could finally close my laptop for the day, quickly change clothes, and head to a yoga class. Having moved closer to Matt during his illness, I was able to drop in to see him frequently, but when I let the thoughts creep in—that time was running out, the disease was advancing, treatment options were dwindling, my brother was dying, and it would soon be just my mom and me from our original family of five—the panic and sorrow would overwhelm me. I'd retreat to my apartment, and either smoke weed and watch TV, or take a shower and cry for a much-needed release. At the hospital, there was nowhere for me to run to get away from what was happening to Matt or my feelings about it. I was stuck.

Mom and I each took turns sitting with Matt while the other stepped out to make phone calls, take a walk, or get food. Mom called the answering service for Matt's oncologist in an attempt to get some— any—orders that would better inform the hospital staff of Matt's case and pain management needs. I called family and friends, sharing updates and seeking emotional support. Matt mostly tried to sleep to escape his agony. Periodically, he would wake up a little disoriented.

When the patient in the neighboring bed groaned, Matt awoke and turned to face me. "Huh?" he mumbled weakly.

"What's up?" I asked.

"What did you say?" Matt inquired.

"I didn't say anything," I responded gently.

"Mom?" he persisted.

"Mom's out making a call," I said.

"Who's talking?" Matt asked.

"Oh, it's the guy in the next bed," I said.

"Is he ok?" Matt probed. I couldn't believe that my exceedingly sick brother was still so empathetically attuned in his state.

"Yeah. I think so," I said. "He's recovering. He'll be ok." I watched Matt's breathing start to regulate as he fell back asleep.

With his lungs covered in tumors, Matt's breath had become labored, and he experienced deep and extended coughing fits before he'd even arrived at the hospital. The week before, our mom rented an oxygen concentrator to help facilitate his airflow. She'd brought it to the tiny granny flat Matt shared with his girlfriend. Their place was small, and the droid-like machine gobbled up precious square footage. I visited Matt on the day Mom dropped it off. He was livid. "How the hell am I supposed to live with *this*?" he snarled, kicking the side of the machine with his bare foot. "It's like having another person in here!" He wasn't wrong, but I had to stifle a giggle in response to the emotional outburst from my normally even-keeled brother.

I understood that Matt felt our mom was imposing on not only his space but also his independent decision-making. After witnessing our father's terminal journey with cancer, Mom openly feared that Matt would share his same fate. This morbid expectation was hard for Matt and I both to swallow. Matt for obvious reasons: he was fighting for his life. To maintain his energy and keep going even as his body betrayed him, he needed hope from the people closest to him that he would survive. And me? Well, Matt was my big brother and the one person in the world that knew me better than I knew myself. If he needed me to believe he would survive, then that's what I would do. Our sibling connection deepened while Matt was sick, which I wasn't expecting. We were united in opposition to our mother's cynicism and fear. It was a bond I cherished, and a bond she seemed resentful of. I tried to console Matt that day, telling him we could return the concentrator if he really wanted to. The thing was, it improved his breathing and stamina, and before long, he was using it all day, both while sleeping and awake. He actually *did* need it, though he never admitted it and I never brought it up.

Back in room 112B, Matt wasn't supplied with an oxygen line, and his coughing fits returned with a vengeance. It was during one particularly prolonged coughing fit, that he started to gag and then choke. My stomach dropped and my head spun in a frenzied cyclone of panic and dread. *"This is it,"* I'd thought. *"This is how it ends. He's going to suffocate."* There was no time to alert the medical staff. Standing at his bedside with my hand on his leg, I was entirely present for what was surely the horrific end to our long, painful journey. As Matt struggled for air, I tearfully blurted out all the things I thought might bring him peace, and ease his suffering. "It's okay," I said. "Just let go. It's okay. We'll be alright. You don't have to fight anymore. Just let go."

Without the fit letting up, Matt spat out between coughs, "I…want…a…PHYSICAL…EXPERIENCE!" It was a supernatural moment hearing such strength and rage in his voice despite his debilitated physical body. As if my shoulders were shoved by an invisible force, I stumbled backward away from the bed wide-eyed and stunned. Throughout his illness, Matt always insisted that he wanted to be alive to experience the world no matter how compromised his physical body might be. Matt didn't fear death; he simply loved life too much to accept that it was coming to an end for him. In the hospital that day, it was as if Matt's ego came forward, grabbed my face between its two hands, and spoke to me directly, telling me that his soul would not be "crossed over" into the next life by me or anyone else. The air in the room was thick and charged with the emotional intensity of Matt's assertion. Simultaneously awestruck and terrified,

I said nothing to Matt or my mom before quickly fleeing from the room just as the coughing fit began to pass.

My face was hot and my chest was tight as burning tears streamed down the sides of my nose, and I sped down the hall to the elevator. When the doors opened I dashed in, jamming my finger into the "L" button to take me down to the lobby, frantically hoping that there would be no stops and no one to see me on the verge of falling apart. Arriving at the ground floor, I escaped out the sliding doors into the hot summer sun and called my Aunt Bernie from my cell phone. Out of my dad's seven and my mom's five living siblings, Bernie was the one who checked in on us the most even though she and our Uncle Joe lived in Ohio. She was and is a lifeline for me. Gasping for air between body-shaking sobs, I tearfully shared what just happened in Matt's room. Bernie encouraged me to connect with a hospice nurse. "They can tell you what to look for in the body, so you'll know when the end is near. He's not ready yet," she said. Before I could respond, my phone signaled that my mom was calling. I told Bernie I had to go and clicked over.

"Where are you?" she asked calmly as if I were simply running late returning home from a grocery run and had not just been roared at to mind my own goddamn business by a lion living in my brother's body. I told her I had to get outside. "Are you coming back up? Matt's asking for you. He doesn't know what happened." I made my way back up to Matt's room, and sure enough, he had no recollection of what had just transpired.

When Monday rolled around, and Matt's oncologist finally came to check on him, we were all relieved. The weekend had dragged by with just the bare minimum of care for Matt. After reviewing his chart and assessing his symptoms, Dr. Lee wrote orders to have Matt transferred to a floor with other cancer patients. That afternoon a team of orderlies arrived to facilitate the move. Upon entering the room, the two young men greeted Matt and worked quickly to unplug the IVs and monitors that would accompany him to the next. Worn out and in a morphine haze, Matt didn't say much. Mom and I walked alongside the bed as we headed to the elevator making small talk with the patient care assistants. As his bed was wiggled into the elevator, Matt came to life with a small surge of energy. He turned to one of the guys. "I have the same cancer that my dad had," he wheezed. "Isn't that crazy?" he continued in a weak voice with almost childlike wonder.

"Uh, yeah," the porter responded, caught a bit off-guard by Matt's re-engagement with the conversation. "What kind of cancer is that?"

Matt had already started to slip back into sleep and didn't respond. "Leiomyosarcoma," Mom answered, as his proxy. "He died in 1990," she said. The young man raised his eyebrows slightly and turned back to Matt while nodding as he connected the dots between what my brother and Mom had just shared. He said he was sorry for our loss in the way that people do when grief hasn't yet touched their lives. It was kind, but also sort of thin and empty.

When the elevator doors opened on the eighth floor, the energy was noticeably different. It was calm and quiet, save for the rhythmic beeping of patient monitors. As we passed the nurses' station, the men and women looked up, gently smiling their acknowledgment of our arrival. It was so peaceful, and just…respectful. It was comforting to finally arrive in the place where we belonged—where Matt would be given the attention and care he deserved by a staff that was trained to work with patients just like him. Matt was given a private room with enough space for both a recliner and cot, so Mom and I conveniently took up residence as well.

I'd been so busy advocating for Matt to receive more dedicated care, that I didn't realize until later that the upper floors in a hospital align with the severity and complexity of the patient care being managed. Mom must have known this because she went through a similar escalation with our father before his passing. Dad had been admitted to the ICU with an infection that developed after his surgery to remove a softball-sized tumor from his abdomen. While there, he'd gone from breathing on his own in a sterilized environment to getting intubated and put into a medically induced coma, and eventually, he died from a cardiac arrest when his lungs filled with fluid and compressed his heart. It was only ten months later when Mom found herself in the pediatric ICU of a different hospital holding my two-and-a-half-year-old sister as her body expired after a drowning accident in our backyard pool. The people our mom loved most never seemed to leave the hospital after being admitted, and she saw the writing on the wall.

"I can't lose him, too," Mom said to me as we waited for the elevator to take us back to Matt's floor after an unsatisfactory dinner in the hospital cafeteria. I tried to offer a different perspective, telling her that helping our loved ones cross over was an honor, but with all of her unresolved trauma triggered, she couldn't receive it. "I can't," she repeated, "I can't do it again." We held each other in the hallway. It wasn't looking like she was going to have much of a choice so long as she stayed by Matt's side. I was grateful that in addition to the specialized care administered to my brother on the eighth floor, the staff was also trained to provide emotional support for all of us. And with family and friends coming to visit Matt, I was relieved to have reinforcements showering my mom and me with extra love and support.

I was eleven and twelve respectively when my father and sister died, and my grief was forever eclipsed by the enormity of my mom's losses. "Your poor mom," was the repeated response to our family's tragedies. "No parent should have to bury their child." "It's not natural." "The loss of a child is the worst pain anyone can go through." With these phrases echoing in my head, I grew up devaluing my own grief, denying the trauma of seeing death up-close and personal while still so young. My mom's twenty-seven-month-old baby drowned within a year of her becoming a widow. Twenty years later, her firstborn child lay dying in a hospital bed, and my grief was again overshadowed. When Matt moaned softly in pain or discomfort, Mom rushed to his bedside, hoisting her hip up onto the mattress next to him, wrapping her arms around him, and laying his head on her shoulder. She'd smother him with kisses whispering that it was okay and that she loved him. Her fear, anxiety, and overwhelming desperation were palpable and I felt stifled. There was no space left for my feelings. I knew I had a right to be present. It was important to me to show up, bear witness, and hold space for all that was unfolding for Matt. I couldn't compete with my mom for the space to be physically close to Matt, or with the depth of the loss before us, so I didn't. I just trusted in the bond I had with Matt, knowing that he could sense my presence.

In the days leading up to Matt's passing, he was in and out of consciousness as a result of the morphine and other pain medications being administered in increasingly higher doses. It also became obvious to me that Matt was accessing a different plane of existence during this time. Skeptics might say it was the drugs he was on, but I witnessed my brother attune his energy to the realm beyond the Earth plane. Seeing his transition led me to develop an indisputable *knowing* that there is indeed life beyond the death of our human bodies.

At the end of a dose of his pain medication's efficacy, Matt gritted his teeth while grunting, "uh uh, uh uh, uh uh" in a low voice, as if he was disagreeing with someone or something. I came to understand that this was Matt's flat-out refusal to give in. Death was beckoning, calling him to submit to the pain of his disease, and using all of the energy he could muster, Matt was saying, "No, I'm not going." He was fighting the pain, the temptation to sleep, and the notion that his body was expiring. He had more music to make, a bucket list of things still to experience, and thirty-five years just wasn't enough time for him to offer and create all that he wanted to in the world.

Matt's ex-girlfriend, April, was living in LA during this time, and she made her way to the hospital to be with us. Matt and April had remained close after their break-up, sharing a love and appreciation for music, both making their living as recording and performing artists. April was also a gifted energy worker and medium: she saw auras and communicated with spirits on the other side. After spending time with Matt in the hospital, she shared that he was essentially straddling two worlds with one foot in the physical plane with us, and one in the spirit realm beyond. I began to see evidence of this myself.

Mom and I were in his room, chatting away from Matt's bedside. As we were talking, out of the corner of my eye I saw Matt start to slowly turn his head from side to side on his pillow. It was as if he were listening to different stereo speakers or conversations on either side of his bed. Remembering what April had said about Matt accessing the spirit realm, I thought maybe he was making connections there. "They're talking to you, huh Matt?" I asked.

"Yeah…" he said softly.

"What are they saying?" I asked.

Matt raised his eyebrows: something he did often when he was confused or questioning. He gestured with his hand to one side, "Well, there's these guys," and he raised his other hand gesturing to the opposite side, "and then there's these guys…." He trailed off.

"What are they saying?" I pressed, desperately wanting to know. But before Matt could respond, a coughing fit took hold and stole the moment. A nurse came in to check his vitals and the spell was broken as Matt came back into the reality of the hospital and his disease. So many of our family members had already passed, and I figured they were lined up waiting for him: all four grandparents, our uncle Tommy who'd died before we were born, and our father and sister. I imagined a receiving line of souls ready to embrace Matt and facilitate his transition.

The night before he died, Mom and I were in Matt's room making up our beds for the night, Mom in the recliner, and me in the cot. A respiratory therapist had just left, and Matt was trying to settle in, taking shallow breaths behind his oxygen mask. In a weak voice, he started to mumble some words behind the plastic face covering.

"We're getting ready for bed, honey," Mom said. "Just try to relax and get some sleep."

This did not placate Matt. In fact, he became a little bit more agitated, his voice growing louder, but his words were still unintelligible.

"It's okay, babe. We're not going anywhere. Just rest," Mom said.

With flimsy and fatigued attempts, Matt raised his hand to his face and pushed at the oxygen mask in front of his mouth all the while vocalizing words we could not decipher.

"I think he's trying to say something," I said.

Mom walked over to his bed, and gently slid the mask down below Matt's chin. "I love," he mumbled softly, his jaw heavy and loose from the pain medications. "I love," he repeated with more clarity and conviction.

"And we love YOU!" I responded, my voice filled with emotion.

"I love!" Matt declared and his lips began to purse together making small pecking motions. "I love!" I lept to the opposite bedside leaning in, just in time to receive the sweetest most gentle kiss on the cheek from my big brother. "I love!" he repeated.

"Hey, what about me?" Mom moved to the other side of his bed.

"I love!" Matt expelled in a small but sure voice, and he turned his head to kiss our mom on the cheek. "I love!" he kept repeating while turning his head from side-to-side kissing each of our cheeks, first one and then the other. At that moment, I experienced the essence of Matt while engulfed by the powerful energy of our soul family connection.

How could I not when he'd declared it to me so clearly so as not to be misunderstood? He loved and *was* love. Without thinking, I instinctually opened myself up at the beckoning of my big brother's tender loving energy. Matt and I had always trusted each other implicitly, so I allowed myself to soften and receive every ounce of the love he was giving. At that moment, Matt's love transformed me.

The next day, with family and friends journeying to the hospital to say their last goodbyes, and knowing the end was near, the nurses moved Matt into a larger suite that included a fully furnished lounge area. Mom and I didn't even get a chance at a better night's sleep on the lounge's comfy couches.

Matt died later that night.

We had gathered together with Matt's fan club of close family and friends. We sat in the hospital waiting room eating pizza, rearranging the chairs, and sitting on the floor. We found some levity in the dire situation by sharing stories and laughs. After we ate, Mom and I headed back toward Matt's room, but before we could get through the door, my mom gently tugged my arm, pulling me back into the hallway.

"I just want to wrap him up and take him home," she said. My body froze, and my mind raced ahead. Matt was so fragile, and he was finally getting the medical attention he needed from trained professionals. Why would we leave that behind and go back into the chaos of trying to manage his pain on our own?

"I know that's what he wanted," I said gently, "but they're taking such good care of him here. He's got all of the medications and treatments he needs."

"He might pull through this," Mom said. She was staring at me, willing me to believe. "We might make it to Brazil," she urged. Stunned, I searched her eyes, trying to understand what she was saying. *Was she serious?* Just three weeks earlier, I'd booked plane tickets, secured visas, and found accommodations for the three of us to visit a controversial healer in Abadiania, Brazil—a Hail Mary in Matt's search for a cure. I still needed to find an FAA-approved oxygen tank and a place to refill it in Brazil for Matt to travel. I hadn't even considered that the trip would actually go ahead after Matt was admitted into the hospital. I'd spent the last few days coming to terms with the end of my brother's life, and now I was being asked to imagine his life going on with so many added complications. It was unbelievable to me at the time, and yet, since I'd learned about Matt's diagnosis, everything seemed unbelievable. It was unbelievable that my beloved brother who had suffered through cancer and life-saving treatments as a toddler would be cursed with another more painful cancer in his adulthood. It was unbelievable that Matt should be diagnosed with the same cancer our father suffered and died from. It was unbelievable that after the deaths of my father and sister almost twenty-five years earlier, I would be facing the loss of another member of my immediate family. Everything about this odyssey had been unbelievable, so when my mom floated the far-fetched idea that this was not the end for Matt, I paused and considered it.

"You really think so?" I asked in a small voice with tears pooling in the corners of my eyes.

"Maybe," Mom said with a slightly hopeful inflection.

As we entered his room, my mind clouded with the risks and logistics of Matt leaving the hospital and then traveling abroad. Standing next to my mom at his bedside, I took in the full scene of what Matt had become, looking at his body, not so much as my brother, but as the diseased vessel his spirit inhabited. So much care and attention were required for it just to maintain its essential functions. His was not a body to disturb, much less to remove from the hospital and put on a plane. I looked at Matt's face, his eyes and mouth were open as he breathed rhythmically. He seemed almost vacant: neither asleep, nor awake, but just suspended in time. His tongue curled toward the back of his throat with each breath, which was also odd, and I pointed it out to my mom. While we stood there together, peering into his face, Matt stopped breathing.

Panicked, I rang the call button for the nurse, "Help! My brother's not breathing!" Time stretched, and the seconds it took someone to jog from the nurses' station into the room felt like minutes we didn't have. Matt had a DNR—do not resuscitate—order on file, so there was no rush for the nurses to revive him with any life-saving measures. They simply took his pulse and watched the monitor as it gently slowed and then stopped. My own heart pounded thunderously in my ears as the medical monitors sounded their shrill alarms. I looked up at the clock. It was 9:28 p.m.

"He's gone," the nurse said.

Tears streamed like water down my cheeks. My mom threw herself into my arms. "It's just us, now," she sobbed.

I held her and wept softly.

———

My brother's death broke my heart but it didn't break me completely. I had been distraught and outraged while he was alive and fighting, but in the weeks following his passing, my anger dissolved and I floated around in a bit of a daze. Friends would ask me how I was managing my grief, but the truth? I couldn't even begin to grieve because it felt like Matt was still with me. Sure, I couldn't *see* him or hug him, or hear his raspy breaths, but I could feel him in places I couldn't have felt him when he was alive. It was as if my broken heart had undergone Kintsugi, the Japanese art form of repairing broken pottery using powdered gold to mend the pieces back together. Witnessing Matt's soul transition toppled the walls I'd built around myself, and reconfigured and expanded my broken heart to be able to feel both the immense joy and horrific pain of being alive simultaneously. With

Matt gone, I felt an increase in my energetic frequency. I was vibrating higher and embracing vulnerability. And I noticed that when I stopped bracing myself and instead softened, my pain and loss more easily passed through me in waves. I felt more integrated and aligned with the essential nature of all souls: love.

Before Matt died, one of our last brother-sister outings was to the Irvine farmers' market on a Saturday. The fifteen-minute, mostly traffic-free car ride along a network of Orange County freeways gave us precious alone time to talk uninterrupted about what we were facing. Matt said that he was afraid of the pain in his head increasing to ever unbearable heights. I told him that I hoped that the universe was merciful enough so that his soul would effortlessly transcend to a place beyond that pain before his body could ever experience it. "I just…I'm just not ready for it to all be over," Matt said, a sob caught in the back of his throat.

"But what if it's not *over*?" I responded gently. "What if it's better? Pain-free," I offered.

"There are just things that I'd miss," Matt countered.

"Yeah," I nodded. "Like what?"

"Like playing guitar and music," his voice picked up slightly at the mention of his natural gifts and passion. "I also really love teaching. Like when something just clicks for a student," he said, snapping his fingers lightly. "I really love that 'a-ha!' feeling."

"What if, in the next plane of existence, you live in that 'a-ha' feeling all the time?" I posed. "Like you're not listening to the music anymore, but you *are* the music?" A vision of Matt's soul extending out beyond his human body and flowing like stardust rings around a far-flung planet out in the infinite universe formed in my mind's eye. I imagined Matt's stardust rings being strummed and plucked like guitar strings by the Divine.

I wasn't able to share my vision before Matt conceded, "I don't know. I'm just so tired of this." He sighed, presumably referring to the many doctors' appointments, treatments, medications, and his body's dwindling stamina. "Something's gotta change." I wholeheartedly agreed that the situation was not at all sustainable, and that change was inevitable.

Matt was the light to my shadow; a visionary. His warmth and generous spirit lit people up. My sarcasm and sharp humor could cut someone to the quick. Throughout all of the unpleasant life changes we endured side-by-side, my big brother consistently evolved and expanded through every experience.

Before Matt died, I'd spent years seeking and collecting tools for healing from our childhood traumas. I explored different modalities of therapy led by various practitioners. I learned how to practice yoga and meditate to focus my mind by observing my breath. As my awareness expanded, I observed the stories I told myself about my experiences and feelings. By looking inward, I created space to honor and dive into the pain of losing my father and sister. Plant medicine softened my rough edges formed by sarcasm and sharp wit. My stone-cold cynicism began to melt away and I could laugh and take myself and life less seriously. I was no longer living at the edge of my skin and so easily triggered. I became more at home with myself.

Matt and I guided one another. As children, I took his hand and led him through our shared experiences in the physical world. In turn, Matt led me on a path back to rediscover and trust my intuition. He embraced vulnerability by sharing his soul through the music he made, and he showed me the courage it takes to pursue your path to a purposeful life. In watching Matt surrender to death, I learned how to surrender to life and allow it to unfold, trusting that I was supported by him and all of our other family members on the other side.

For the entirety of our relationship, I narrated the visual world to my blind brother. On car rides, I'd tell him what places and things rushed by our windows. During movies, I sat next to him, whispering each scene's unspoken actions into his ear. Describing things to Matt helped me practice using my voice and articulating my point of view. Matt taught me to look—not with my eyes, but with my soul—deeper into myself, and others, for connection. Witnessing his transition from life to death attuned me to my soul's purpose. As my journey continues without him, I'm called to chase my dreams of fostering more meaningful connections by using my gift of communication. I want to share my offerings with the collective because Matt had wanted so badly to keep learning, growing, and creating in this human experience. My big brother was there the day I was born to welcome me; I was there the day he died to send him off on the next journey; and today, encouraged by my loving connection with Matt, I'm taking steps toward achieving my dreams just by sharing this story with you.

ABOUT THE AUTHOR

Andrea Birskovich has spent half of her life designing marketing and advertising campaigns, crafting communications and content for a variety of products and services, and infusing brands with value while building consumer demand. In seeking a reprieve from a general sense of overwhelm in her early twenties, Andrea found herself watching her thoughts and counting her breaths in a yoga class almost by accident. Since then, she has continued to journey deeper into herself to awaken and reconnect with her intuition, nurture her innate gifts, and rediscover her soul's purpose.

Uncovering the transformative power of grief offered by the successive deaths of her father and baby sister in her pre-teen years, and her beloved older brother in her early thirties, Andrea has only recently embraced her path as a Resilience Guide. In seeking to make meaning from her pain and facilitate soul growth using a wide variety of kinetic, spiritual and energetic practices, she's grateful for the ability to empower others simply by sharing what she learns. She's currently on a path to use her marketing and communication skills to promote healing modalities that have served her, and shed light on the strength and endurance within all of us.

Andrea currently lives by the beach in Santa Cruz, California, with her chiweenie Stanley Stretch Jones. She shares snippets, snapshots, and sass at @hi.andreanicole on Instagram.

LONNA WHITING

After ten years in search of meaning and peace, I eventually realized Mom's slow disintegration into dementia had been feeding me a unique kind of knowledge, one about bearing witness to someone losing her mind and what my role was in holding the pieces for her. Like the best worst junk food, I just couldn't (and can't) seem to get enough. It was my turn to take on the role of nurturer in this world, for her and for myself, and I'd been doing it all along without knowing it. I was her voice and my voice simultaneously, and at times, when all the conditions were set just right at the table, it consumed me alive over and over.

DINING AT THE
DEMENTIA CAFE

Some people eat to live. They track protein versus carbohydrate intake, hydration, macros, blood sugars, uric acid profiles, potential vitamin deficiencies, saturated fats—all in a quest for ideal body mass and lowered disease risk. Calories go in. Calories come out. It's all about balance, measurement, and the comfort that comes from knowing they've done what they can to be as healthy as possible. Food isn't as much a pleasure as it is a deposit into a hypothetical longevity bank.

I love these people because they make me feel like every time I eat a kale salad I've added fourteen years to my life. I also hate them because even if they're just some wellness influencer I follow on Instagram, they seem to just *know* when I so much as side-eye a powdered donut in the bakery case while at the grocery store— obviously buying kale.

Others live to eat. They take great joy in serving up plates of comfort to themselves and the people they love. Funeral casseroles, family grill-outs, office potlucks, bake sale fundraisers, happy hour appetizers, afternoon teas, Sunday brunches. For those in the live-to-eat camp, food is meant to nurture the soul. Food is a pleasure designed to be experienced in the moment, not in a future where—let's be real—there are no guarantees.

Actually, these are also my people. Food is both medicine for the body and a prescription for experiencing a life well-lived. I might add fourteen years to my life eating that kale salad, but tomorrow I might also fall onto an open dishwasher full of sharp knives—blades up—and bleed out before I can muster my final, embittered words: "Should. Have. Eaten. Powdered. Donut. …"

However I'm feeling about food on any given day (Kale v. Donut), it's not lost on me how strongly food has influenced me over the course of my lifetime. How often have I manhandled a bag of jalapeno kettle chips after a stressful day at work? How many homemade pizzas have I thrown in the oven for guests and celebrations? How many Pinterest-worthy salads-in-a-jar have I tossed together and then tossed in the garbage? A lot. Food has been my best friend and my biggest enemy. I've used it to self-soothe and self-sabotage. I've used food to hurt my stomach and heal my heart. I've experienced binges of delight and purges of regret in equal measure. Almost always, I've used food to give sustenance and meaning to the slow-cooked loss of my most potent source of nurturing: my mother.

For the past ten years, I've had the honor of holding a VIP reservation at The Dementia Cafe, where grief expert Elisabeth Kubler Ross serves me endless platters of her world-famous dishes: denial, anger, bargaining, depression, and acceptance. Every time I've taken a generous pass through the buffet line, moving from the desperation of denial all the way to acceptance, chef Ross is right there standing by the desserts saying, "You haven't had enough yet. Go back for more."

One star. Do not recommend.

This long-haul grief isn't any person's fault. It's The Dementia. It's my mother who got it, or rather, it got her. To be more historically accurate, it all goes back to 2010 when, at age 58, she started showing symptoms. Of course, that's the time of one's life many consider the prime, when she was supposed to be feasting on the fruits of her labors, preparing for retirement, enjoying her grandchildren and imparting the wisdom of her years on the progeny she so lovingly tended to for decades. Only, The Dementia picked my mother's prime of life apart piece by piece. Is it something Mom ate? No. But as my longtime partner Kevin says, it's "a total shit sandwich" nonetheless.

Admittedly, I had strong emotions and unhealthy attachments to Mom The Person, my most devoted companion, my favorite eating buddy, and my greatest teacher. At first and for many years, I took on every single part of her she lost to The Dementia and made it a part of me instead. Just after diagnosis on October 4, 2013, I secured power of attorney, and from then on I made all her decisions. I legally and emotionally became her. Put another way, when The Dementia managed to swallow her autonomy seemingly overnight, I reached into its mouth and snatched what I could right back. *Mother, I am now you. How am I doing?*

When The Dementia came for what was left of her independence, I found her a place to live at an assisted living facility. *Mother, you're safe and clean. There is nothing else to be done.*

And when it took her personal history, I held onto the people she loved the most. *Mother, your dad's name was Bob. He was a good man.*

When The Dementia devoured my name from her tongue, I spit it out for her again and again and again. Mother, *I am your daughter. My name is Lonna.*

When The Dementia chewed up her own name, I fed that right back to her. *Mother, your name is Beth. You are beautiful.*

When The Dementia inhaled her ability to walk, I wheeled her around. *Mother, the world is still going by. You are still a part of it.*

When The Dementia sucked up her laugh, I laughed for her. *Hahahahahahaha.*

When The Dementia ate her smile, I smiled for the both of us. *Mother, do you know how much I love you?*

One star. Do not recommend.

That's not to say that every waking moment of the last 3,300 days (who's counting?) since Mom's diagnosis has been all about repeatedly circling the seven levels of Dante's Inferno. There have been many good moments with Mom, even in the end-of-life version of her I witness today. And there's always been food, which was our thing since I can remember because Mom and I were ride-or-die best friends. Before The Dementia took the driver's seat, we became quite the culinary explorers together. Food gave our pre-dementia adult relationship with one another a rich sustenance. All the pre-D food experiences we created and consumed gave us adventures we wouldn't have otherwise had.

"Let's go to Chicago and eat a bunch of Ethiopian food," so we took the Amtrak and went to Mama Desta's.

"I want to try a New York slice for my thirtieth birthday," so we flew there and ate our way across the city.

We learned how to roll dolmades and California rolls on the same kitchen counter I sat on as a child while she rolled out sugar cookies. We made vegan lasagna with paper-thin slivers of zucchini and homemade marinara. Not all our adventures were successful. One time, Mom tried making tea rolls from scratch and ended up with inedible rocks we tossed outside for the birds to pick apart. I overcooked $200 worth of wild-caught Alaskan salmon at our family's lake cottage one drunken summer weekend. During one particularly creative collaborative effort, we almost burned down the house making from-scratch calzones for Kevin's birthday.

But the best food always took us back to the basics, the family favorites. Egg bakes on Sunday mornings. Beer cheese soup (one brick Velveeta, one can cream of mushroom soup, one can Miller Lite), ground beef casseroles with cheese topped with tater tots, chicken Kiev and mashed potatoes, spaghetti and meat sauce, plates toppling with buttered garlic toast.

And of course, futschki at Christmas.

What is futschki? Great question. Some families make Christmas ham. Others get takeout Chinese food. Ours had futschki, an eastern European peasant dish made of little gnocchi-sized bread balls and gobs of sauerkraut browned in pounds of salted butter. And milk. Because nothing says "Happy Birthday, Jesus!" like a plate full of soggy bread balls soaked in fermented cabbage, grease, and hot dairy.

The process of making futschki began several days ahead of the yuletide feast and put my mother in a foul mood. It never occurred to any of us to help her assemble the deceptively simple dish, which by the way, has no origins other than speculative, which is that some great-great-great grandmother of ours concocted it out of necessity and called it "futschki," pronounced 'foo-tsch-kee,' which I *totally* think sounds like a German lady trying to say "fuck" while sneezing.

Unfortunately, there came a time for every young woman in my family to learn how to make futschki in order to perpetuate the venerated holiday meal for generations to come, and also because the senior matriarchs eventually tired of stirring sauerkraut in the kitchen while everyone else played cards and drank beer in front of the TV. They, too, wanted to watch "A Charlie Brown Christmas" and win a hand of gin-rummy. So at age thirteen, a moment in my moody, hormonal, greasy-faced teenage years that couldn't possibly have been chosen at a worse time, Mom yanked me from my angsty bedroom bunker and said, "Time to make the balls."

In the kitchen she had everything set up. The oven was preheated and ready to go at 350 degrees. The pans were greased. The loaves of frozen Rhodes bread dough had been thawed and were resting on the counter like little baby buttcheeks squeezed together. The first step was cutting the bread dough into quarter-inch squares, then rolling them in our palms until they were perfectly round and the size of large marbles.

As we went along, Mom explained the origins of futschki and some essential rules.

"Futschki is made with bread. Haluschki is made with potatoes."

"You have to get the bread balls nice and stale or it won't turn out. That's why we start a week ahead of Christmas Eve."

"Only make haluschki if you have potatoes that need using."

"You don't have to like futschki, but you have to at least take a bite or Grandma will think you want her dead."

Since then, I've made futschki one time and it was a disaster not worth repeating. Plus, there are other reasons I don't make futschki that have nothing to do with my distaste for them and instead have to do with one of the first times I noticed something wrong with Mom's mind. It was two Novembers before diagnosis and just ahead of our final "normal" Thanksgiving and the holidays when she called me on the phone.

"Will you come help me with the futschkis this year?" she asked. I assumed she was just planning ahead, which looking back on it now was odd because Mom wasn't much of a planner.

"We've got time," I told her. "What's the rush?"

The next day she called me again to inquire about making the balls. "We're going to have to make futschki soon. Can you help?"

Instead of acquiescing to her repeated requests, I yelled at her in frustration. "We'll get the balls done! Don't worry about it." Then I hung up on her and never did help her make futschki that year—or ever again.

Whenever I wonder how much longer someone can survive for as long as she has, I think about futschki and learning how to make it. Today, it seems like a miracle Mom ever knew how to work her hands through a loaf of bread dough, or how to brown butter, or how to heat up the milk just so without scalding. It seems like a dream, because in her present self, Mom has retreated in her shell, like an oyster dropped too long in water. I know she is still my mother, but she is also not. I know she is still beautiful, but she is also not.

There were many food-related dementia warning signs that should have tipped me off more than they did, but all my denial kept things comfortable, like eating at Olive Garden. The endless soup, salad and breadsticks are *comfortable*. Consistent.

But she hadn't been consistent in a while. Several months earlier we were out for pizza. Mom: "I just can't figure out what to order."

Then we went for drinks and appetizers. Mom: "How do I calculate this tip?"

Then we went for Indian food. Mom: "Let's go get that one food. You know … um … that spicy stuff with the cheese in it."

Lying to myself was comfortable, like a lukewarm Olive Garden breadstick dipped in minestrone. I subsisted on this denial for a long time.

But then I found a full plate of nachos in her cereal cupboard.

Then she forgot how to feed the babies under her care at the daycare she'd operated for thirty-seven years.

Then she voluntarily entered a psych ward where she failed a mini mental exam.

Then she called me and whispered two words: "It's dementia."

It was the first time of many that I heard Elisabeth Kubler Ross whisper in my ear: *Move over, denial. Time for some anger!* That anger fueled a hunger inside of me, for answers, of course. But something else, too. Aside from the *Why her? Why me? Will I get it?* questions that followed, there was a need to conduct a life of normalcy like my peers. But Mom's illness changed the future I thought was in front of me. I got fired from my copywriting job, I drank too much, I emotionally abused myself and Kevin.

The anger lasted for years and came out in odd ways at odd times, like when Mom lived with us briefly before she moved into assisted living in December 2013. She had progressed quickly that summer and she wasn't safe on her own at home. There was no money for luxuries such as in-home care service or a live-in caregiver, so she moved in with us for a few months. Having her stay in our spare bedroom was a fine solution for a time, but I was never cut out for being a full-time caregiver. I would have killed her. Then myself.

Cooking an evening meal—such a simple and methodical activity of daily living I typically enjoyed—brought out the worst in me. One night, I was chopping stir fry vegetables while I kept Mom busy at the sink rinsing bell peppers under cold water. I crushed some garlic using a butcher knife when she leaned in and asked, "How do you do that?" She'd lost her way in a most familiar place: the kitchen. The place we'd made so many meals. Shared so many laughs. Rolled so many futschki balls. Hearing her say, "How do you do that?" forced me to understand my Mom was going missing, or had at least wandered to a dimension wholly inaccessible to the rest of us. One where the familiar turned unfamiliar. Knowing shifted to unknowing. Remembering turned to dust. I also realized The Dementia had gifted me with two shadows, hers and mine, neither of which I wanted.

That's when, while stirring garlic tamari sauce, I lost it and slammed a wooden spoon onto the counter until it splintered in two.

I screamed at my mother. "Get the fuck away!" Her cheeks burnished in shame as she said, "You're mad." She shuffled out of the kitchen, found Kevin in the TV room, sat down and cried.

As I watched her shadow behind me get smaller and smaller, my memories came to me larger than ever. All those futschki balls. My berating her for not remembering the name of our favorite Indian restaurant (Saffron). All the forgetting and confusion. The denial. The clues. All of it came to me then in a rage that continued to slice me to pieces for years.

Long before where we are now on our journey at The Dementia Cafe. Long before this sigh of acceptance, and the end-stage calm and the quiet evenings when I now visit to feed her soft-boiled eggs, banana custard, and rub her scalp with leave-in conditioner, and get low to her ear and whisper, "I love you. I love you so much." Long before she lost the word for mom, for daughter, for love. Long before my rage and self-harm, my drinking and denial, her diagnosis, her early signs, our dinners out, my New York birthday, our train trip to Chicago, our dolmades and vegan lasagna. Long before I got myself down to 103 pounds on a diet of Saltines, Coca-Cola, and Marlboro Mediums. Long before her comfort casseroles and beer cheese soups and spaghetti with towers of buttered garlic toast. Long before I recognized the scent of my mother whenever I peeled an orange. Long before all that living, Mom taught me about how food was also fuel for shame.

I was four.

My quintessential '80s mom, with her '80s perm and high-waisted jean shorts, had bought some very '80s weight-loss regimen from a mail-to-order catalog. The diet program consisted of vials of vitamins and supplements that smelled of plastic and the milk bones we gave our dog Sam.

Mom took her vitamins and supplements in the mornings with a cup of coffee and a half grapefruit sprinkled with Sweet'N Low. She was very crabby. I've kept a polaroid of her from around this time. It shows her standing in her bedroom wearing her bra and underwear. On the back of the photo, she'd scribbled, "Beth, 1983. 160 pounds." She looked shy and ashamed, but to me she looked more beautiful than ever. Curly brown hair cut short, oversized, thick-framed glasses, creamy white skin, lightly glossed lips. She was my mom. She was a miracle.

I suspect the diet also had something to do with wooing my father, too. The affairs were already well-documented after he'd crashed a friend's van and shattered his foot while drunkenly cruising around for other women. Like a lot of people I know, when we're starved for love and affection, we hurt ourselves rather than nurture ourselves. "Here, eat this dry grapefruit with gross fake sweetener on it," the diet gurus said. "And don't complain about being hungry because your husband is going to ravage you with lust once you finally get rid of all that baby weight!"

The diet program also came with special snacks, such as assorted rice cakes and crackers to satiate the appetite and sugar-free lemon drops and mints to quell the desperation.

Around the time "The Young and The Restless" came on the TV, Mom would pull out her special diet crackers for a mid-afternoon snack. She'd neatly place five on a small plate and dolloped a little cottage cheese on top of each one.

Oh, how I wanted to try one of her diet crackers! Often, I stood next to her chair and watched her eat them while "The Young and The Restless" played on the TV. I'm certain I'd reduced myself to the level of our dog Sam, begging at the side of the table for whatever scraps were mercifully tossed to the floor. But I didn't care. My focus was on the crackers.

Then one day my efforts paid off.

"Just one!" she said.

Mom begrudgingly pulled a cracker out of the box and handed it to me. If she was any good at diets, she knew how many crackers were in that box and just how many were in her budget for the day, but of course I didn't come to this understanding until later in my life when I knew how to count calories better than I could do any other math, which is saying a lot because I'm shit at math.

I took a nibble. It was delicious and tasted like the buttered toast my grandpa made for me when I had an earache, which was often because my dad was an unrelenting cigarette smoker. As in most situations when good food is present, I wanted more of it, so I climbed onto my mother's lap under the guise that I wanted to snuggle, only I was really going after the box of crackers. I slid my arm across my mother's stomach, sighed, reached for the box and slipped my hand in to nab a treat.

She violently slapped my hand away. "No more!" she yelled. It was the first and only time she'd ever hit me.

While the incident gave me my first taste of food shame that's lasted my entire life, since she got sick, I've fed my mother whatever her heart desired 100 percent shame-free because I knew the outcome in the end would be the same: The Dementia would win no matter what I did or didn't let her eat. So if anyone would like to argue with me, "Well, there are studies that show a ketogenic diet can reverse signs of Alzheimer's and dementia," or "Just give her a tablespoon of unrefined coconut oil with her morning oatmeal and she'll pop right back to life," I can certainly regale you with the research I've collected during the past ten years that shows the number of people cured of dementia or Alzheimer's by following a certain diet or protocol. Actually, I'll save you the time. It's a whopping zero. There are zero survivors of Alzheimer's.

For all the times she ate diet crackers in her life, none of it has mattered in the end. None of that self-imposed food restriction did Mom any good. In the end, the appetite goes anyway, which I learned in 2019 when Mom quit eating for the first time. At that point, caregivers at her memory care facility attempted to entice her appetite back to life with her favorites: cheeseburgers, spaghetti, beef stew, cheesecake, strawberry shakes. "She's just not eating," they said right before she was admitted to hospice.

It didn't take long before she lost fifty pounds, reducing her once-generous frame to bones and sagging skin. As she transformed into this end-stage Alzheimer's version of herself I see today, she slowly started to look more like me than ever. For the first time in Mom's life, she had visible cheekbones like mine. This is something I did not like at all. People said, "Wow, you look like your mom," more and more often than ever before. To me, that translated to, "You're going to end up just like her. Wasting away. No mind left. Alone." When my head goes to that place of fear, which it does often, I tell myself:

As long as someone makes sure I'm lotioned head to toe every day!

As long as someone spoon feeds me vats of Ben and Jerry's!

As long as someone remembers I'm still here!

Eventually, the time came when I fed my mother for the first time. We'd gone a year and a half without seeing each other in person because of the pandemic, and by the time I was allowed back into the facility for visits, The Dementia had purloined her ability to walk, talk, and feed herself.

Our countless virtual visits made it seem like Mom was doing better than she actually was, maybe because Bonnie, the activities director in charge of family Zooms, had a way of getting Mom to smile and occasionally say something during our calls. Maybe it was also because by nature of experiencing Mom's progression from behind the screen, I was being fed only as much reality that could be revealed on a thirteen-inch computer screen, which wasn't much. Either way, the virtual visits were better than nothing and almost always involved a cheerful topic about the facility's daily food menu.

"It's been a good day," Bonnie would say to Mom. "We had taco in a bag for lunch and some yummy carrot cake just now. Didn't we, Beth?"

For a while Mom would respond with a simple "Yes," but as the months went on she stopped saying words completely, something I didn't actually notice until hospice sent me her updated medical chart that listed her as "nonverbal."

"That sounds delicious, Mom!" I'd yell at the screen, trying to pry her attention back from the void. "I had split pea soup, so definitely not so good." And then I laughed, Bonnie laughed, and Mom stood up out of her chair and shuffled out of view. That was always my cue the call was over, so I'd say my "I love you" to a screen showing an empty chair and half of Bonnie's PPE'd face, then go back to work. Most calls lasted less than five minutes and I was left craving futschki of all things. Given the opportunity, I would have shoved those buttery balls with sauerkraut down my gullet with gusto. Hell, hand over the diet crackers, too.

About the time she lost weight and went on hospice, all of her words left, then her cheerful laugh went next, another gut punch among countless over the years courtesy of The Dementia. I lost track years ago how many times I've asked, *"What could you possibly take next, Dementia?"* And then it would take another slice of my mother, and as a consequence, a little bit of me, too.

After several months of these virtual visits, the facility called to tell me I could physically reenter the facility under new criteria called compassionate care visits reserved for family members with residents on hospice whose life expectancy was predicted at less than three months. I also had to be fully vaccinated and wear a mask and a face guard. They told me they'd supply the PPE, but that I'd have to ring the security door, sign a statement that to the best of my knowledge I was not showing symptoms of covid, nor had I been exposed to covid in the past fourteen days. I had to have my temperature checked upon arrival and sanitize my hands.

Also as part of the compassionate care allowance, I had to commit to performing at least one activity of daily living on behalf of my mother. Obviously, I chose feeding.

Feeding felt like the easiest way to contribute to Mom's daily care, and by some small miracle, she could still chew and swallow without trouble most of the time. In my opinion, the residents prescribed pureed diets had it the worst. Essentially, kitchen staff took whatever was on the menu for the able-to-chew crowd, and stuffed it in a blender with some chicken broth until it was the consistency of no-longer-a-choking-hazard. Over the years, I'd seen all sorts of meals pulverized into soup that should never be made into soup. Cheeseburgers and fries, eggs and toast, hot dogs and buns, spaghetti and meatballs, fish and chips. One time, an entire pepperoni and cheese pizza.

My compassionate care visits were confined to her room (for the safety of staff and other residents). Staff delivered her dinners to us on a cafeteria tray with a bib (for necessity) and a cloth napkin (for posterity). The first meal I fed her was a one-time family favorite Mom used to make often during the cold winter months: hamburger hotdish, otherwise known as a goulash of stewed tomatoes, ground beef, and elbow macaroni. For a side, they'd buttered a piece of whole-wheat bread, and dessert was banana cream pudding with a spray of canned whipped cream on top. It was no futschki, but I was happy to have one last way to connect with her. In fact, I craved it.

Feeding Mom was more difficult and messy than I'd imagined. Bits of hamburger fell off the fork, butter from the bread melted into my fingers when I held it up for her to take a bite. She didn't always chew everything, so I was constantly on edge about her pocketing food in between her cheeks and risking a choking incident.

I spilled. A lot. "Oh-shit-sorry-Mom," came out of my mouth on a number of occasions. As did the following:

Did I even make that into your mouth?

Why is this beef gray?

You must like this food or you wouldn't eat it.

How did that entire English muffin get in my shoe?

What if I accidentally kill you?

Fear of potentially committing matricide aside, giving her water was the hardest. I must have missed that day in Dementia Caregiving 101 when they explained food and beverage as a choking hazard. Nobody told me how to tip the lip of the cup just enough to wet her tongue but not too much that she'd choke. The result was me basically waterboarding my own mother the first time I helped her take a drink. *Oh-shit-sorry-Mom.*

"Maybe let's try a straw next time," I said to her. To my surprise, she responded to that by laughing, probably at me, not with me. But still. The act of feeding her created a new language for us that we could share, a kind of connective tissue that brought me incredible joy and peace. Knowing that calories, carbs, fat content, sugar, all that bullshit just didn't matter anymore was a bonus, and soon I was bringing her Big Macs and fries, shakes, tacos, shrimp baskets, and helping her eat as much as she wanted completely guilt-free. She would never ever have to eat another diet cracker in her lifetime.

Because The Dementia takes away literally everything, Mom continued to lose weight despite all the high-calorie, hyper-palatable foods I fed her. Sometimes I think she'd be so pleased to know she's down to 115 pounds. "Mom, you're finally a size small." And then I remember that she's lost every single bit of who she once was and she's never getting it back. Like the pleasure of washing your own hair and brushing your own teeth. The joy of a conversation with a good friend. The freedom of driving a car. The sensation of getting out of a chair and stepping one foot in front of the other and feeling the earth beneath your feet. The freedom of making a decision for yourself. Using a fork. Drinking from a cup. Gone. Gone. Gone. Gone. Gone. Now her appetite comes and goes. She'll eat breakfast but sleep through lunch. She'll want half a dinner and then a late-night snack, or nothing at all. When her world has become so small, I imagine eating a meal takes a lot of energy out of her. I know she is tired. But I also know she's still ready to tuck into an Oreo or two. Most of the time.

Because it's not too late for me to slow the progression or prevent my own dementia, I am more often than not choosing kale over donut. I've curtailed the consumption of most comfort foods, aside from the occasional homemade pizza or post-long-run plate of cacio e pepe. I quit drinking alcohol, not only because it was absolutely destroying me, but also because it's a known neurotoxin. I run a lot because what's good for the heart is good for the brain. All these tactics could save me, or they could be all for naught and only time will tell, but if I do end up like my mom, I can say I did my best with the knowledge I have. This effort matters, even if it's futile. Trying gives me a little hope when faced with a disease some refer to as "a fate worse than death."

Not too long ago, I visited Mom during regular dinner time. On the menu: chicken and rice with black beans, cornbread, peach cobbler, and ice cream. By this time, I'd been helping her eat for two years and considered it a point of pride that I rarely needed to put a bib on her anymore. After much trial and error, I'd figured out just how she liked to eat and what kinds of foods she needed to cut up a little extra, like chicken or a hamburger. Over that time, helping Mom eat had become the greatest source of connection I'd had with her for years. It provided me with a chance to give her nourishment, and in turn, she nourished me with a rare smile or a tapping of her foot. "This is delicious, thank you very much," she seemed to say. We'd once again developed our own kind of connection through food. Our tools: bowls of beef stew, corn bread, succotash, apple pie, tacos, mac and cheese, ice cream sundaes, and many, many cups of ice cold apple juice.

Then, after I had just forked a piece of cooled-down chicken into her mouth, Mom started choking. Not just her typical needed-to-clear-her-throat coughing fit, but a real choking like I'd only seen in CPR training videos or hospital dramas. I watched her for a few seconds until her face started to burnish. When she started turning purple, I grabbed Bonnie from her office across the hallway.

"I think she's choking," I said in a surprisingly calm voice that didn't sound like my own. We pulled Mom up by the armpits to get her more vertical, which was difficult. The contracture made her stiff and reminded me of trying to bend a Barbie doll into a seated position.

Bonnie started swatting Mom's back and I just stood there in the way—the exact opposite thing you're supposed to do in an emergency situation. In fact, I'd been through first aid training a while back and the most important PowerPoint slide in the deck, the one that spelled out what *not* to do in an emergency situation, listed in bold, red letters: ONCE EMERGENCY PERSONNEL ARRIVE ON SCENE, GET OUT OF WAY.

But it was my mom, and if this was it, I was going to be there for it as I'd promised. Inside, though, all my anxiety dropped to the pit of my stomach and my heart thumped so fast I thought I was going to throw it up. *This is it. She's going to die from choking on a piece of dry chicken and I'm going to watch every agonizing second of it. In slow motion because it feels like an eternity since she took a breath and now she's looking at me for the first time in months. Straight at me and we're mother and daughter all over again, and Elisabeth Kubler Ross is yelling at us, "Acceptance! Acceptance! Acceptance!"*

I was terrified. Not only because Mom looked terrified, and rightfully so, but also because in the forty seconds it took to clear her airways, I both wanted and didn't want it to be the end. What would the next moments look like if we couldn't jostle her airway clear? Would she keep looking at me, so scared and helpless? Would she grant me some mercy and just close her eyes so I didn't have to look into them? Maybe she'd say one final word, her personal favorite, "Shit!" and then slump over in her Broda chair. It would have been a brutal conclusion to a ten-year journey to die from choking on dry chicken, but it maybe would have been okay. I mean, it would have had to be okay.

We eventually cleared Mom's throat and I stayed with her until she could breathe normally and was willing to take in a few bites of a chocolate sundae. I was relieved, naturally, that I didn't have to watch her die right then and there, but I was also disappointed. *How much longer can this go on? How much longer can she take? How much more can I take?*

Your mind will go to odd places in a life-or-death crisis, like watching your mother choke. Aside from the existential dilemma of potentially watching someone take their last non-breath before being ushered into the next plane of existence, while Mom was choking, Mayo was on my mind. Not mayonnaise, per se. The Mayo Clinic in Rochester, Minnesota. The place Mom got her formal (super unhelpful) diagnosis of "Dementia, Not Otherwise Specified." The clinic is named after the world's most contentiously debated condiment (mayo). Actually, it's named after a doctor, but it's pretty much impossible to not think about mayonnaise because nobody ever says "Mayo Clinic." It's always just "Mayo" or "The Mayo." Like, whenever I say, "We went to Mayo," or "She saw doctors at Mayo," I end up craving a tuna sandwich.

If only it was Miracle Whip Hospital instead and there was some groundbreaking treatment, like "Make one ham sandwich, lather it in as much Miracle Whip as it can hold before it turns into a soggy mass of bread and deli meat. Eat. Repeat as needed until memory is restored." Maybe if it was Miracle Whip Hospital, we might have had a chance in hell of fighting anything. Anything at all.

Except it didn't go that way at all. Dementia feeds on grief all the way to the last bite and there's nothing that mayo the condiment or Mayo the clinic can do to fix it. After ten years in search of meaning and peace, I eventually realized Mom's slow disintegration into dementia had been feeding me a unique kind of knowledge, one about bearing witness to someone losing her mind and what my role was in holding the pieces for her. Like the best worst junk food, I just couldn't (and can't) seem to get enough. It was my turn to take on the role of nurturer in this world, for her and for myself, and I'd been doing it all along without knowing it. I was her voice and my voice simultaneously, and at times, when all the conditions were set just right at the table, it consumed me alive over and over. But not in a bad way. Just consistently, like in an all-you-can eat soup, salad and breadsticks from Olive Garden way.

Since the near-choke incident, I've committed to visiting Mom less. Not because I want to, but because I have to. I have to start extricating myself from her or I worry I won't ever find myself again. I'll be lost in the desert for good, probably without any dessert options. Mom wouldn't want that. I certainly don't want that. I can't keep saying "I'll take the trip after Mom dies," or "I'll move away once she's gone," because I've been saying that for a decade, and if dementia knows how to do anything, it knows how to take its damn time.

The abundance of time, energy and resources I've poured into her must come back to me, and the only way that can happen is by taking it back for myself. So now I visit once a week or less, and when I hold her hand and pop fried potato coins dipped in nacho cheese sauce in her mouth, it's still about the connection it provides, but it's also about telling her story and leaving plenty of word count left over for myself. This time is more sacred than ever. I've had a decade to figure out how to heal and I think I'm only just figuring out how. For me, that begins with understanding that even in loss, I can find the abundance I need to at least move on. I shall eat the kale and then the donut. And some diet crackers, too.

Besides, during my seemingly eternal rounds at The Dementia Cafe, I have memorized our journey forwards and backwards. I don't need to taste futschki ever again to know Mom once knew how to make the balls. What's important is it happened and I have the absolute honor of documenting everything about her. I get to talk about Grandpa Bob and his homemade cologne. I get to tell her she's always smelled of oranges, cheerful just like her. I get to whisper in her ear, "I love you. I love you so much." I get to use the wooden spoon I once slammed into the counter until it splintered. "Please forgive me, Mom, for being so cruel. For turning my back on your shadow," I think. Maybe most importantly, I get to start telling my own story.

Even though I'm turning down the volume on her voice, I'm doing it so I can turn the volume up on my own. I am learning to feed myself first and Mom next because she won't be hungry for much longer and I'll still be here afterwards. Still hungry for life and thinking, "Let's go to London for fish and chips," and then I'll go because she'd want me to eat that most basic ingredient for living, which is just love. So simple. So sweet. So essential.

Five stars. Definitely recommend.

ABOUT THE AUTHOR

Lonna Whiting is a freelance writer, editor, and communications consultant who lives in Fargo, ND. She holds a Master of Fine Arts in Creative Writing from Minnesota State University Moorhead and writes frequently about her experience as a caregiver to her mother who has been living with early-onset dementia since 2010. You can follow her on Instagram @lonnawhiting.

GIA MARIAM HASAN

**This chapter contains sensitive content
pertaining to sexual abuse.*

*In my desert of abandonment, I couldn't see the whole context of
my life. I existed in the wasteland and void where the options were
limited. Once I could see my humanness, I could take accountability
for how my hurt affected me and those around me. This admission
and accountability softened me further, and I could access a space in
myself where reimagination was possible. I could make new choices
about my life.*

THE
ORIGINAL
WOUND

My father never wanted me.

This isn't a story of blame, but simply a fact of my origins. Or more precisely, what I have chosen to be the beginning of the story: conception. I was to be the fourth child, born after three sons, and yet another unexpected pregnancy for my mother. Her whole heart was invested in this unborn child, but my father didn't share the same eagerness. Instead, he condemned his pregnant wife and insisted she "take care of it" because he couldn't raise another child. He didn't speak to my mother for three months, in the hopes that she would extinguish the earliest whispers of my existence. Her determination outweighed his demands, and I was born five weeks premature into the open arms of my mother. It took me decades, and plenty of therapy, to understand that this feeling of being unwanted and disposable began in those early developmental stages, and it's taken a windy, treacherous road to connect the dots.

I could tell a lot of stories of the several wounds of my childhood, but beneath them all is the original wound. The story of abandonment, of not belonging, of not mattering. Ironically, or not so ironically, both my parents have deep experience with this wound. The genesis of epigenetic and intergenerational patterns and pain is too challenging to trace back to the beginning, because, where is the beginning? Do we really know where to map this and find the starting place? For me, I had to begin somewhere. My brain wanted a starting point to make sense of when the harm set in, so I intentionally placed this original wound in my own formation: in utero. The contradictory emotional climate of my home was my first birthmark; being both unwanted, and wanted.

My childhood was bleak in many ways, marked by persistent childhood sexual abuse, rape, grooming, bullying, racial abuse, emotional abuse, a cocktail of health issues, eating disorders, self-harm, anxiety, and depression. It was also filled with roaring laughter, and three older brothers who played in-house comedians. We had simple family fun, birthday traditions, and the warm embrace of my deeply affectionate mother. I spent my childhood between school and the shop floor, a relatable story to children of immigrants with full-time working parents. I went to fulfill my job duties at my mum's business after school each day, while my peers would go home to play.

Nobody had time at home. My parents immigrated to England for more opportunities. My father came on a scholarship to undertake a Ph.D., and my mother accompanied her entrepreneurial family; her father was a hotelier, and opening a location in England was exciting and held promise. My parents married in the U.K., quickly had children, and busied themselves with life as working parents. Building a life in a new country took its own form of survival; this became the fabric in which my brothers and I were raised.

These factors of my home environment have been the building blocks of my identity. Being shaped by immigrant parents who were traumatized by colonization and partition, I was taught that being exceptional, self-reliant, and focused on achievement were the keys to the door that led to the place everyone wanted to be: free. This self-reliance messaging wasn't overt. However, in the ecology of my childhood home, nobody had developed the vision to see another one suffering in silence, because we were far too busy trying to achieve. In our lives, achievement was one way of coming out of survival and into freedom.

I certainly didn't know how to see my own pain. It was there, in me, so present and palpable. I wasn't just sorting through the confusion of being a third-culture kid, I was frozen by the grooming, violation, and abuse I experienced as a small child. I had unknowingly developed many ways to cope; namely disordered eating, hiding my pain behind a nervous smile, and showing up as the "good girl." I was always obedient and stuck in a cycle of appeasement. And then there was meditation. The meditation was both a healing space and a hiding place. I just didn't know it was a hiding spot until I grew up, when I faced the aching realities of my pain, and committed to looking at the cobwebs I have spent a lifetime sweeping into corners. Now, these very practices serve as guides and excavators for my well of shit.

The shit that originated in the earliest years of my life.

I have no memory of the first time I was raped. For many years I couldn't even say the word rape. I silently identified as someone who had been sexually abused. I certainly did not feel like a survivor. The cognitive understanding that something violating was happening to my body, at the hands of my adult male cousin, came into my conscious memory around the age of three.

I never found the voice to tell my mother what was happening as a small child. In spite of my love for her and my need for her comfort, I had neither the language nor the understanding. More importantly, I didn't feel safe enough to say anything. This man hadn't only been raping my body, but my confidence and voice. Years of rape, in those early childhood years, wired my brain in trauma. The cascading effects of these years continue to impact all areas of my life, without exception. Not only was it such a terrifying and lonely experience, but eventually, the weight of the secret was too much to bear. It took me three years before I would tell my mother. I wanted to every single day. We would all be at the dinner table eating, in the living room watching football, in the car on the way to school, and I would constantly be thinking, *shall I say it now?* But I couldn't find a way to say anything, and I wasn't sure I wanted my brothers to know. What would they think of me? I felt the increasing pressure of the shame and secret.

I finally said it when it was just my mum and me in the car, on the way home one evening. She had finished work, and we were commuting home. I was ten, and she decided it was time to give me the "talk" about the birds and the bees and my changing body. As she began, I could feel my body tighten. Then she said the word *sex*, and without pause, I blurted out, "I already know what sex is. *He* did it to me." She was driving; I was shaking uncontrollably in the passenger seat.

Her exterior remained calm as she asked me follow-up questions. "How many times did he do it?" she asked.

"A million," was my reply.

She asked me to report it to the authorities, to which I screamed, pleaded, and begged her to not say a word, to never speak of it again, to never tell a soul and to just let it go. I felt I had done my part to tell her.

We never really spoke of it again until I was seventeen. There was one mention of it the day I started my period. I was thirteen, and came home from school and told my mum the news. She was congratulatory and I was perfectly annoyed. Then I mustered the courage to ask her my biggest fear: would I now be pregnant? She assured me it wasn't possible, but no further action was taken. She was shattered by her daughter's abuse, and I was engulfed by the dark ocean of silence I was drowning in. I had spent the years prior to my period planning my escape, sure I would be growing an unwanted child, uninformed about the workings of the human body and trapped in a nightmare. Once my mother stated pregnancy was not possible, I exhaled the years of strategizing and felt I could finally live. It would be years until I would enter the story with my brain again, but my body's memory was constantly voicing the trauma.

It felt like I was on auto-pilot for years, dissociated and disembodied, fulfilling cultural and societal expectations. I worked all the time under high demands from school and home. We didn't vacation as a family, so there weren't any breaks for shared pleasure and joy beyond meals and movies. My parents were invested in our education and achievement, so they sacrificed all their time for work and to put us through private school.

Being raised in English private schools in the eighties was harsh, to say the least. If you've seen *Matilda*, you'll understand why (think Agatha Trunchbull). Punitive measures and physical abuse were still legal at some schools, so my siblings and I had some haunting experiences of authority. I went to an all-girls private school in the city of Manchester; we lived in the countryside between meadows and farms at that time. As idyllic as the countryside was, it was the site of ongoing violent racial abuse for my family and me. Between home and school, not many places felt entirely safe. I remember being a seven-year-old, and the headmistress of my primary school calling me into her office. As she character-assassinated me, ripping into me with words like knives, she cut me with phrases like, "you will never amount to anything, you are nothing," sending tears down my cheeks, etching shame and pain into my little second-grade heart. There were neither comfort nor apologies; instead, she chastised me, growling, "don't expect me to give you a tissue." I never shared the ongoing teacher and student bullying I faced in those years of my life. I knew my parents worked hard to put me through private school and I wasn't prepared to tell them. So I would silently take the abuse and shrink, as one does when they are obliterated by the adults in their lives. I was already holding in the biggest secret of my life, so what was one more?

As with the early part of my childhood, my teen years were silently turbulent. On the exterior, I was obedient and conscientious. In the quiet, I was clinically depressed and would rebel by sneaking out and cutting class. Nobody noticed my suffering at school or at home. I was harming myself in a myriad of ways, and I spent two years fatigued and wiped out by chronic insomnia. I slept no more than one hour a night, if that, using those moonlit hours to scribe poetry and prose. I despised school, which is funny because I love to learn. But the container of school was problematic for me.

College was a brighter time in my life. I had promised myself I would travel when I left my parents' home. I had plans to adventure and break away. There was always this part of me that wanted to uproot and leave where I was, and those college years and new-found independence nourished my inner nomad. I had access to free therapy, which I took full advantage of. I spent time traveling and working in the Middle East as a reporter and copy editor, and at refugee camps. I felt alive in ways I never had before in my life. Even though I traveled alone, I felt less lonely, infused by the sense of awe and adventure of being on different land, and feeling connected to where I was and to my work. I was open, experimental, and daring. I dyed my naturally dark hair blonde and had my eyebrow pierced. It was the first time I liked the way I looked. Not many people understood the piercing choice. To voluntarily put metal in my face was met with some very pointed questions: "*Habibti*, were you in an accident? How did that metal get into your face?" My inner rebel felt seen, and I absolutely marveled at these interactions.

Before I could blink, I had moved internationally again, now living in the USA, married and pregnant with my first child. Pregnancy changed me entirely, and with no support system, established friendships, or even acquaintances, I committed to parenting this growing new life. Everything in me wanted to ensure that my children would have a safe and secure upbringing. Life was dynamic. Big things were happening, births and new homes, but beneath it were the echoes of pain that were ready to be voiced. I lived out a lot of the conditioning of my heritage and our cultural and social expectations. This felt like the ultimate compromise of myself. While parts of me seemed content, there was a burgeoning volcano of grief and anger that needed attention. It was only a matter of time until it would spill over and erupt.

I made the choice to heal at thirty, but I wasn't prepared for how ugly it would be. My thirties were about breaking down, breaking through, and learning to recover. It was a purge and a power struggle, a helplessness and a hopelessness that hurt all parts of me. It didn't matter who I was around, I felt isolated, alone, and utterly abandoned. Did my pain not matter? I had spent my life in a survival response that was unconsciously curated to ensure nobody could penetrate the facade and see the mess beneath it. I could see the way I was unhinged at times, and it was both volatile and exhausting. Those who lived with me over time saw the cracks, and the moments of despair more than anyone else. One of my three brothers used to joke that I was a pendulum of emotions, and would swing between every human emotion in a fifteen-minute cycle. It took me years to know what this meant in my body and to understand the metabolic cost of this. I was hardwired in deep distress; getting raped under my older brother's bed and then eating dinner with my family five minutes later made it possible for me to become skilled at holding a vast amount of agony and violation in secret, all alone.

But I wasn't ready to feel it all just yet. I was titrating between honesty and denial. I didn't know how to discharge the heaviness of all that I was holding. I had neither the skill nor the courage, and was afraid of being seen as a victim. The first lies I told myself were to me. I bypassed the chaos and convinced myself I was fine, wearing a warm smile to prove I was happy. The betrayal was tormenting me. I wanted to choose to heal, and I did. It took me some time to accept that the healing chose me, too.

And so this is why I broke down. I mean a full-on, could no longer walk with the weight of the world and unexpressed trauma, need-to-check-myself-in-for-help type of breakdown. I felt I suffered this alone yet again. I did not know how to ask for help nor did I understand how help from anyone else could move me through this. It felt like the loneliest time in my life. All that stuff I wasn't paying attention to crushed me, and not just in that moment. But for the next ten years.

Motherhood became a container for healing that I never expected. The mirror my daughter provided me with was a key to seeing myself outside of my experience. I was able to relate to the childhood trauma with less shame. I distinctly remember looking at my daughter at the age of four: it was just after bath time, she was so fresh and clean, so perfectly pure and innocent, and suddenly it was like I was seeing my own little body that had been so violently violated. I was igneous, overheating from the anger and the injustice of it all. Not just for me, but for all the children who endured this choiceless pain. I was infused with the motivation to do something about it, to right this wrong. So I started being open about parts of my story. While I convinced myself I was strong enough and ready to go public with it, I would routinely shut down, and feel the lead-like heaviness of the vulnerability hangover. I wasn't sharing for catharsis, I was sharing to build community with other survivors and to feel less alone.

I was also trying to place myself in the world as someone who could serve the betterment of our culture and society, to find ways to subvert this harm and violence. But I was ill-equipped. I was so good at performing strength through survival, showing up strong, that nobody could see what was plainly happening before them: I was falling apart. Everyone told me I was so resilient, and believed I was resilient, too. But I didn't have the resilience I needed just yet. I was still existing in survival mode.

In 2015, I watched a TED talk by Dr. Nadine Burke Harris on adverse childhood experiences. I was in the throes of the turmoil, having buried the hard things I couldn't yet attend to. Yet there they were, bursting out of me. I don't know what called me to watch the TED talk, or how it was on the "playing next" cycle, but there I was in my living room, alone, watching this talk, pausing it every few minutes to find scrap paper, a journal, a pen, anything to make notes. I rewound it over and over, just to get the points driven in. *What was that she just said about the correlation between childhood trauma and chronic illnesses?* Followed by a flood of understanding that left me swimming in a pool of: *well shit, I'm doomed.* Resolution followed with a deep decision: *No, I'm figuring this out—I'm* choosing *how to do this.*

At this point, I was approaching thirty-four, steeped in motherhood, and tripping up over the threads of all my pain that I didn't want to see. I was frantically reading everything, trying all the ways to fix myself. I tried to eat my way to healing. I became too staunch about eating, swinging between extremes and telling myself:

Perhaps if I stay super clean and healthy I can hack my body systems and I'll be ok. My trauma won't cause me to get sick. Fail. Another potent life lesson I learned was I couldn't simply hack the body, and diet culture was not a pathway to true well-being. The body is an interconnected and sophisticated system. Healing is complex and functional and requires working *with* the body. I was trying to imprint an external goal onto my well-being as a way to feel good, but it wasn't the wisdom I needed. It was a temporary solution, and I would find myself in relapse. I kept recycling through a pattern of appraising myself for my issues, making a plan to assuage the pain, feeling good, and then new things would show up. And often, these things would come with a new texture of fury and heat.

I needed to reconnect to myself, to become embodied, and get to the root. Everything I had been doing was a Band-Aid solution. As I mapped out my life, trying to uncover the origins, I ardently threw myself into the study of trauma and adverse childhood experiences. I needed to build the capacity to even make the choice to reprocess the abuse, and all the persistent trauma thereafter. My whole self was calling to me to reintegrate all the parts of my life. I was tired of waiting, I was hungry for wholeness and saturated with impatience. And about to learn that being in a hurry was hindering my well-being.

There are chapters to healing; it's important to note it doesn't have to be a page-turner. I let it be boring, slow, and seemingly unproductive. I am still learning to do this. I walked through life with little guidance, without a compass or map, and finding my way through the thick, overgrown forest of confusion meant taking time to orient myself. It meant getting back to my own roots in many ways and connecting to my ancestral practices of yoga and meditation. Building and refining present-moment awareness, and practicing equanimity gave me the courage for my next steps. Meditation was once a hiding place because the object of my awareness used to be a narrative around my pain or living in a much-needed fantasy. It was my escape. Meditation became transformative when I was practicing mindfulness of the breath, body, and emotions, simply being present: coming back to the moment, over and over. What enhanced my healing was education beyond my own meditation practice, and this carved out my path to working in integrative wellness and resilience. Studying both the spiritual practices of my lineage and the psychobiological implications of trauma taught me about myself, how to hold the humanity of others, how to lean into the heart, and not abandon the self.

Immersing myself in texts on trauma bestowed upon me some new insights and clarity. Trauma robbed me of even knowing myself on a basic level. What did I even enjoy? Childhood trauma disrupts neural pathways, and the function of survival becomes paramount. All that brain circuitry is doing something based on some really dark times and impacts the sense of safety everywhere. This is true for trauma at any point in life, but in cases of early childhood trauma, and in my lived experience, I didn't have a data point for not living in survival. So how was I really able to know myself? If my psychobiological experience, the functioning of my brain and perception was deeply distorted by this trauma, then how could I know myself? And who I was innately, before it all?

Healing has become a form of getting to know myself. Taking all the study and integrating it into my life has meant building quite the toolkit. Applying the principles of both new and ancient teachings to my experiences has been about building new neural pathways, and learning to be in a relationship with myself outside of my trauma. If I cannot balm the wound and it still weeps, then it is the thing that takes most of my attention. No amount of distraction can take that away. It has taken me a while to understand that my pain owned me when I could not look at it. It was all-consuming, lurking in the shadows, the unexamined driver behind most of the things I said and did.

I had normalized living with secret pain. I endured a level of aching in order to remove what was hurting: throbbing, stabbing pains, burning, the texture of sandpaper, rough, with hard or sharp edges, the dullness of an ache. My nervous system hadn't found a space of recovery and chronic stress was the ongoing climate of my body and mind. The more I practiced presence of mind and body, the more gaps I found in the stress, the more moments of recovery. The cumulative effects of these small moments served me in ways I never expected. I felt lighter, freer, more intuitive, and less afraid of conversations I was once terrified to have. I was supporting others with their stress, resilience, trauma, and disease recovery. I was getting better at boundary work, and my communication skills and relational intelligence were growing in positive ways. I was reconnecting with myself and others because I had the space to explore.

What I was doing on this microcosmic scale for myself was radiating outward. What others were doing to heal and recover was simultaneously helping me. I felt plugged into something so much bigger than the wound. I was exposed to more wisdom teachings, absorbing the words of those who had overcome tragedy, and those who work towards collective liberation. I became a student of complexity. As complex and dynamic beings, we contain multitudes. Because of our different histories, our needs are not always the same. All of this helped me to cultivate the courage and capacity to live with more intentionality, and to enter the many shades of reclamation: pleasure, self-care, laughter, unapologetic joy, community, as well as quiet contemplation, solitude, and walking barefoot on the earth.

Not being able to look at my own disconnect was doing more harm to me than the abuse had. Building my capacity to look at all the inner wounds wasn't easy. I hit all the hardness and sharpness, the sting of that truth, looking at the most human parts of my own self. But what I didn't expect was how arriving here would give way to something more beautiful: softness. I like to think of the process like composting; taking the muck and with the right conditions witnessing it transmute into something fertile and rich. This insight has become clearer as my own vision has expanded. It's okay to be human and to see it. There is so much more to what we can see at any one time. In my desert of abandonment, I couldn't see the whole context of my life. I existed in the wasteland and void where the options were limited. Once I could see my humanness, I could take accountability for how my hurt affected me and those around me. This admission and accountability softened me further, and I could access a space in myself where reimagination was possible. I could make new choices about my life.

I even had to reimagine my dad. If I decontextualize my father, I paint him with only one color. However, he, too, is complex; once a deeply neglected child who was brought up in a war-torn country, suffering in silence in a culture that didn't support males to cultivate a relationship with their hearts. His unexpressed trauma turned to narcissism, only doing more harm to the family ecosystem. Placing him in the context of his own hurt does not mean that I exempt him from the affliction; we all must practice accountability. And when accountability is absent, so is the heart. Our family was built on weak foundations, split apart by actual harm plus really toxic narratives that drive us to stay apart.

In reclaiming my body, my voice, and my power, I am more self-assured now. I have the resources and the willingness to revisit the broken spaces and to see if it's possible to build bridges. Returning to the site of pain isn't for everyone, but my intuition is guiding me to something that I now have the resilience for. I have the self-trust, and the sensory capacity to listen to my body and know when I need to let go of something, or when I can potentially rewrite the story. I have completed some very hard cycles, leaving the pain of isolation, and finding my way up the mountain. My curiosity keeps me on this trail. Practicing harm reduction, generative conflict, and compassionate listening with my family is revolutionary because we can co-author our family story with consent, kindness, and understanding. We can have new visions for healing together. While this has been the truth in my experience of trauma and healing, I am aware that my way isn't the only way. Creative and intentional living can take infinite expressions.

I want to investigate why we hurt each other. I yearn to get to the origins. Trauma for me has been a way of breaking me and my heart over and over and over until I get to rebuild my life creatively, honoring as much of me as possible. I might even make mistakes rebuilding, but I get to rebuild over and over until I know what I'm building is my truth. The imaginative process of this rebuilding and reclamation is the ongoing journey of befriending complexity through keeping my heart *open*. Thus far, heart-openness is the ultimate lesson from my life, and potentially the most challenging one to practice. That is because it is a subversive act to keep my heart open when I'm hurting. It is a protective instinct to retreat into my shell. The cost of closing my heart is the loss of connection. It is the repetition of the original wound, of isolation. The antidote then must be to love and love hard. Radically love.

What is it to radically love? Radical, as abolitionist Angela Davis states, means "grasping things at the root." What are we doing if we keep scratching at the surface and spackle and paint over the damage? If the foundation is weak, no amount of redecorating will stop it from crumbling. I know this for sure because I crumbled. My relationships crumbled; I lost friendships and partners, some ruptures too big to repair. My relationship with my father is fractured. What I have discovered on my own ascent up the mountain is that radical love encompasses the repair, and the letting go. It holds complexity, ambiguity, and opposition without condemnation. Radical love is understanding, accountability, and mutuality. It is love that is infused with compassion for the self and others, and celebrates the richness of diversity, the full expression of our humanity. Much like cultivating a garden, the rose will not expect the lily to be a rose. Radical love is nourishing, that comes from the same ground, and it allows that which grows upon it to blossom in its glorious expression without conforming or compromising.

Ancient wisdom teaches us that the greatest illusion is separation. If the original wound is anything, it is not seeing our own connection to each other. Abandonment comes from this idea of separateness. But nothing is separate. The earth mirrors this to us. All parts are interconnected and interdependent, so the longer we buy into the separation, the longer we keep the wound open. In this time of injustice, where so many people are heartbroken by the perpetual cycles of trauma, we can choose to call each other in, to reduce harm, and to honor each other's humanity with the respect and dignity all beings deserve. It is in the re-connection to ourselves and each other that we find the magic. Together we can hold and transform much more than we can hold in isolation. As bell hooks, who was one of the most luminous voices on healing, love, and community says, "rarely, if ever, are any of us healed in isolation. Healing is an act of communion."

ABOUT THE AUTHOR

Gia is a coach and facilitator, working with people across ages and sectors in stress, resilience, nutrition, and overall well being. As a survivor of childhood sexual abuse, Gia dedicates time to working with and for other survivors and people needing supportive tools for recovery and healing. Born and raised in England to South Asian parents, Gia moved to the USA 18 years ago, and currently lives on Piscataway Land (Alexandria, VA). She is an eternal student, and is particularly interested in trauma, resilience, somatics, and complexity. With a love for earth wisdom and earth medicine, she is currently fascinated by all things mushroom related.

Gia loves to feed people and creates new recipes in her kitchen lab, where she compiles her own cookbooks for clients and friends. Her ethic is firmly rooted in love, and she works with local organizations on diversity, equity, and belonging. She loves the power of reinvention and reimagination, and is committed to collective liberation. You can find out more about Gia at www.urbansanctuarywellness.com, www.pangaeaplus.com, or follow her on social media @ relativelygia

SHAINA PHILPOT

*This chapter contains sensitive content pertaining to physical abuse, sexual abuse, and suicide.

I was about to go from being a go-getter who knew who she was and what she wanted, to someone who just simply stopped caring. In the moments before that hello, I cared about so many things: making an impact in my community, being professionally successful, my grades—I was a straight A student—and in a matter of months, everything I cared about dissipated into blackouts on his living room floor.

And it wasn't just the alcohol. I didn't know what to call it then, but I would find myself in confusing situations where I was being forced to do all kinds of things I didn't want to do. I would say no. He would not care, and he would do what he wanted to me anyway.

WHERE DO I BELONG?

It's hot and dry in California this afternoon again. The radio inside the police car screeches at a low hum. I am being detained, waiting for the policeman who is staring at me in amusement to answer. *How can these handcuffs be so tight? My wrists are tiny,* I wonder. I try to adjust my body to get more comfortable, but there is nothing comfortable about being in the back of a police car, the back of my legs sticking to a metal seat. My eyes tear up as I twist my hands back and forth, watching as the cuffs dig deeper and deeper into my skin. I lift my right leg up a little for some relief and hear my skin as it sticks. I'm wearing a short, blue, spaghetti-strap dress covered in flowers, and it offers very little coverage. I'm starting to smell my own sweat as I try to move around to get more comfortable. No luck.

As I sit there pondering how I ended up in this mess, the officer sitting in the driver's seat looks up at me in the rear-view mirror and says something to the effect of, "So, what do you do?" I can't make eye contact because he's hiding behind his sunglasses and I miss his smirk when I answer.

"I'm a master's degree student."

He looks sideways at the other officer sitting next to him. There is a pregnant pause, then they both burst into man-sized giggles as if to say, "That's hilarious!" And he replies, "No seriously though, what do you really do?"

"I'm a master's degree student." I repeat it again. Irritated. Half because they don't believe me and half because I keep repeating the same thing. I hate repeating myself. Especially to men I don't know.

"Interesting," is all he says. In one word, I could hear what he really thought: "Someone who is getting a master's degree doesn't belong in the back of a cop car." One word, but the message, it's so familiar. I don't belong here alright. I don't belong anywhere. He should know. He's a man of the law.

Belonging. It's a common theme in my life. I am the middle child. My older sister, Brittney, and my younger sister, Meghan, both look like my parents, particularly my father, who is Native American, an enrolled tribal member of the Hopland Band of Pomo Indians. I did not grow up on my reservation; I am what many call an Urban Indian, someone who grew up off their reservation and in an urban community. My sisters and I are also enrolled tribal members of the Hopland Band of Pomo Indians, however, no one ever questions whether my sisters belong to the tribal community. Me? I came out looking like I had just stepped off the snowcapped mountaintops of Norway—blonde hair and blue eyes—the only one who never looked like I belonged. Growing up, people mistook me for a friend of the family and were surprised to find out I was actually related to all of them, as my parents have dark brown hair and brown eyes. My family always made me feel like I belonged to them, but with outsiders, it was a constant struggle.

Because no one ever believed that I was Native American I developed the need to prove myself. As I entered college, I was afraid I would be lumped in with the "box checkers"—people who checked the box because they assumed they would get free money for being Native American, but they weren't Native American at all—so, I dyed my hair brown. I didn't want my new college friends at the Native American Recruitment and Retention Center to think I had just checked the Native American box on my college application to get money, which, by the way, is a stupid stereotype: all Native American students don't get to go to school for free. I have the student loans to prove it.

It wasn't until I started college at the University of California, Berkeley that I felt like I truly belonged in an academic setting. It was such a relief to be in a place where people didn't question or judge me based on the way I looked or my tribal affiliation. I was finally surrounded by fellow Natives who supported me, and I jumped right into being involved with the Native community on campus. I helped put on our annual pow wow, a social gathering of Native peoples to celebrate our culture. I was the first Native American resident assistant in the residence halls and led the pilot program for a Native American-themed housing program. The very next year after I graduated, it became an official theme program that stands to this day. I loved being surrounded by my community and giving back in any way I could. After I graduated, I took a year off to apply to grad schools while working on campus mentoring Native American students. I loved my job and was excited about my future. I received a fellowship at a university back home in Southern California to complete my master's degree, and I gladly accepted it. I was ready to come back home after being away for three years.

While I found acceptance in academics, there were still pieces of me that didn't feel accepted. Those parts often outweighed the sense of belonging I had found in my academic surroundings. I had just broken up with my fiancé, whom I had been with for seven and a half years. I was on track academically, but I felt alone because I no longer had a connection with someone. I moved back home for grad school, and all I wanted was to feel like I belonged. We all know how this story goes: Where does a twenty-one-year-old go to find connection? A party. And what does a twenty-one-year-old find at a party? Booze and boys, baby!

In between shots, I spied the cutest boy I had seen in quite some time, and all I could think was, *I need to know his name.* He was younger than me, a high school dropout, and worked at the local liquor store. As I was floating around in a vodka haze, he knew exactly what to say, at just the right time. I wouldn't know it then, but everything was about to change.

I was about to go from being a go-getter who knew who she was and what she wanted, to someone who just simply stopped caring. In the moments before that hello, I cared about so many things: making an impact in my community, being professionally successful, my grades—I was a straight-A student—and in a matter of months, everything I cared about dissipated into blackouts on his living room floor.

And it wasn't just the alcohol. I didn't know what to call it then, but I would find myself in confusing situations where I was being forced to do all kinds of things I didn't want to do. I would say no. He would not care, and he would do what he wanted to me anyway.

It started off with him telling me everything I needed to hear. He gave me the attention I so desperately craved and filled my void of loneliness. Although I was from the same town, I had been gone for three years, and I felt like I was the new girl all over again. He invited me to parties with him, knowing all I wanted was to fit in and belong.

My period is a few days late. Since I am on birth control, it should have been as regular and on time as the clock on the wall. I am in the bathroom at his place, staring at myself in the mirror, watching as the terror overwhelms my body. What the hell am I going to do if I'm pregnant? I know I don't want to be a mom, not now, not ever. I have to tell him though. If I am pregnant, it would be his and we need to talk about our options. I walk out of the bathroom and see him sitting on the couch; he's eating a bowl of cereal, engrossed in some reality show. He looks up at me with a look I can't read; I never know what he's thinking.

"I'm worried. I haven't started my period yet." The words hang in the air, until he moves it by getting up off the couch.

As he walks toward me my body relaxes into the anticipation of comfort, maybe a hug. Instead, his fist lands straight into the middle of my belly. He's so close I can smell the cereal on his breath as he shouts, "You better not be pregnant!"

As I collapse into myself and find air to get me through the pain, all I can wheeze out is, "What the hell was that for?!"

He picks up his cereal bowl and changes the channel. "Well, if you are pregnant, you aren't anymore." And he just keeps watching TV. My period came three days later.

I was on a crazy train that took me from constant pain "down there" to forcing me to get my tongue pierced for his pleasure. It took me too long to realize I was no longer an active participant in my own life. It should have been crystal clear when he forced me to go down on him while my tongue was still throbbing. I was a slave. His slave.

If he told me to go and jump off a bridge, I would have. I was doing everything for him. My need to belong, combined with this deep fear of being alone, made me believe that if I didn't do what he told me to do, he would leave me. And I could think of nothing worse than that. Even with all the horrible things he made me do, it was still important to know that I was his. And above all, that I wasn't alone.

The abuse became so normalized, he stopped caring who could see it. At one point, at the height of it all after he had moved in with a friend, there was a "celebration" in which there was too much of everything. I found myself heaving in the bathroom and was met with screaming insults and pounding fists to, "Open it up, Bitch!" meaning the door. Fumbling with the lock, I no sooner heard the click, when he nearly collapsed on top of me in his blacked-out state. Instead of steadying himself on the wall or the sink counter, he found my head and grabbed me by my hair. Over and over, he slammed my head against the counter, shouting obscenities over the loud music. No one within earshot came to my rescue. As I choked on my own tears and vomit, the beating came to an end. He dropped me in a heap in the corner, took a piss, and then left me there for dead.

All we did was fight, and yet somehow I kept believing that maybe he would change. He was controlling. I couldn't talk to any other men unless they were his friends. He was constantly calling me names. His favorite: Bitch. I was constantly being told I wasn't pretty enough or skinny enough and I had been beaten into believing him. I would never be enough for anyone else, he said. To me, this was proven, over and over again: like on the afternoon when, during a heated argument that had grown physical, he pushed me down the stairs and I landed in a pile of my own shame, at the feet of his roommate. I'll never forget lying there, silently begging him for help. He just looked at me and walked away. In that moment, I internalized the lie that I deserved to be treated this way. If someone could watch me be pushed down the stairs by my abuser and walk away, then I must have done something to deserve it, not the other way around. I chose to be in this relationship in the first place, right? All three of us on that stairway knew I didn't have the guts to leave. If he was going to do this to me while we were together, what would happen if I actually did try to leave? I had been too beaten down to try to find out, and besides, who would want me now? After all this?

————————————

"Answer me!" I push send so hard it sends a jolt of pain up my finger. If he's going to ignore my texts and phone calls then I decided I'm going to go over there in person so he can't ignore me. I enter the house and no one is downstairs. "Are you here?" I say it loud. No response. I go up the stairs—the same ones he had pushed me down just a few weeks before—and push open his bedroom door. His sheets are strewn across the floor and there's a woman draped over his body.

All I can see is red. And finally, FINALLY, I snap. "What the fuck is this? What are you fucking doing?"

A woman I have never seen before rolls off his naked body and to my astonishment, they both just stare at me and laugh. "I don't care about you. No one does," is all he says before she rolls back on top of him. The jeering continues as I grab his phone and scroll through multiple text messages to other women showing parts of his body. Clearly, he has been cheating on me for months. Like a tidal wave about to take me out and drown me in the sea, the reality of where I was, and who he was, emboldens me enough to lift my hand and slap him across the face. As our bodies make contact this one last and final time, I can finally see the truth.

I can't fix him. I can't fix me. We are both broken.

"Fuck you," is all I can manage.

I walk down the stairs, feeling my way as I weep from the deepest part of my broken soul and decide I don't want to live anymore.

I wake up the next morning feeling sick to my stomach. I go to the bathroom and get sick, staring at the four walls which are my reality, walls that don't even belong to me. All I can think about is how much I hate my life. I can dye my hair so I look more Native American, I can pierce my tongue to make him happy, I can pretend I'm okay and put on a fake smile…but none of it is ever going to be enough. I'm never going to be enough for anybody. I'm never going to belong to anybody, even to myself. So why even stay? Why am I here on this earth? To be somebody's punching bag? I can't do it anymore.

As I stare at myself in the bathroom mirror, I decide I'm done with it all, and then I make a plan. I will take my car out into the middle of nowhere, find a tree, and drive headfirst into it as fast as I can. No one else will get hurt except me, and if I drive fast enough, I will crash hard enough so that it will kill me. I will be out in the middle of nowhere, so no one will find me. I get ready one last time. I do my hair and apply eyeliner; my hands are shaking, and I have to keep redoing it. I put on a flowery blue sundress with spaghetti straps. It's my favorite. I want to look at least halfway decent as I go out. I get in my truck and drive. It takes me fifteen minutes to find a field with a few trees around. It is off the beaten path and I know it will be a while before anybody finds me. I sit there, the engine idling. This is it; I can't live in this pain any longer. I send one last message to my ex-fiancé declaring that I am done with everything. I put the phone on silent as it signals calls from my parents, my sisters, a friend. I ignore them all. It's too late to change my mind.

As always, I make one exception, because he's always been my exception. I hate him for what he did to me, but seeing his name pop up on my phone gives me a rush of feeling that he actually cares about me killing myself. I want him to care. Even in that moment, I still want to feel like I belong to someone, anyone, even if it was him.

"I don't want to talk anymore; I am fucking done." I look at the tree and make a promise to myself. I'll be back later.

As I walk through the door of his place, there he is, standing in the kitchen. He is leaning up against the oven. Immediately, he picks up his phone and makes a call. "She's here," he says, and then he hangs up. I'm frantic. Somehow, I make out that my parents have called the police. As I stand in the kitchen with him, my plans to kill myself have not changed. I grab a knife to stab my stomach, but before I get there, he pries it from my hands.

"I can't be here anymore," I sob.

"Just stop it," he says. I look at him, then down at my hands. Clenched so tightly I am beginning to break the skin with my fingernails. "You did this to me!" I wail. "Just let me go!"

He steps aside and motions toward the door. "Fine, then go!" he shouts angrily.

I break free through the front door and just start walking. I can't get in my car and drive because I know the police are on their way and they know my car. I make it about a block before they find me. My tears have stopped, and now I am angry that the police were called. I can feel my cheeks growing redder by the second. They park their car and two officers make their way towards me. One is taller than the other, and both are wearing sunglasses to protect their eyes from the California sun. They explain that I am being held on a 5150: for being a danger to myself. Because I have a taser with me at the time (something my father had given me to protect myself) I am classified as armed and subsequently arrested.

I'm taken to the police station where they finally uncuff me and force me to remove all my piercings. I'm placed in a cell with a crappy stained mattress in one corner and a dirty toilet in the other. I am so pissed. And I think again about the date I have with that tree. I'm mad at everything and everyone. Mad at my parents, myself, him, life: the world.

As I'm gauging how long I can hold it before I have to break down and use a toilet in front of the entire police station, I am notified an ambulance has arrived and I am being transferred to a mental institution. But I'm not crazy. Am I? I look around as I am ordered to lay down on a cot and wheeled into the ambulance. For the entire hour-long ride I stare out the window, not knowing what to think or how to feel. I take in what I'm seeing. The cars, the lights, the trees, the roads, people changing lanes. So this is what it feels like to lay it all down.

We arrive at the regional mental health facility and I am escorted inside. As long as I live, I will never forget what I witnessed. A patient is screaming at a wall, banging. Very sick people are walking around talking to themselves while hitting themselves. "I don't belong here," is all that is running through my head. Suddenly, I am scared. My anger diffuses and turns into fear and a need to get out of there and survive. I sit in the waiting room in gruesome wonder.

How did I end up here? After hours of waiting, a nurse finally comes up to me.

She pulls me aside so we can speak one-on-one with a little more privacy.

"Sweetie, how did you end up here? Tell me what happened to you."

I break down in tears. She's so kind, so compassionate. And suddenly I have words for everything I have endured for the past year. I tell her about the abuse: that my abuser is not even a high school graduate, and until I met him my life trajectory was so bright! The words pushing, shoving, and hitting all ended with the statement: "I don't want to be alive anymore."

She looked at me as she took my hand.

"Oh, Sweetie." There was so much authentic sincerity in her voice, I started to cry again. She continued, "But don't you see? You are up here!" She put her hand up over both our heads to indicate a level of height. "And he's down here." The same hand moved below both our waists, parallel to the floor. "You are about to get your master's degree! That is incredible! But you have been through something you never should have gone through. And I'm sorry about that. You don't belong here. You are beautiful, you are young, and I guarantee you this: You are going to stand as a symbol of women's empowerment. I am going to see you on television one day telling your story. You are going to do so much with your life. You remember that."

As her words of encouragement dab at the wounds of my broken spirit, I sob uncontrollably. I don't know much at this point, but I do know this angel was sent from above to save my life. I have no doubt in my mind about that. As she holds me in her arms, she just whispers over and over again: "You are going to do good things, Sweetie, great things." I wipe away the tears and nod my head.

As I collect myself, a doctor walks in and conveys a similar message. I am not a danger to myself, I am a victim of domestic violence, and I don't belong here.

The words of this nurse had landed deep within my soul. As I sat there half listening to the doctor, all that kept repeating on a loop inside my head were her words: I'm up here, he's down there. I'm up here, he's down there.

He's not worth my tears.

He's not worth the pain.

He's certainly not worth my life.

"So how are you doing now?" I break out of my trance and see the doctor staring at me expectantly.

I point at the nurse and reply with more certainty than I've felt in months, "Your nurse just saved my life. I don't belong here." She smiles and so does he.

I have always gotten tattoos as a way of symbolizing different defining moments in my life. Deciding to live was tattoo-worthy for sure. It took me no time to decide on what to get. I walked right into the tattoo shop and told the artist I wanted the word "EMPOWERMENT" forever printed on my arm.

As I watched him dip the needle into the ink, and then make the color permanent on my bicep, it felt as if I were writing a contract with myself, one that I would see every time I looked down at my arm.

This was a promise I was making to myself—to my voice, to the Universe, to life—that I would stand as a symbol of women's empowerment. After he finished, as I flexed in the mirror and admired the work, I marveled at how I felt. I was alive, I was free, and I was going to make it.

I spent months in therapy talking with my doctor about what had happened and how I felt about it all. I was put on depression medication, aka my happy pills, and I was no longer suicidal. I was able to finish my master's degree and pass my master's thesis defense. I went from lying on the cold, bathroom floor, drunk, alone, and abused, to walking across that stage with my head held high, degree in hand. I am living proof that just because something is broken, it doesn't mean it can't be put back together again.

For the next few years, I still struggled with my self-confidence, with feeling like I belonged, and finding love in all the wrong places. I decided all men really wanted from me was sex. I kept partying and drinking. Although I was no longer suicidal, I still felt that I didn't deserve love. It wasn't until two years later that I met the man who would later become my husband. I do not know how else to explain it, but after our first date together I knew he was my soulmate. It's like his heart was on the same wavelength as mine. He was able to speak to my soul the way the angel nurse spoke to my soul—he *saw* me—and I knew I belonged. After six months of dating, we got married. We moved to Japan together, where the Navy stationed us. We have now been married for eight years and it really is the happiest I've ever been.

I have certainly had ups and downs, as being a military wife is no easy feat. However, I have learned that there is so much joy in this life. I have learned that life is worth living, despite setbacks and challenges.

The look on my students' faces when they finally get a concept they have been struggling with or the phone call from a parent who tells me their sixth grader received their first A on a math test because of my teaching and support: those are all things I could have missed. The students who stop by my office solely to see my face and say hello as they walk to their next class period, and the feeling of love and support I receive daily from my husband, these all make life worth living. I have learned that there are good people out there, you just have to find them. I have learned how important it is to surround yourself with people who will uplift you and cheer you on, not people who will tear you down. And although I still struggle with self-love, I have this depth of knowing that I can do anything. I can accomplish whatever I set my mind to and I can be whomever I choose to be. I am the one who gets to make choices about my life, no one else. From lying at the bottom of the stairs and looking up at my abuser, believing I had chosen that, to now choosing myself over and over again.

So, what does it mean to belong? It means to feel at home, to feel supported, to feel wanted, to know you aren't alone. And belonging can come in different ways: I belong in my job, I belong with my husband, I belong in my body, and my voice belongs to me. I think you have to find this in yourself first: you have to decide that you are going to stay and explore, feeling the depths of sadness and moving through the pain, even if it feels scary and you are afraid. You have to decide you aren't going to run away. In those last moments, when everything feels lost, when your voice is worn out from crying and screaming and just living, I have found, there is a place, if we just wait out the pain and are willing to work to feel better, where our voice will find its home. Within me, I belong.

After all the suffering, I survived. I landed my dream job, which I love, and am about to receive my doctorate. I have a beautiful relationship with my parents and the rest of my family. I focus more on my mental health now than I ever have before. Self-care is a daily part of my routine. I participate in monthly online FLOW challenges, where I am surrounded by a community of supporting humans from all over the world who cheer me on throughout all my endeavors. This helps me manage anxiety and focus on self-love as if my life depends on it, because it does. It has helped me to overcome the trauma of my past by focusing on the present moment.

With my job, I have the pleasure of serving Native and Indigenous students. I have the great privilege of giving back to my people by honoring my ancestors with my advocacy. I strive to be an advocate for Native and Indigenous students, who are still fighting to be recognized for something other than "Other." I am a role model for my tribal community and other Native students, so they can see that a Native American woman can grow up, survive abuse, and still become successful.

Affirmations are one of the most powerful tools I have used to propel myself forward on my journey of healing. This is my favorite one.

I am strong.

I am brave.

I am courageous.

I am smart.

I am intelligent.

I am beautiful.

I am loved.

I am worthy.

I am enough.

I am a BADASS.

And so are you.

ABOUT THE AUTHOR

Shaina Philpot (she/her/hers) is an enrolled tribal member of the Hopland Band of Pomo Indians. She received her Bachelor's Degree in Native American Studies from the University of California, Berkeley, her first Master's Degree in Public History with a subspeciality of Native American History from the University of California, Riverside and her second Master's Degree in Teaching from the University of Southern California. Shaina co-authored a chapter in the book titled, The Indian School on Magnolia Avenue: Voices and Images from Sherman Institute (OSU Press, 2012), which focuses on the off-reservation boarding school experience at Sherman Institute in Riverside, CA. Shaina spent many years in various roles in the field of education, including teaching and working with tribal communities. She is also currently a doctoral candidate in the Ed.D in Leadership in Higher Education program at Northcentral University. Her research centers on American Indian students' sense of belonging in higher education, specifically comparing American Indian students' sense of belonging between predominantly White institutions (PWIs) and Tribal Colleges and Universities (TCUs). When Shaina is not working and researching, she is a dog mom and enjoys watching anime and traveling with her husband. Shaina hopes her story will inspire other women to continue living. You can follow Shaina's journey on her Instagram: @s_philpot.

CATHY GABRIELSEN

This chapter contains sensitive content pertaining to references of suicidal thoughts.

It was just there. Suicide. I knew, as I dragged on another breath of nicotine, I was hitting bottom. Head over heels, I was tumbling down, down, down into emptiness because I had nothing left of myself to give. I had run out of me, and I just couldn't pretend anymore. The gig was up, and I still hadn't figured out what my gig was. I was a woman who had it all but couldn't be the woman with it all, anymore.

A LIFETIME
OF DYING

There were leaves everywhere on the wet road. The only sounds I could hear in the car on that gray morning were the rain splatter on the windshield, the swoosh of the wipers, and my quiet whimpers that had turned to uncontrollable sobs. I wasn't driving anywhere in particular, but I was searching desperately for a safe space to cry. A panic attack was coming on and I was desperate to have it in private.

There was always a signal in my body, a message warning me that panic and anxiety were on their way. Tears would always follow and all that would be running through my tired mind was that it was time, time to hide. I would begin to feel the pull of a tightening in my chest followed by an awful sensation, the unbearable need to stretch my neck and shoulders. The panic had no preference where I was when it came. It was a shadow, always lurking, that brought enough darkness with it to block out the sun.

Maybe it was my teacher's fault, this desperate need to cry alone. The day I accidentally spilled my milk, when cookies and dairy were a thing. I am crying, but not making any noise. I am five and sitting in front of my best friend Heather, our small desks facing each other to form a table. Each desk has our name at the top, on a large white rectangular card, written in thick black marker. Below it, there are numbers and various shapes in different colors. I watch in horror as my spilled milk turns my cookie into soggy crumbs and crawls toward my napkin, smearing my name. As the spilled milk runs like a small river toward Heather's cookie, she too is left with a soggy, soaking mess. The milk finally finds a reservoir, and it drips into the belly of my desk, leaving my large scented crayons to turn sour in the puddle. I am devastated. Embarrassed. I can't move or make a sound. I stand still, waiting for my teacher to comfort me.

In the time it took for my milk to make inroads into my desk, I waited expectantly for my teacher to hug me. I waited for her to wipe my tears and assure me it was going to be ok, that "accidents happen." I predicted that she would explain, "there is nothing to be embarrassed about." More than her understanding, I was hoping for a new cookie, a dry napkin, some fresh milk, and new scented crayons. But instead, as I held my breath, my five-year-old self realized I wasn't afraid of the mess the spilled milk had caused, I was afraid of her. Her eyes were dark and glaring, and her voice bellowed as she screamed from the top of her lungs, "Stop those crocodile tears!" Startled, shocked, and confused, I was ordered to the bathroom as if I had committed a crime. I was only allowed back into the classroom after I "got my act together". And the bathroom was where I finally stopped crying, alone.

I knew why I was crying. I was doing what five-year-olds do: crying over spilled milk. I was crying because my red crayon would no longer smell like cherry. I cried for my cookie, for my friend Heather and the sour smell of milk on her nametag, and I cried because I was sad, ashamed, and embarrassed. That day, I learned an important lesson that would become a light guiding me in the wrong direction for years.

I learned that I was expected to stop crying, which translated to stop feeling. And if I couldn't? Well, then I should be ashamed. That was the day the lesson turned from learning about numbers and letters to how I should control myself. I did what I was told; I cleaned myself up, got my act together, and walked into the rest of my life.

Back in my car, I was frantically searching for a place to get my act together. The rain beat down, and my heart pounded as I lit a tear-soaked cigarette, cracked the window, and took in a dragging breath. The wipers were swiping at their fullest speed, the road was flooding, and I was determined to find privacy. And then I heard the word. It freaked me out. I wanted it to go away—I needed to stop seeing it, in my mind's eye. I had never before considered how I would do it, but I heard the word again in the car as loud and clear as my sobs. It was just there. *Suicide.*

I knew, as I dragged on another breath of nicotine, I was hitting bottom. Head over heels, I was tumbling down, down, down into emptiness because I had nothing left of myself to give. I had run out of me, and I just couldn't pretend anymore. The gig was up, and I still hadn't figured out what my gig was. I was a woman who had it all but couldn't be the woman with it all, anymore. I had built a super life but could no longer be the superwoman who managed it. I was tired, empty, and sad. I had lost my strength, energy, and the power to do the simplest tasks. I could no longer get my act together and clean up the spilled milk.

Rain-drenched leaves continued to fall, clogging the wipers, and the windshield became difficult to see through. The dying leaves always triggered the memory of my first near-death experience at eighteen years old. Damp, dreary, and dark November days would bring my awareness back to the bottom of the mud and leaf-filled ravine. The front of the blue and tan Eddie Bauer Ford Bronco is smashed into the hole in the ground. It would be the very first time I can remember screaming, but I didn't yell for help. I look to my left, and my boyfriend is lying over the crushed steering wheel, moaning, desperate. I don't help him, because I can't. I am paralyzed by fear. It's hard to see clearly. Blood drips into my eyes and down my face. In front of me is broken glass. Some has landed in the car, and most of it is stuck in my flesh. There's a man next to me, explaining he will get help, and then he disappears.

Between my boyfriend's moans and my screams, I lay back and look up at the stars and the light. I choose to cross the veil to the life after this one. I want a safe space to go to. The light envelops me, and it heals me, it empowers me. I am told I am to come back to earth, but before I return, the angels and my ancestors heal me. I receive a clear message that I am to return to help others heal. I come back from heaven and wake up in a hospital bed. That night, alone in the ICU, I lay awake. I am aware of my pain, but it is overshadowed by the experience I've just had. My pillowcase is wet from tears because I am so afraid. I'm not sure if my boyfriend is still alive because no one will tell me. I stare out the window, into the dark star-speckled night, knowing with such certainty that there is life beyond. I consider the healing that took place and the healing I would have to do for others.

The nurse comes in and checks the bag on the metal rod next to me. I study her and wonder if she is safe to tell. Will she judge me? Will she look at me like I am crazy? Will she confirm what I suspect—that I am not worthy of such an experience? Will she demand that I get my act together, and stop with the crocodile tears? I open my mouth but the words won't come. I want to tell someone, anyone, of this new awareness. I want to describe the angels, the Master Healer, and my ancestors who are all alive. I have had a life-saving and life-changing experience but I cannot summon the inner power to share. I am too scared of what people will say or think. And so, I decided to bury the memory. It's better to keep it to myself and not say a word.

I later learned my boyfriend had suffered a horrific and traumatic brain injury. But instead of expressing my fears and pain, I silenced the terror I experienced and pushed it way down deep into a part of me that would never be excavated. I would be fine. It was time to help heal my boyfriend. I got my act together, stopped with the tears, covered the cuts on my face with bronzer, and took my post at his bed. I genuinely believed all I needed to be okay was for him to be okay.

Taking another long drag of my cigarette, I grieved the memories and pain of the past. The blurring of my tears made it difficult for me to see the road. I had to slow down or I was going to end up in another accident. But there it was, like a beacon of something: the small, creepy, dirty, white church. It gave me a shiver. There was a large sign in front with big black letters spelling out, "FAITH, HOPE, and LOVE; the greatest of these is LOVE." I pulled into the empty parking lot, parked next to the sign, and just cried. I cried because I knew, deep down in that place that always tells the truth, I had no faith that life would get easier, no belief that Source was with me, guiding me. I was completely hopeless and believed I was all alone. All my life, I had been able to get my shit together, do my shit along with everyone else's shit, and all without a single problem, until now. As I stared at the sign my eyes wanted to rearrange the letters as I quietly and privately lost my shit. *Love?* It was easy to love others, easy to give love, But love to me, from me? I didn't know what that felt like. How could I love myself when I didn't even know myself?

I emptied myself out then lit another cigarette (a habit I picked up to, you know, help with the anxiety). I smoked a few more in silence. The *word* had been pushed out. What had taken its place was greater than all of these things: it was love. I pulled out of the parking lot and got back onto the road, headed in the direction of home.

I looked at the clock: almost 5:00 p.m. It was time to cook dinner. Even though life had emptied me out, I would never ask for help. I would never ask for anything. When my heart begged me to lay down and rest, I did what I had always done, I listened to the five-year-old who controlled my voice, the girl who was afraid to speak up, existing in the fear of not being loved. "No. Not today, I can't help you," I longed to say, twenty times a day, but the words were stuck in the back of my throat like a wad of bubblegum, unable to release. And I was choking.

Help me, I need a break. My throat ached to release my requests, but I couldn't or wouldn't make them come. I had been diagnosed with breast cancer when I was a young mom of two boys. They were just three and one, and wanted what babies always want from their moms. They wanted me to hug and hold them, to lay with them until they fell asleep every night. I never said no. How could I? I would hide the wince when I laid down and avert the tears when I got up. I would sneak off to pop Motrin so I could get through a game of Power Rangers without passing out. In reality, I know now, it was me that needed to be held, but I didn't ask for help, because I needed to be the one who was wanted, I wanted to be the one who was needed, I had to be the one who was loved. I needed to rest, I needed to heal, but I didn't know how.

On the day I came home a breastless woman (I was just hours post-surgery), I did what I only knew how to do: I packed the blue and yellow Vera Bradley diaper bag with extra gauze, wraps, and pumps, and headed to Chuck E. Cheese. The sounds, the blinking lights, the moms talking in small groups, and the screams for more pizza made my head spin, and my pain meds wore off too soon. I longed for my bed, but I wouldn't take myself there. I had the warped belief that it was okay for me to hurt if that made my kids feel better, and so I pretended. *It's fine. I'm fine. Everything is fine.*

I had to do for others to feel better. *You want to feel loved? Then play some games and eat some pizza. Go to the bathroom, wipe your face, and put some lipstick on that smile. Get your act together, Cath.* So I did. Until it killed me—again.

I knew I was dying because I had died before. And I knew I was dying because I hadn't cared for myself. It was after my eleventh post-cancer surgery. Because I was an old hat at all this surgery stuff, instead of going home and taking to my bed, I packed, planned, and self-tanned for an upcoming family trip to Florida. It didn't matter if I felt good, it mattered that I looked good. I hit the gym and hid my drains and the pain under a sweatshirt.

As I wandered through the beachfront hotel, the corridors seemed to never end, and I continued to get lost and confused. I kept trying to shake nausea and fatigue while I went to grab some small cereal boxes and milk for the kids and coffee for my husband. I made it back to the room, placed what they needed on the dresser, closed the door quietly, and went to save the perfect seats by the pool and then head off for my run. The early morning Florida sun wasn't enough to keep me warm, and I lay shivering on a pool chair. *I'm just going to take a few more minutes before my run,* I told myself. But I never made it on my run. I woke up, hours later, still on the pool chair. My kids were standing over me holding their swim toys, calling my name and I met my husband's concerned eyes. I didn't have the strength to pretend I was okay anymore. I stumbled back to the hotel room where I collapsed in my own urine on the bathroom floor. It was time for the hospital.

I was in and out of consciousness, but I knew my body was shutting down. I was too weak to talk, to focus on what was happening, I had lost control of the situation. I was being prepped for surgery, and I held my breast, an indication to my surgeon, *please don't take it again.* It didn't matter. I had no voice, no power. My options were life support or removal of the infected breast. I watched as the anesthesiologist injected the port in my wrist, and the nurses hustled around me. My husband's fear turned to sadness as he left the room. He stopped to take one last look at me.

As a Mind, Body, and Soul Healer, I help my clients release the blocks that are in the way of their light. I help them embrace their inner nature and connect them with their own divinity. In the hospital that day, I had not yet discovered my soul. I had not been introduced to my spirit. I had not yet been acquainted with my light. I had not yet understood that my life's challenges came for me, they didn't happen to me. They were opportunities to step into my purpose and my meaning for existing in this lifetime. They were opportunities to initiate higher levels of consciousness and awareness. Instead of forgiving life and forgiving the experience, I stayed in the energy of the challenges by holding onto the emotions that were attached to them. I was holding onto fear and anger, shame and guilt. Those negative emotions, brewing inside of me for so long, manifested into the illnesses and diseases I had experienced over my lifetime and into the raging sepsis that moved through every crevice of my physical body.

Emergency surgery was performed, and when I returned to my hospital room, I spent most of the days and nights that followed hovering above my bed in what I later learned was an out-of-body experience. I would see myself below in the bed, weak and tired, struggling to breathe. I knew I was dying. I knew, because I had died before, all those years ago in the car, and felt the same light pulling me in. It was right there. The light was right in front of me, calling my name, beckoning me to come. But I was also being pulled by my family; I needed to be with them. After spending a week in the hospital in this state, I checked myself out so I could get back to them.

When I arrived, I was so happy to see my kids and quickly hit the default button. I was trying to act as if nothing was wrong with me. I let them lay next to me in my bed. Their eyes closed with smiles on their faces. I lay right between them, terrified. I was afraid to close my eyes.

Once again, I was struggling to breathe. I was torn by a mother's duty: I didn't want them to know I was feeling sick, but at the same time, I didn't want to die in between them in that bed. As I drifted off, I prayed that my lungs would open, so I could keep breathing. As they slept, a tunnel of light appeared right in front of me. The opening kept getting wider and its pull stronger. I took one last look at my babies in the bed, and then I went in.

I crossed the veil from the earthly life to the life after. As I joyfully connected, once again, to my ancestors and angels, I floated in the comforting light amidst the sound of seraphim singing and I made my way to the arms of the Master Healer, his mother was right above. I rested in the comfort of his arms and his voice was soft and reassuring as he spoke of the good I had done so far in my life, and then he said simply, "My daughter Cathleen, you still have more work that you need to do." He didn't rush me or push me away. I never said any goodbyes, I just soaked in the sounds of the heavenly music and bathed in the peace and love that was the light. And then I came back, once again.

I walked back into my house, after the experience at the creepy church, feeling the same inside, as if I had never left. The panic attack had passed, and as I fried chicken cutlets on the stove, cleaned dishes, answered homework questions, and sipped my wine, I remembered the word I had heard earlier in the day and knew what was true: *I needed help.* The words were now gagging me. *Help. Me.* Needing help terrified me because everyone would know I wasn't perfect.

As I sipped and stirred, I realized the suffocation of my life was killing me and I knew I was the only person who could fix it. It was do or die, and I didn't want to die to live. I wanted peace, love, and happiness within me. I wanted to live a life where I was my priority, and where I mattered to myself. I had purged in the parking lot, and I knew

I hit the floor. I also knew I had to get up. There was something within me, a light that sparked, a clearing from the tears that turned my despair into a desire. As I served dinner that night, there was a wallowing within me, a cry deep inside an unfamiliar voice I had maybe heard before. *Speak up, speak your truth. Speak up so you can manifest and create.* I knew it was time to spit out the words or choke on them.

I had to shift my thinking; it was that simple. And also really, really hard. The belief that I had to perform to be loved had stunted my emotional growth. The belief that I had to do something in order to be seen, that I had to give in order to receive, that I had to sacrifice so that I could experience satisfaction, and that I had to look good while doing it, had to go. I had to let go of the belief that I was only lovable if I was a good girl and that it was best to be seen and not heard. I had to shed the belief that my own opinions didn't matter. I had to shed the idea that it was okay to be stepped on if it meant lifting someone else, and the belief that I didn't know better. I had to let go of what was holding me back and keeping me stuck in a state of anxiety, depression, and PTSD.

If I wanted to find my voice so I could live my life based on my soul's aspirations instead of others' expectations, I had to find the reason I created the block in the first place and heal the wounds of my inner child. I had to right my path and get into alignment with my soul. It was time. If I wanted to heal myself I needed to get to know myself. And that was my first step toward healing.

The house is quiet, and I am alone in my room. It is time for self-compassion and contemplation. I silently ask myself four basic yet critically important questions in this practice: *Who are you? What do you want? What do you need? What do you like?*

The bright light of the morning sun peeks through the slats of the wooden blinds, and slivers of light bring my attention to the pictures on the table next to me. Photos of loved ones gone, of me, as a child. I pick up the black and white picture of my sisters and me in the bathtub. We all smiled even though tub time was no fun time back then. I was one of five siblings under five and a twin. My mom didn't bathe us; she cleaned us, scrubbed us, almost till the skin, especially behind our ears, was raw. She was firm, but her cleaning, her tough tub time, was a sign of endearment. I sat staring at the picture of me, wondering who I was then and who I was now. I sat in silent awkwardness in my room for a while. It felt unnatural, but I was desperate to get to know myself. I began to pray, which was easier than being silent, and found myself growing sleepy. I closed my eyes and repeated the questions to myself: *Who are you? What do you want? What do you need? What do you like?* Images of a child cut through the quiet. I heard one word. *Pink.* I laughed out loud and saw in my mind's eye bright pink clogs, my summer shoes, a childhood favorite. *Aha! There it is! My favorite color is pink!*

Suddenly, more scenes came into my awareness, scenes of summer, my favorite season. I watched as I wandered the small forest behind my childhood home, my favorite place. I swung from the vines and climbed onto my favorite very large rock. I stood on the top with my arms crossed as if I had just conquered the world. From the top of the rock, I surveyed the trees all around me and all the pathways through the forest that I could take. Right there, in my room, in that silence, I sensed the power of that little girl as I remembered her, watching as she wandered in her pink shoes, in her favorite place, picking the path of her choice. I opened my eyes and grabbed my journal. I began to write what I saw and list all of the other favorites that came to me: mint chocolate chip ice cream, the kind with shaved chips, not chunks; a plate of spaghetti; and crispy french fries with a heaping side of Heinz ketchup.

As I continued in my quiet times of self-compassion, I healed and rediscovered myself. I began to shed the negative emotions and attachments to my past and the anxiety, depression, and PTSD. It was as if I had taken a rake and begun to clean up the dead leaves, the stagnant beliefs, memories, and dark emotions that no longer served me and blocked my spirit. I cleaned my house by removing all my dark emotional debris. I decided to be quiet more often, during times in my car, on a walk, in nature, and in meditation. During the silence, I would hear guidance from Source, my guides, and most importantly, my soul. It was in the silence that my wall of perfection was finally broken down, the veil of pretending was lifted, and the real me would step forward. My life would never be the same.

I had found myself. I mattered, my voice mattered, and the child within me mattered. One morning I grabbed a stack of post-it notes and wrote out: *I know what you are inclined to do, but you will not do it today.* I filled an entire stack with my new commitment and went through my house, sticking the notes everywhere: on the refrigerator, the sink in the bathroom, on the mirror, and above the kitchen sink. I needed to permit myself and remind myself that I don't have to do it all, I don't have to be it all, that I already am…it all. As I brushed my teeth, I would stare at myself in the mirror and say my mantra as toothpaste dripped from the corners of my mouth, *I know what you are inclined to do, but not today. Not today, not today.* I wiped my face and looked in the mirror and smiled.

I smiled because I knew I had gone from sitting in a parking lot, smoking cigarettes, popping Ativan, and contemplating suicide, to discovering how to heal. I connected with myself, the child within me; I knew what I was inclined to do and would no longer do it, and I knew the anxiety, the PTSD, and the panic were all fear. If I wanted to be free of fear, I had to find it, feel it, forgive it, and let it go.

When I walked into my office that day, I had no idea Spirit or Source would hand me such a cathartic and healing exercise. I sat down, intending to make a journal entry, listing things I was afraid of, but instead, I found myself drawing a stick figure on the paper. I drew a picture of myself, looking empty and frail. I stared at the picture as all the fears I had in my life circulated in my head. I recalled the very first fear I could remember. The fear of getting a spanking. I wrote that fear at the bottom of my stick figure self, right next to my stick figure foot. I thought about the experience and how it made me feel and it led me to the next fear I had, spilling that milk, and the next fear, using an eraser in first grade, and the next fear, raising my hand, and the next fear, and the next fear and the next. And from bad breath to boys not liking me, from not having a clean house to not being the perfect wife, I realized the fears shared a common theme. It was like I had just cracked a code. My greatest fear was that I would live a life that would let someone else down. And if I let someone else down, I couldn't be loved. I paused, then put the pencil down, closed my journal and I walked out of my office. I was a changed woman. In the following days, I would pause, look at the stick figure surrounded by a list of ridiculous fears, and find my power.

Getting to know myself, understanding what I was inclined to do, discovering my fears, finding my voice, and pausing in life, were all necessary steps toward my healing journey. I had finally shed the medications, and given up the cigarettes (they never really helped anyway). But it was the act of forgiveness that would be my final step in healing. The act of forgiving released the grasp anxiety had on me so I could feel alive. I had to forgive life for making it so difficult to survive. I had to let go of the emotions that were attached to the painful experiences I had. I let go of the anger, the pain, and the fear. I had to forgive myself and everyone who came through my life that had challenged me, hurt me, disregarded me, or let me down. I had to forgive myself for ignoring myself for so long. I had to forgive it all enough, just enough, so that I could move on.

In my near-death, I chose to return to this life and get back into alignment with myself, so I could live. And not just be alive, but truly *live*, with meaning and purpose. Source filled me with extraordinary gifts of healing when I was in the life after this. I realized I came back from my near-deaths to heal myself so that I could help others, teach them and guide them to healing their mind, heart, body, and soul. I plan to live a long life of healing and when the gate opens and the light of love pulls me in next time, I will enter clad in pink. When I arrive I will invite my ancestors, the angels, and the saints, I will invite them to the table with all the Divine Women and Source. I will call for a celebration. I will sit with them and I will slurp the spaghetti and sip the fine Chianti. I will share the crispy fries and the side of ketchup and I will share my gratitude for having the opportunity and journey to have come alive.

ABOUT THE AUTHOR

Cathy Gabrielsen is an Intuitive Healer, Spiritual Teacher, and number-one best-selling author of *Dying to Live: Surviving Near-Death*. Cathy is also a Graduate Teacher of Energy Medicine and the founder of the Gabrielsen Healing Center. Cathy offers in-office and Zoom private healing sessions. Cathy is also the founder of Connect Thru Cancer, a nonprofit supporting families with cancer. To find out more about Cathy visit www.cathygabrielsen.com, or connect with her over Facebook at Gabrielsen Healing Center or on Instagram @cathy_gabrielsen.

GENTRY JONES

*This chapter contains sensitive content pertaining to references of suicidal thoughts.

Then, before I could catch it, the disappearing act went darker. As I sat there biting the inside of my cheek and fiddled with the black ponytail holder I always keep around my wrist, I stared at the garage door in my rearview mirror. What if I closed it, left the car running, and just…fell asleep. I was so drunk, I wondered if it could even be ruled an accident and my boys would get my life insurance money. It felt like it really only would be finishing the job of converting my flesh to match my already dead spirit. Honestly, the fear of them being left without insurance money, as it would most likely be ruled a suicide, was the only interrupting thought that this wasn't a sound idea.

OVERGROWN IVY

A paralyzing force rushed over me. It felt as if thick ivy grew over my limbs and pinned my entire body down to the seat of my car, like in a scene from the movie *Jumanji*: punishment for yet another failed attempt at sobriety. I felt sentenced to wallow in judgment forever, held back by the vines of self-pity for the wreck I had become. I sat there, numb, staring at the small black bag in the passenger seat. All gas stations seem to use the same black bags to carry your items. They hold all the fun, unhealthy things that are potentially killing you slowly like chips, candy, fried food, energy drinks, and in my case, Mike's Hard Lemonades and Limaritas. I thought of it as "The Black Bag of Death."

I sat there, broken, envisioning the mom I wish I could have been. I pictured her dancing, laughing, and being a strong, reliable, motivating force in her boys' lives. I mourned her. There was no way I was her. There was no way this drunk-driving, lying, manipulative, depressed girl sitting behind the steering wheel of her minivan and staring down at the Black Bag of Death was going to be able to come back from how far she had gone. Today would be the straw that broke the camel's back. I watched my future shatter into a million pieces.

At this point in my drinking, my oldest son was already giving up on me. There comes a time in every child's life when they realize their parents are not perfect. From the time they are born until they make this realization, they look at you like you are a superhero that can save them with magical kisses. Letting your kids see you and accept you as imperfect isn't a bad thing; it's necessary and an opportunity to teach them how perfectly imperfect we all are. The difference for my sweet little second grader was that not only did he realize I wasn't perfect, but he was also coming to see that he couldn't trust me, that he couldn't rely on me, that he did not want to be like me when he grew up.

Getting pregnant with my oldest son was not planned. I was only twenty-one when I found out and had just gotten out of rehab a few months earlier. I had checked myself in only six months after turning the legal drinking age with the simple goal of getting the alcohol out of my system. I fiercely wanted to believe I could just remove the booze and all my problems would go away. There is no doubt removing an addictive, brain-altering drug from your system is going to benefit your life, but taking it away wasn't going to get to the root of my addiction.

Twenty-one days later, I was alcohol-free, but still so lost and desperate for love and connection. It was no surprise that I latched on to an unhealthy relationship even though dating in the first year of sobriety is strongly discouraged. When you start drinking, your emotional maturity essentially stops, so for me, that meant I had the emotional maturity of a sixteen-year-old. As exciting as it might sound to feel young again when it comes to glowing skin and athletic ability, going back to the hormonal years of emotional immaturity is not great for romantic relationships as an adult. Getting sober requires an intense amount of emotional work to catch up and relationships can complicate the whole mess, but (insert sarcastic tone) *this was love*! I naively forged forward through the red flag forest, determined to create a "happily ever after" storyline for my life.

It was a good ol' restaurant employee romance. He was the bartender and I was the waitress. I did not get pregnant on purpose, but looking back now, I feel like subconsciously I didn't really care. Maybe I wanted this dramatic love story or maybe I hoped it would bring me that love and connection I was craving or maybe I truly was just too irresponsible to remember to take my little white pill consistently every day. (Side note: It is a scary paradox when the result of irresponsible pregnancy prevention brings another human life into the world. But hey, here we are.) Shortly after accepting the shock of pregnancy, I was forced back into the reality that I was not in a fairytale romance and couldn't bring a new baby into this dysfunctional environment. I ended the relationship and moved back home.

While all that fell apart, I did meet my subconscious goal of gaining love and connection when I welcomed my first son Beckham in 2010. Here was this beautiful, perfect child. From the very moment I could feel him move I knew he needed me. And most importantly, I needed him to need me. His dependency on me became necessary for me to feel worthy and capable of cleaning up my act. I relied on him to believe in me so that I could one day truly believe in myself. It was an incredibly unfair, selfish burden to put on a sweet, innocent child.

Before I gave a shit about the importance of being socially "cool," I spent my elementary school recesses playing basketball with the boys and would occasionally attempt to connect with the girls. When my parents separated in fifth grade, I was just starting to fit in with the girls, which resulted in me going boy crazy. I turned to the boys for attention and acceptance, only to be met with cold shoulders and gossip. I had never quite felt like I knew where I belonged, but that realization hit hard in fifth grade. I was an emotionally intense, attention-seeking, creatively overthinking tomboy. One day, I made a suicidal comment that promptly landed me in the principal's office accompanied by two crying parents. I had no actual plan or desire to die, but I was frustrated and confused by this inner whirlwind of emotions and pain I was feeling. As if I wanted to simultaneously punish and provoke acceptance from the people hurting me the most, I created drama to make them see and feel my pain.

My parents did the best they could and probably did better than most in navigating my moods and changes. I understood suicidal comments were a bad idea, and my friends apologized, and boys eventually liked me, but that feeling of being left behind, not good enough, never left. The poisonous seed of self-doubt had already been buried deep in the fertile grounds of my heart.

When my son was young, he had this block toy he absolutely loved. It was a box with different-shaped cut-outs on each side and corresponding blocks cut to match each shape. Every time I played with him and that toy, I could see it so clearly. It was as if my son's love was a circle and my self-love cut-out was a square. I might be able to get the circle through the square hole, but that wasn't where it belonged and it didn't completely fill the void. I think of all love this way.

So there I was, sitting in my old Dodge minivan with its wind-down windows, staring at the mountain of unorganized and broken toys in the garage that symbolized my life. I saw only two options for moving forward. I could accept that my kids were going to be raised by a mom who would be drunk for most of their childhood, or I could just disappear. Option one meant I would continue letting my kids watch the train wreck I had become, and pray they learned what not to do from my poor example. As I sat there, considering, I wondered how I could set up a "therapy fund" for each of them because they were surely going to need it. I could accept that I was doomed to be a drunk mom and that I couldn't change that, but I could try to figure out how to be the best drunk mom there had ever been. Option two meant complete removal from their lives. Maybe I could run away and let my family raise them: I was good at that because clearly, I'd been running from most of my addiction-related problems my whole life. It seemed like the motherly thing to do would be to spare them from having to watch me slowly kill myself with alcohol.

But before I could catch it, everything went darker. There *was* a third option. As I sat there biting the inside of my cheek, fiddling with the black ponytail holder I always keep around my wrist, I stared at the garage door in my rearview mirror. What if I closed it, left the car running, and just...fell asleep? I was so drunk, it could even be ruled an accident and my boys would get my life insurance money. It felt like it really would only be finishing the job of converting my flesh over to my already dead spirit.

This wasn't my worst drinking day. I had racked up embarrassing moments the way most girls collected shoes. I had passed out in the dorm bathroom and landed in the hospital with alcohol poisoning, or there was that time I was found wandering around, completely naked, at my boyfriend's parents' house—by his parents. There was that time I was taken advantage of in a house full of college guys that sent me straight into an AA meeting the next morning, head hung in shame. There were countless nights at house parties where I would be found crying hysterically, curled up in the fetal position, screaming, "I wanna go home." No, this wasn't my worst moment, but it was my most hopeless. Just nine months before, I had been found passed out drunk in my running minivan in 100-degree weather with twin infants in the backseat. Phone calls were made and I had a house full of family and friends by the next morning. Nobody quite knew what to say, but they all unanimously agreed: my behavior was scary and unacceptable.

The crazy thing about addiction is that I knew it was completely unacceptable to be drunk and passed out with my babies in the backseat. I'm not stupid. But as suffocating as the guilt and shame were, they weren't necessarily motivating. After two weeks of beating myself up and feeding my self-doubt and self-pity—the self-destructing seed had now turned into overgrown vines—I felt like I couldn't breathe and resorted back to the only coping mechanism I trusted.

My first drink after that two-week break was a flood of endorphins. It was like I had been holding my breath for all those days, and with one sip I was finally able to grasp the air and fill my body with oxygen. I started drinking again with the understanding that I just needed a break from all these feelings. I needed to numb and check out but I would (I promised myself) get to sobriety later. This moment in the garage was different, though. I was out of hope of ever recovering. It felt like the alcohol doctor had just walked into my hospital room and dropped a truth bomb: I was a stage-four terminal alcoholic with no more treatment options or experimental trials available to make me well. I don't remember leaving the car. I don't remember turning the engine off or going inside. The next thing I do remember is waking up in my bed that evening and hearing my kids laughing down the hall as their mom spent another night passed out, drunk, in bed.

However, at some point in my blacked-out, suicidal state sitting there in my minivan, I did do something remarkable: I chose to live. I had been at work earlier that day. They hadn't known how bad I was struggling, but I had already been taking swigs off a water bottle full of vodka to keep me from feeling sick. I was on a three-day binge and would sweat uncontrollably if I stopped. The binge had to end, though, because the next day I was getting a breast augmentation and wasn't allowed to eat or drink anything after midnight. I had always been insecure about my ta-tas. They were like sad, floppy puppy dog ears. And that was before I nursed four babies and those pancakes turned into crepes that had to be practically rolled up and clipped when it was time to put on a bra. I had promised myself that if I was done having kids by the time I was thirty and still hated my boobs, I would get a boob job. So at thirty, I had four beautiful boys and great equity in my house, so Haylie and Baylie were getting a makeover.

I was constantly over-explaining why I deserved them, and desperately wanting to avoid being judged for my decision. At the time I felt extremely selfish for dropping thousands of dollars of our family money on something as vain as my boobs. I am a CPA-licensed accountant and though I don't fit the stereotype of a classic accountant in many areas of my personality, I do when it comes to being cheap. Everyone I worked with knew I was getting a boob job and that I would be out of the office for a few days recovering. We decided to go to lunch to have a fun going-away party for my depressed chest and we were given the okay to have margaritas. This was perfect since I was already buzzed. Now, people would be seeing me drinking and I would have an excuse for my unpredictable behavior. Unfortunately, while everyone else was getting a small buzz at a work lunch, I was already getting sloshed. I had this arrogant belief that I was capable of hiding my drinking as long as I wasn't blacked out, but with every sip, I was getting closer and closer to that darkness, and I was starting to panic. I knew I couldn't be there anymore.

I made it through lunch and went back to a friend's house for another shot of fireball, just for good measure. But once back at the office, I finally made my move. I knew I would receive more forgiveness for leaving than being there drunk, so I walked out the front door with a quick, "I'm going to the scale house!" The scale house was a building on the property I would have to drive to. I had already snuck my purse out the side door so that I could easily grab it after walking out. I jumped in my car and headed toward the scale house knowing damn well I was about to drive right past it and head home. I don't remember the drive, but I know I made a stop at the gas station because the evidence was clear to see: the black bag of death in the front seat of my car and an open Mike's Hard Lemonade in the cup holder.

They know. Damn it, Gentry, now they know. It's not going to take them long to figure out this past year of bizarre behavior is all tied to you being an alcoholic. My coworkers' opinions of me were about to shift, because up until this point, I used the postpartum period after the birth of my twin boys, Brewer and Brixton, as the excuse for my anxiety attacks, meltdowns, missed work, lack of focus, and emotional instability. This wasn't a complete lie. I was tired and overwhelmed, and my hormones were raging. I felt incredibly trapped in motherhood, marriage, and my life. The problem was, my addiction saw a window of opportunity in my vulnerable state, and with each false promise of relief alcohol gave me, it only dumped fuel on the fire that was burning down everything to ash inside.

I had been in a similar situation in my professional life before when I was arrested for a DUI in 2014. I was heading home from a bar with my husband on a Saturday night. It was the first time we had gone out since I had stopped breastfeeding my second son, Brody, who was born in the summer of 2013. Upon being pulled over, I blew a .235, which in Washington State was over three times the legal limit. The officers were debating on whether to take me to the hospital for possible alcohol poisoning because I was so obnoxiously drunk. Being that intoxicated and still having the arrogance to get behind the wheel made it pretty difficult to plead this was just a horrible mistake. But I was a first-time offender. In fact, according to Mothers Against Drunk Driving, the average drunk driver has driven drunk over eighty times before their first arrest, and I can definitely attest to that being true.

Being arrested in a small town of only about 3,000 people meant my boss was most likely going to find out. I was working as a tax accountant in an accounting firm in my home town, and so I made the only decision I could; I decided to take the angle of being honest. This wasn't my first time driving drunk, and I was willing to admit I was an alcoholic who needed help. And it wasn't an angle, it was the truth. I was ready to get help, or so I thought. I took this DUI "rock bottom" very seriously and was determined to get sober for good. Also, remember, cheap accountant here, and DUI's are not cheap. This one hit me hard. Not only could someone have gotten killed, but the financial consequences shook me. I enrolled in the required outpatient classes and installed the mandatory breathalyzer in my car. I went above and beyond to prove to the court I was going to get and stay sober. My DUI charge, with a BAC three times the legal limit, got reduced to reckless driving, and I was allowed to exchange the typically required twenty-four hours in jail for community service.

I want to take a moment to acknowledge my White privilege in all of this. During the court process, I researched what would be required of me by the court so I could start checking off the requirements before they had the opportunity to ask. I had several people write letters of recommendation, including retired, well-respected law enforcement, I wrote a letter of recommendation for myself sharing my accomplishments and apologizing for my actions. I quickly got to work volunteering with my dad's high school girls' basketball team, which was a piece of cake. I got to hang out with my dad and play basketball, two things I love. I had the privilege of possessing all the confidence in the world that the court would see my efforts and believe I had good intentions to truly do better. I believed (and had proof) that I would be met with empathy for and faith in my addiction and recovery. Not once during this process did I have to consider if I would be viewed or treated any differently because of the color of my skin or the way I looked and presented myself in court. I was a pretty white girl with pretty white girl privilege. While I did everything in my power to appeal to the court, I could do so because I had the confidence backed by years of reassurance that if I just smiled and worked hard, things would almost always work out.

After the DUI, I stayed sober for five months. Reflecting on why I would always come back to drinking again after I repeatedly pledged to quit, I realized it was my uncanny ability to not only cosign my own bullshit, but convince others to cosign it too. Five months after my arrest, while on a family getaway, I was struggling with not being able to join in on the drinking fun. I started rationalizing with myself, *I'm not driving, so maybe just drinking and driving is my problem? I'm surrounded by responsible people, nothing would get too out of control. If I can stay sober for five months, maybe I'm not an alcoholic? I've been doing so good, I deserve a reward.* On some level, I knew if I could get just one partner in crime to cosign me breaking my sobriety I would feel okay about it because I had their permission. So I manipulated someone close to me to agree that I *did* deserve that drink and persuaded them to secretly pour real beer into a cup I had been dumping my non-alcoholic beers into. No one else knew I was drinking and because I had involved someone else, I could pass the blame. But with every single sip, drunk, depressed, piece-of-shit Gentry started creeping back in.

While reflecting on all my failed attempts to get sober, I concluded that if I could convince people of one of the following three things, my addiction would feel justified in continuing its slow weave of ivy around my neck, choking the life out of me. *I'm not that bad.* This was always accompanied by my shoving the dark ugly parts and empty bottles into the back of the closet and under the bed. I would compare myself to people who were "worse" than me, which gave me a necessary illusion of control. I would post pictures of myself showing up for my kids and make people delete any photos where I had a cocktail in my hands. The façade that at least I was better than "them" was nothing but bullshit my drinking buddies loved to cosign. When that stopped working, I reverted to: *Poor me! I'm a victim of addiction.* This one blamed unacceptable behavior on my addiction. Every time I did this, I was able to deflect responsibility at all costs and invoke pity from my codependent army. They would inevitably cosign my bullshit with sympathy for my ill-fated disease and make excuses for my misconduct. "It's not your fault, you have a disease!" they would tell me as they refilled my glass with sympathetic nods. And when that didn't work anymore, my go-to was always expressed with a heartfelt half-truth that sounded something like, *I* am *trying.* Sure, I was willing to admit fault, but it was cloaked in a false sense that I was also willing to take responsibility for the agony I was inflicting on myself and everyone around me. This one played on people's hope for change, and somewhere inside me, I guess I hoped I could too. I interchangeably used these three manipulation tactics for years, depending on which codependent soldier I was targeting.

It wouldn't be until I committed to starving my codependents that I would be able to make some progress in my sobriety journey. I decided I could no longer feed them my toxic bullshit and could not be responsible for guiding them to a healthy relationship either. I couldn't have a healthy connection with them until I had one with myself, and their codependency recovery was something I couldn't force on them. I was swimming in a sea of addiction and codependency and every time I tried to drag them to safety along with me, I was only drowning more. If they didn't want to drown, they were going to have to swim out themselves.

The day after the incident in the garage, I got up and went to my scheduled surgery. New boobies were something I had spent ten years waiting for but instead of being excited, I was incredibly sick, physically and emotionally. I wanted to die. I spent the next three days laying on my couch, high on pain pills, hit by waves of complete numbness, and then, out of nowhere, I would be overcome, inconsolable with emotions I couldn't identify. I was so tired of running. I didn't want to run away from my kids. I didn't want to run from another job. I didn't want to start over. I didn't want to keep pretending like I was okay and like I wasn't getting pulled down into the pit of despair by a jungle of my own making. I was running intending to break free from those vines, but running only tripped me up more and I was exhausted. I didn't want to keep turning my back on my self-doubt, I wanted to finally stand strong and tall and face it.

When I finally went back to work, I had a sit-down with my boss and the general manager to explain my behavior. I was so incredibly broken. I cried hot tears of shame as I repeatedly apologized for my actions. I got a stern warning and it was made very clear that if it ever happened again I would lose my job. Typically, this would have been my cue to start job hunting so I could continue to repeat my addiction patterns, but I was done running. On my lunch break, I drove myself to a local AA meeting hall, which I would continue to do for the next sixty lunch breaks.

There was something about that most hopeless moment in the van that finally gave me hope. I didn't want to die, I wanted to live. And if I wanted to live, I was going to have to surrender to the discomfort of change. I was going to have to commit to facing that overgrown jungle and put in the slow, methodical work of healing and manicuring its overgrowth. I had to walk toward it alone and take responsibility for how out of control it had gotten. I had to accept that it was going to take time and all I could do was take it one step, one vine, one day at a time. I had to face the fact that I am not someone who can be content with mediocrity in my life. I had to commit to re-exploring things that used to light my soul on fire, like acting, performing, athletics, motivating, writing, and just dancing and playing with my kids. I had to fall in love with all those things again, but this time, do it alcohol-free. If I was going to do this, I couldn't panic and demand results, I had to have faith. With each small step I've taken, I've grown and my life has improved. My son no longer looks at me through eyes of hurt and distrust. In fact, he just recently told me while we were playing a game, naming inspirational people, that I inspire him the most. It didn't happen overnight, and I cannot change the memories of the person I used to be, but I can create new ones. I choose to have faith that by continuing to prove myself as a reliable force, triggered responses to my actions will continue to improve.

The three biggest lessons I learned from the journey out of my desert were that I control my response, I control my actions, and I have absolutely no control over the outcome. It was time to understand that I control every step of the journey of my life. I spent a lifetime watching the world around me and always felt a self-inflicted, insecure pressure to fall in line. I compared myself to others to judge how I thought I should feel about my life. I begged others to fix my problems for me and then blamed them when they couldn't. Deep down, I've always known what my purpose was and would try to take steps toward it but would eventually be faced with a paralyzing fear of walking alone and losing that sense of belonging. Once I finally submitted to taking full responsibility for my life and actions, I had to go back to when I was a kid, reignite those dreams and that purpose I once had, and bring them back to life. If I truly wanted to give to the world what I knew I was made to give, I had to be the version of myself I knew I was meant to be. Instead of mirroring what I thought others wanted and needed from me, I was going to have to look in the mirror and be satisfied with what and who I had become.

Every failed attempt at sobriety knocked me down harder than the last and instead of having faith in the journey, I childishly pouted as I scooted back down the side of the mountain, wallowing in self-pity. If I am really honest, I didn't get sober because I stopped drinking on May 1, 2018. I got sober because I took that first step up the mountain by walking into an AA meeting in 2007. I didn't get the desired outcome when I went to rehab in 2009, or in 2014, when I got my DUI, or in 2016, when I got pregnant again, but every failed attempt was a step toward the mountaintop I was longing to reach. I have built an unwavering faith that, as long as I take control over my responses and actions on my journey, I will land where I am needed by the universe. To take that final step to the mountaintop of sobriety will forever be one of the greatest accomplishments of my life.

ABOUT THE AUTHOR

On May 1, 2018, Gentry drove into her garage broken, defeated, and convinced there was no way to stop the train wreck she had become. It was in that moment of feeling like there was no way out that Gentry finally submitted to the only way out. After struggling with alcohol abuse for over ten years, she surrendered to sobriety. Since that day she has been dedicated to learning as much as she can about her addiction, mental health, and personal development so she can use her voice to help bring support and community to others suffering. Gentry built her social media platforms around her life as a sober single mom and sharing the joy and confidence that can come after addiction. After receiving so much love and support from sharing her journey online, she wanted to do more to give back to the sober community and became trained as a certified life and recovery coach. Being from a long line of well-respected educators and coaches, she's using her natural abilities and continued education to teach others how to get and stay sober and reclaim their lives. A few months before getting sober, Gentry decided to only focus on making small habit changes. She started by making her bed every day and strongly believes habits helped get and keep her sober. She has since created a twelve-week healthy habit bootcamp to help other men and women experience their own transformation to a happier and healthier life. Gentry is dedicated to inspire, entertain, and end the stigma of addiction. You can follow Gentry under the handle @lifewithgentry on all social media platforms. You will also find links to her twelve-week course on those platforms as well.

RUTH HETLAND

*This chapter contains sensitive material pertaining to child sexual abuse.

He gets up, and before I can move he swallows me into the hug I have been dreading. I can't breathe. This is way too close for me, and he stinks, like dead fish. He sits back down and pulls me onto his lap. I don't want to be here! I look around the room for someone to rescue me. But I know if I say anything, I will get in trouble for being rude.

So I sit, like a good girl. It's only for a minute, I tell myself. It's not like he's doing anything wrong, I rationalize. Except it feels wrong, and a voice inside me, my voice, is telling me to get away. A minute passes. I brace myself and try to leave his lap, but he holds me tight, his arms and hands forming a noose around my stomach.

NOTHING REALLY HAPPENED

Today is Tuesday. I know it's Tuesday because my mom is getting ready to leave for Rotary, and she goes to Rotary every Tuesday. She doesn't go to the meeting, because women aren't allowed. She helps other women prepare and serve lunch to the men in Rotary. They cook lunch in the kitchen, then pass plates piled high with food through big windows to the men meeting in the dining room. My mom usually brings home leftovers. *Please let it be something good today,* not *lutefisk.* Thinking about that putrid fish makes me gag more than usual today. I should be at school, but I am home sick.

I am in my parents' bedroom. I came in here early this morning when my mom was still sleeping. Sharp pains in my stomach jolted me awake, and I barely made it down the stairs to the toilet before I puked. My eyes drift upward, to the clothes hanging above their bed.

My parents have so many clothes, too many to fit into the built-in closet next to the bed and the rolling wardrobe that spans the wall on the other side of the room. My mom has turned the shelf above their bed into a makeshift closet by hanging clothes along the edge. Lying here, looking up at my dad's shirts and my mom's dresses, taking deep breaths to try to calm my churning stomach, I think they look like people, headless and legless, floating above me.

My mom comes in to check on me. She peeks into the ice cream pail she gave me to puke in, but I haven't had to use it yet. I might soon though. My stomach feels like something is twisting and squeezing it, telling whatever is inside to get out. It reminds me of how my mom wrings out a dishrag to get the water out. The churning had eased up earlier but returned in full force when she reminded me it was Tuesday, and I realized I would be home alone, with him.

"Do you need anything before I go?" she asks as she pauses at the door.

I ask her where he is.

She arches an eyebrow. "He's in the living room."

"Can I come with you?" I ask, in my soft child voice, knowing her answer before she says it. "Please don't go," I beg again, already knowing her answer. Part of me wishes she would ask me why I don't want her to go, to leave me alone with him. But she doesn't. She just tells me she won't be gone long and everything will be fine. As she leaves the room, she tells me to stop biting my nails. "That's probably why your stomach hurts," she scolds.

I stop and study my hand. I didn't realize I had been biting my nails.

I hear my mom leave the house. I am now alone with him, and my hand finds its way back to my mouth. I stare at the closed bedroom door, studying the handle. This door doesn't have a lock. None of our bedroom doors do. Our bathroom door does, so I could lock myself in there, but it's our only bathroom. He will need to use it before my mom gets back, and I don't want to get in trouble for locking him out. I wish this door had a lock! If he knows I am home and in here, I can't do anything to stop him from coming in. I shrink deeper into the blankets, wishing I could become invisible.

Maybe I *can* do something. Somewhere in the back of my memory, I see someone on a TV show my brothers like to watch using a knife to stop a monster from opening a door. That could work. I just need a knife. But I'm afraid to move. The bed springs squeak easily, and my stomach might decide it's had enough of the twisting and let go again. I finally force myself to move, slowly scooting back to the side of the bed by the door. I stop after each small movement to listen for footsteps, my eyes focused on the door handle, willing it not to move. When I reach the edge of the bed, I peek over the side, hoping there is a discarded butter knife in the mess on the floor. Surprisingly, there isn't.

I take a deep breath and uncover myself from the blankets, thankful I am wearing full pajamas instead of a nightgown. It's not overly warm in the house, and I feel safer in full pajamas. Turning the door handle slowly, I pull the door open just enough to peek outside, checking my path. The kitchen is straight ahead of me, past stacks of boxes, clothes, and other items that make the hallway much narrower than it actually is. I don't see or hear him, but my heart is beating so loud I am sure he will hear me. I turn to grab my puke bucket in case I need it, open the door the rest of the way, and step into the hallway. I duck between clothes hanging from a high shelf outside the bedroom door, another makeshift closet. I tiptoe in my bare feet toward the bathroom, pausing after each step to listen, stepping carefully around scattered papers and other discarded items that have made their home on the floor. I peek around a dresser, piled high on top and on both sides, to check inside the bathroom. He isn't there. I keep moving toward the kitchen.

Not everything in our kitchen has a place. In fact, few things in our house do. Counters, tables, chairs, couches, and floors are stacked with things that don't belong. Ironically, our silverware is one of the few things that can be found in a place that makes sense. Unlike most everything else in the kitchen, it is also well organized, into separate, specific spaces for each utensil type. I am grateful for this, because I know exactly where to find what I need and I can do it quickly.

Lifting up, I carefully pull out the silverware drawer. I know that if I don't do it just right, it will squeak like a mouse and make my presence known. I quickly select the top butter knife from the stack and put it in my bucket. Grabbing the drawer handle again with both hands, I push it back to its original position. Suddenly, all the hair on the back of my neck stands up. I slowly turn around, expecting to see him there, watching me. But he's not. Releasing breath I didn't realize I was holding, I quickly retrace my steps, weaving around the giant obstacle course of junk lining and littering the hallway. I duck between the clothes, step through the door and push it closed. I sink down to the floor with my back against the door and grab the butter knife from the bucket just in time.

I feel better after puking, but I'm worried he heard me. As my stomach spasms subside, I listen for footsteps, but it's quiet, except for my ragged breathing. Weak and shaky, I recall the scene from *Night Gallery* and put the blade of the knife against the door. I wriggle it inside the gap between the door and the frame, as far as it will go. I step back to inspect. The knife stays in place, with most of the blade between the doorframe and the wall. I do a test, turning the handle and giving it a strong pull. The knife stays in place, and so does the door. I feel safe, or at least, safer. I hope this works like it did on the TV show, and if the monster tries to open the door, this knife stops him. Sitting at the edge of the bed, I brush off crumbs, dirt, and other debris that accumulated on my feet during my walk. Then I lie down, scoot back to the wall, and cover myself with blankets. Curled up like a barn cat waiting for my mom to come home, I reflect on how much safer I used to feel before he moved in with us.

Before

My family is packed into the car, on our way to visit my grandparents. My dad is driving, and my mom and little sister are in the front seat with him. My little sister is lucky she gets to ride up there, where there's more space. My older sister and I are packed like sardines in the back seat, between our two older brothers. It's sticky hot, and our car doesn't have air conditioning. The windows are open until we get to the gravel road and the dust makes us cough so hard we need to roll them up.

My sister and I are fighting about whose shoulder gets to be on top. It started out as a game, but the longer we play, the pushier we get. Dad tells us to knock it off or he'll stop the car. We look at each other, remembering the time he stopped the car when our brothers were fighting, forced them to get out, and drove off, shouting at them to walk home as dust rose from the tires and swallowed them. I stop moving my shoulder.

When we arrive at my grandparents' farm, we pile out of the back seat and start running toward the house. I am excited to see my grandparents, and my cousins will be here soon. With lots of people around I should feel safe, but beneath my excitement is a gnawing fear, knowing he will be here too.

My grandparents live in an old farmhouse that smells like a fireplace. They have a big wood-burning stove in their kitchen that heats the house when ice covers the ground and wind instantly freezes your face. The stove is also where my grandma cooks and bakes. As I step into the house, the smell of warm cinnamon hits my nose and

I run to the kitchen. My grandma is taking a pan of cinnamon rolls from the oven, her long gray hair tied back in a bun as always, wearing a flowery cotton dress that reaches her ankles. She gives me a warm hug, then points to a plate of rolls on the table and instructs me to take one. I select a golden, butter-topped roll from the plate and take my place on the long wooden bench leaning against the wall. This is my favorite spot, close to my grandma and close to the stove that warms me in so many ways. My sisters join me on the bench with their own rolls, crowding in beside me. There isn't much room, because half of the bench is piled with stuff.

As I savor my cinnamon roll, I observe the scene in front of me. Across the kitchen, past where my grandma is working, is a big porcelain sink. Unlike our house, water doesn't come from a faucet here. My grandparents pump water from the well outside into tin pails they carry into the kitchen, and my grandma heats water on the stove to wash dishes. Buckets of water are lined up along the wall, and chunks of wood are stacked beside the stove. My grandma is never far away from her work, as her bedroom doorway is right beside the kitchen sink. I have a perfect view of the bedroom, which is terribly messy. Heaping stacks of clothes leave space for a narrow path to the bed. I am unsure if the heaps are all clothes, or if there is stuff underneath. I wonder why there are so many, and why they aren't in dressers or closets. Were there dressers and closets in there, and slowly, they got buried? Was there another bed in there, now lost and forgotten? I shift my gaze to my grandma's cotton dress and wonder how she found it today. How did she get it out of the stack, taller than she is, without everything toppling over and burying her alive? I ponder these questions every time I am here, but I don't ask them. Instead, I enjoy my grandma's treats and the stove's warmth.

Predators

Across the living room from where my grandpa is sitting is a bedroom. I hate that bedroom, my uncle's bedroom. Thinking he might be in there is terrifying enough, but even when I know he's not, I know something else is. Inside the door, on top of a dresser, is a lynx, a wild cat, shot, killed, stuffed, and standing guard. With one paw lifted as if taking a step, it sends a warning message of danger to anyone who comes near. I know this lynx is not alive, but it looks like it is. Its eyes follow me wherever I go, and its slightly open mouth seems to be smiling, reminding me of the way Herman watches me and smiles.

Herman is a dark, constant presence in my life. Like a lynx, he lurks in the shadows, watching and waiting to pounce. He terrifies me. He is mostly bald, and the hair he does have hangs in long, thin, messy strings around his scruffy face. He has a horrible habit of grabbing me to give me whisker rubs—scraping his rough, stubbly face against my soft, smooth one. He thinks this is tremendously funny. I don't. It hurts my face, and his shrieking hyena laugh and foul-smelling breath haunt me long after I escape his grip.

I hear the sound of his teeth before I see him. He is obsessed with pushing his false teeth out of his mouth and sucking them back in. The sound it makes reminds me of someone trying to pull their foot out of thick, sticky mud.

He steps out of his bedroom wearing a white, long-sleeved, underwear shirt, like he always wears. His belly is big and sticks out in front, making him look like he is pregnant with a giant baby. His pants, as always, are hanging way too low. He wears suspenders to hold them up, but the straps aren't tight enough, and I know when he turns around I will be able to see his butt crack. It's always there, on display, like he's proud of it. He is wearing his big black boots that he hardly, if ever, laces up, making him sound like a horse as he walks.

Clomp, clomp, clomp.

Suck, suck, suck.

Shriek, shriek, shriek.

Scrape, scrape, scrape.

Everything about him makes me cringe.

We are predator and prey. No matter where I am, if Herman is there, I try to disappear. My only goal is to get as far away from him as possible, to survive. Like a frightened rabbit, I can sense him, the lynx, always nearby, stalking me. I know I am unsafe, and yet I can't make a sound.

My mom chastises me for biting my nails, ordering me to stop. I take my hand from my mouth and move to stand behind her, out of Herman's view, and reach.

My cousins are here, and we're playing outside. I need to pee, which is unfortunate because my grandparents don't have a bathroom. My choices are to use the outhouse or the white ceramic pot my grandparents keep under their bed. The porcelain pot feels safer because it's next to my grandma. But there's no door, just a curtain to slide closed. Even with the curtain closed, I always feel like Herman can peek in and see me, either under the curtain or from outside, through the window. I scurry inside to the bedroom, slide the curtain closed, and quickly use the porcelain pot.

A while after my cousins leave we come inside. I stop abruptly as I walk into the living room, realizing my mistake. Herman is here, and he's seen me. He and my parents are eating fish from a white paper package, fish he caught and smoked. He offers me a bite. "Have a treat," he says. I shake my head no, unable to speak. I don't like smoked fish, and it's not a treat. I know what it is; it's bait.

He gets up, and before I can move he swallows me into the hug I have been dreading. I can't breathe. This is way too close for me, and he stinks, like dead fish. He sits back down and pulls me onto his lap.

I don't want to be here! I look around the room for someone to rescue me. But I know if I say anything, I will get in trouble for being rude.

So I sit, like a good girl. *It's only for a minute,* I tell myself. *It's not like he's doing anything wrong,* I rationalize. Except it feels wrong, and a voice inside me, my voice, is telling me to get away. A minute passes. I brace myself and try to leave his lap, but he holds me tight, his arms and hands forming a noose around my stomach. As I struggle, he hyena-laughs his dead-fish breath into the back of my neck. My ears are ringing, and my stomach hurts from the tight grip he has on me. Finally, after several attempts of trying to get away, he lets me go. I run to the kitchen, to my spot on the bench, the safety of my grandma, and the warmth of the stove.

It goes on like this for years, me getting snared, me desperately trying to escape, him finally releasing me. And here I am again, child prey caught in Herman's trap. *Be a good girl,* I tell myself as I count down to my first attempt at escape. Everyone else is huddled around the kitchen table, finishing their angel food cake, chatting about who knows what. I can hear them, but I can't see them, and no one can see me, or Herman. This time his right hand moves from my stomach, where it has always stayed before, to my chest. Suddenly I know why I have been afraid of him for so long.

Like in a nightmare, everything about me stops working. I am frozen, like the hamburger my mom took out of the freezer to thaw before we left. All I want is to get away, to go warm myself in my safe spot in front of the stove. The voices of my family have been replaced with a loud, thumping noise. I realize my heartbeat is all I am hearing. And then suddenly, I hear that voice inside me, my voice, telling me not to be a good girl. She is shouting at me: *get away, save myself, flee.* I try to move. My muscles, still thawing, stubbornly obey. I expect him to stop me and for there to be a struggle. As if surprising us both, he lets me go right away.

As I run to the safety of the kitchen, I take a quick look back to see if he's following me. He's not. He's walking toward his bedroom. Horrified, I find my spot on the bench and my hand finds its way to my mouth. I knew that room housed two predators. Now I know the one will never truly let me escape.

Invaders

Over several years, our house has been transformed from a home into something I can't quite describe. It started in my parents' bedroom, with stacks of boxes, clothes, and other items that didn't have a place. As I grew, so did the stacks, increasing in depth, width, and height. My parents' bedroom started to look alarmingly similar to my grandparents' bedroom, and as my older siblings grew up and moved out, they left space that should have been filled with us younger ones but was instead filled with stuff.

The stacks spread into the main areas of the house, even as we, the remaining siblings, tried to stop them. We worked quickly to clear the main areas one day when our mom was away, taking turns hiding things that didn't have a place out of sight in unused bedrooms, piling them on top of stacks that were already too wide, too tall, and too deep. I tried to picture how surprised and grateful my mom would be when she came home and saw how hard we had worked and how nice things looked without the overwhelming clutter. I also worried she might not like what we were doing, because, for some unknown reason, she seems to feel comfortable in all the mess. I'll never forget finishing and taking a look around to admire our work. It wasn't perfect, but it was an improvement. I could actually see the floor, sit on the couches, push the chairs up to the table, and set a glass on the counter. When our mom returned, we greeted her at the door to reveal our surprise. I was right to be worried. Anger flashed across her face as she hollered at us, demanding to know where we had put everything. "I won't be able to find anything!" she screamed. When she finally finished ranting, I slunk away to the bedroom I shared with my sisters.

Sad, confused, and hurt, all I could think was: *How could you find anything before?* A few days later, I came home from school and everything had found its way back to where it had been. I pictured her, pulling things out from where we had stashed them, undoing all our hard work. Defeated, I managed to withhold my sobs until I reached my bedroom. *Why does she want us to live this way?*

The stacks continue to expand because my parents bring things in but never take anything out. What was once our home has become a maze, a construct of walls made from boxes, clothes, papers, and other items that simply don't belong. I have grown used to it: desensitized, immune. I hardly notice when my parents bring in more stuff, until the gray afternoon I find my mom clearing out a bedroom we don't use anymore. They are bringing in something so monstrous it will dwarf the mass already surrounding me and spread throughout all remaining space, filling every nook and cranny. They are bringing in Herman. I am slowly being buried alive.

Trapped

I haven't told anyone what happened in my grandparents' living room. I have tried to tell my mom Herman scares me, but she doesn't want to hear it and dismisses my concerns. Now that I know why he scares me, I should be able to tell her, but I remember hearing a story of my cousin, and Herman trying to touch her breasts. "She's a liar," my mom had said. "She likes to make up stories to get attention." So there's my proof. No one is going to believe me. No one is going to protect me.

We're in the living room, just me and Herman. The TV is on, but neither of us is watching. My mind is laser-focused on where his hands are because once again I have been pulled onto his lap. In fairness, there aren't many available places to sit amongst the clutter on every available surface, but that's not why I am here. I am here because the predator has once again snared me in his lap trap.

I am wearing my favorite top. Made of crisp, light blue cotton covered in tiny, colored flowers, it has elastic around the top and waist, and a ruffle around the bottom that covers the waistband of my shorts. Matching straps go over each shoulder, like a bra. It's my favorite top because I made it, and I wear it a lot.

Terror engulfs me as I dwell on the danger I am in. This time there are no voices in the next room. No one else is home. No one will help me if I can't escape, and no one will hear me scream.

His arms are wrapped around my stomach, holding me again in a tight noose. His hands stay put for a while, and I start to relax, thinking maybe this is all that will happen. And then, just when I think I might be able to get away unharmed, his left arm tightens as his right hand moves up, from my stomach to my chest. Through my top, he finds my right breast, which is barely more than a mosquito bite. *Please make him stop*, I plead silently. He starts to move his thumb up and down, up and down, over a breast that still belongs to a child. I am petrified, unable to move. The voices on the TV drift away. I hear only my heart, pumping in my ears, and his rough breathing behind and above me. Both are getting louder.

He moves his hand again, back toward my stomach, and I think it's over. This is it. He'll let me go now. But I'm wrong. When his hand reaches my stomach it doesn't stop. It keeps moving, over the elastic waistband of my top, past the ruffle, and past the pocket of my shorts. My body is rigid as his hand continues its torturous descent. His fingers reach the frayed edge of my shorts, nearing the inside of my thigh. He moves his pointer finger along the bottom edge of my shorts and tries to get beneath the elastic of my panties. That voice inside me, *my voice*, screams at me: *you need to stop him.* Summoning all of my strength, I push his arms away and remove myself from his lap. Backing away, I say firmly, "I am going to bed," expecting him to pull me back down. He doesn't.

I quickly turn and leave the room and head upstairs, to the bedroom I share with my two sisters. I pull off my top and shorts and hurriedly put on pajamas, full pajamas. It's hot up here, but I am so cold I can't stop shaking. I crawl into bed and bury myself in the covers, trying to warm up. I can hear the TV, and then it goes silent. Then I hear him. He's clomping toward the stairway. He's coming for me! But the clomping continues, past the door, and eventually there's silence. He went to bed. I feel relieved, but only for a moment.

I can't stay here. He knows where I am, and if he comes looking for me, I will be trapped. I get out of bed, tiptoe across the room, carefully make my way back down the stairs, quietly open the door, and peek out. It takes my eyes a few seconds to adjust to the darkness. I slowly step out of the doorway and creep back to the living room, to the couch tucked against the wall. This feels safer to me than being upstairs because he won't expect me to be here. After clearing out a space big enough for me to fit, I cover myself with a blanket I find on a nearby stack and try to make myself as invisible as possible. After what seems like forever, my brother comes home, and I feel safe enough to sleep.

Something jolts me awake. My bedroom door is open, and someone is going up the stairs. I stay still, barely breathing, waiting, and listening. It's Herman. I can tell by the clomping. He's trying to find me; had I stayed in my room, I would have been trapped. Several minutes later, he comes back down the stairs. He steps out of the stairway, his hair wildly tangled, and looks around the room. I don't think he can see me, but I shrink deeper into the blanket.

What he does next is bizarre and terrifying. He starts clapping, not fast applause-like clapping, as if commending himself for a good job, but slow, deliberate, taunting claps that break any stillness in the air. He brings his arms out wide to his sides then swings them together, hands connecting like cymbals in a thunderous clash, out in front of his big belly. The clap is so loud it hurts my ears, and it keeps going, and going, and going. I try not to jump, or scream, praying he doesn't come toward me. He doesn't. He turns around and closes the door to my room, evidently satisfied he's accomplished what he came to do. It's dark. I can't see him, but I hear his big, untied black boots clomp away, through the dining room, past the kitchen, down the hallway, and into his bedroom. I stay here on the couch, wide awake.

After

I tried to stay awake, but I couldn't. I wake up in my small spot on the couch to my mom and brother talking in the kitchen. I go in to see what they're doing, and my mom tells me to get dressed. They are going out to butcher chickens, and I need to help. Seriously? After my night, this is my day? The voice inside me, my voice, urges me to tell my mom what happened last night, but I think back to her calling my cousin a liar, and I ignore the voice. Instead, I obey my mom and head up to my bedroom to get dressed. As I put on a baggy t-shirt and shorts that almost reach my knees, I stare at the discarded top and shorts I wore yesterday lying on the floor—my favorite top. I'll never ever wear those clothes again.

Later, I tell my little sister if she ever feels unsafe, hide in the clothes. There are so many clothes to pick from, stacked and hung throughout our house. A perpetually messy house has a few advantages.

By some miracle, I manage to avoid Herman the rest of the time he lives with us. It gets easier to avoid him when he moves out, back with my grandparents, and even easier when I leave for college. I don't bite my nails anymore. I tried to stop many times, but I couldn't, until late in high school, when Herman was no longer living with us.

I try to forget about what happened, telling myself I was lucky, it could have been so much worse, and that nothing really happened, I shouldn't feel so violated. But something *had* happened. I had been tremendously violated. Not just my body, but my mind, and my emotions, and in the place I should have felt safest, my home.

My parents did not provide a safe space for me in many ways, and certainly not to use my voice to express my fears about Herman. I promised myself I would be different for my daughter and from early on, I told her she could and should tell me if she ever felt unsafe around someone, anyone. I wanted her to know she could trust me to listen and protect her, and eventually, I told her why.

I have been an avid watcher of *Law & Order: Special Victims Unit* for years, empathizing with the victims and admiring the detectives and attorneys who stand beside them. After watching so many stories of sexual abuse, many of which brought up familiar emotions, I was drawn to help those in our community experiencing similar trauma. I completed an intense, forty-hour training program with our local Rape and Abuse Crisis Center and served as a volunteer advocate for a year, taking after-hours crisis calls.

Sadly, I am far from alone in my experience with my uncle. According to RAINN (Rape, Abuse & Incest National Network), the largest anti-sexual violence organization in the United States, every nine minutes, child protection services substantiates a claim of child sexual abuse. Darkness to Light, a non-profit committed to empowering adults to prevent child sexual abuse, reports that one in ten children will be the victim of sexual abuse before their eighteenth birthday, making child sexual abuse one of the most prevalent public health issues facing society today. We need to do better. We need to bring more awareness to child sexual abuse. We need to know and watch for the warning signs, and we need to listen to and protect children who need our help.

Mountaintop

My journey from the desert has been long. I buried these secrets for decades, allowing myself only brief glimpses back and sharing very little with others, even those closest to me. I started to reach my mountaintop when I decided to share not only these secrets but the details behind them more openly and widely. I listened to the voice inside me, my voice, telling me to take that step, no matter how terrifying it might be. I embrace the saying: "Be brave enough to help people by speaking your truth, even when it's scary."

I knew the path would be difficult, forcing myself to unearth long-buried secrets and painful memories. I also believed there would be healing along the way. I couldn't share with my mom. I was afraid she wouldn't listen, believe, or understand me, and I carried shame that did not belong to me for decades. As I unpacked these secrets and started to share what I uncovered with those closest to me, I worried some wouldn't believe or support me. Instead, many shared their own experiences, confirming the unfortunate fact that child sexual abuse is far more prevalent than we know. I also found these words by the renowned researcher on shame, Brené Brown, to be true: "If we can share our story with someone who responds with empathy and understanding, shame can't survive."

If I could go back in time and rewrite my story, I would give it a much different ending: As I run to the safety of the kitchen, I take a quick look back to see if he's following me. He's not. He's walking toward his bedroom. Horrified, I throw myself into my mom's arms and she asks me what's wrong. I tell her, and she listens, she believes me, and she and my dad protect me. Herman never moves in with us, and he never has another opportunity to put his hands on me or anyone else. I also ask her to get help with the hoarding, before it gets worse. She listens and understands how her problem is affecting me. She puts me first. She and my dad seek help and move the stacks out of our house. With these invaders gone, our house returns to the clean, safe home it once was, and I return to the joyful, carefree girl I deserve to be.

I can't go back in time and rewrite my story, but I can do something. I can use my voice to bring more awareness to child sexual abuse. I can advocate for children in order to prevent these experiences. I can help rewrite their stories. It may have taken me decades to reach my mountaintop, but as I approach the summit, the sun is bright and warm, and I am weightless and free.

ABOUT THE AUTHOR

Ruth Hetland grew up on a small dairy farm near Pelican Rapids, Minnesota, seventh in a family of eight children. She, her husband, and their daughter now live in Fargo, North Dakota and also enjoy spending time at their lake home near Battle Lake, Minnesota. In high school Ruth was a cheerleader and still considers herself one today. She loves to cheer for and celebrate others as they accomplish great things! Ruth earned her Bachelor of Science degree in Mathematics from Minnesota State University, Moorhead and her Master's degree in Business Administration from the University of Minnesota, Carlson School of Management. She is a Project Management Professional (PMP) and a non-practicing Certified Information Systems Auditor (CISA).

Ruth enjoys warm weather outdoor activities, including hiking, running, biking, waterskiing, and paddleboarding. She also enjoys reading, listening to audio books, jigsaw puzzles, yoga, dancing, Halloween and any other opportunity to dress up, and of course, writing! This chapter is Ruth's first publication.

Follow Ruth on Instagram (@ruthahetland) and LinkedIn (Ruth Hetland).

NATHALIE CHOLETTE

I never once regretted making the jump. The only times I have held regret, however, are the instances when I chose not to jump.

MY JOURNEY
HOME

It's a cold, wintry Canadian morning in January. I'm abruptly woken up by my 5:00 a.m. alarm. Feeling exhausted, and with the dreadful thought of my endless daily work commute hovering on the other side of my morning, I inwardly groan as I force myself out of the warm cocoon of my bed. In the dark stillness of the house, I focus on getting myself ready first, knowing all too well that last minute, unplanned things can easily come up once the morning is in full swing. I wake the girls, ages ten and twelve, and then proceed to the kitchen to prepare breakfast. As I flip eggs attentively, I'm on standby for anything that comes up that might require my attention: tasks I had forgotten yesterday, last-minute requests from the girls for help with their hair, or unplanned work messages. The pressure is intense; every minute of every morning needs to be precisely accounted for so that everyone gets to their destination on time.

By 7:00 a.m., the girls are on the school bus. I'm depleted and tired so I go into autopilot mode. I pull out of my driveway and head towards the highway for my routine hour-and-a-half commute to work on North America's busiest highway. "Please don't let there be any accidents today," I whisper to no one in particular. I dread this long, crazy groundhog-day commute. Gridlocked highway traffic has been the one constant in my life these last few months. It has slowly turned me into someone I don't recognize: an angry, bitter, critical, and frustrated woman. Day after day, I count on being stuck. I count on feeling misery and anger. I count on darkness waiting for me within the confines of my car.

With each morning that I find myself driving into the grayness of my life, the anger grows bigger, darker, turning the gray into a solid black void. It slowly seeps into my pores and unapologetically takes refuge in every little corner of my body like a poison. It doesn't ask, it just takes and it cannot be stopped. Woven into this tapestry of dark emotions is one connecting thread: shame. Because really, if I'm honest about it, I have a good life. I actually love my career as a Speech-Language Pathologist (SLP) supporting children with communication difficulties. I'm a wife and mother to two bright and compassionate pre-teens. I have a network of supportive friends. I own a house in Toronto, Canada's biggest and most expensive city. I successfully escaped the confines of the small Northern Ontario town in which I spent the first twenty-five years of my life. On paper, I have it all.

With each passing kilometer on my unending commute, I shame myself with chastising thoughts: *There is so much for which to be grateful! You've checked all the boxes of a successful life by society's standards!* And yet, despite all my accomplishments, I have never felt so utterly alone, so completely unrecognizable to myself. I am lost at sea, adrift. I can't find an anchor. Every morning, anger and darkness are waiting for me. I feel like I have no control over my mornings and commute. I've become a slave to the car, wasting my best, most productive time of day in a prison made of metal that holds me hostage. My numerous attempts at finding a faster, alternate route have failed, and the highway remains my only way to and from the office. As each kilometer creeps by, the truth of the powerlessness I feel becomes sickeningly obvious. If I'm honest (what else can I be at this point) my life is already unraveling at the seams. I feel claustrophobic, stuck, with no escape from a life that everyone else says I should love. And it has nothing to do with the drive.

I feel like I have no control over my marriage. It's not working for either of us. I always feel sad, alone, empty, and confused. I can't quite figure out the reasons why, and I languish in a state of defeat from failing at making any improvements within this relationship. I feel like I have no control over who I am. In the process of always doing what has been expected of me, by my family and society, I have completely lost myself. I feel untethered. Despite my constant and valiant efforts, I am failing at being perfect in each of my roles.

The messages I receive in my marriage about not being good enough fuel my deep insecurities and fears, as do the societal pressures of doing everything perfectly as a woman. So, I try harder. I commit more time towards being perfect, leaving even less time for me to be human. The more I sacrifice, the more sweat and tears I put in, the more I feel like a failure. The effort never equals the outcome. At the end of every night, I collapse in exhaustion next to a total stranger and I wonder: *Why can't I get it right in the same way other women around me can?*

I'm a perfectionist, overachiever, and over-planner, so having no other solutions available is terrifying. Up to this point in my life, I had always made things work. Or so I thought…the positive, smiling bravado I plaster onto myself is my armor, and for the first time in my entire life, it isn't working anymore. It has worn thin and can't protect me. Being confined in my car for countless hours forces me to really look at myself and dig deep into my beliefs about my life, myself, and what I truly want. I have to acknowledge the truth. I am unhappy. Like deep down in my soul, something isn't right, unhappy. And I am petrified.

As I signal and pull onto the highway for what feels like the millionth morning in a row, I settle into the silence and suddenly recognize that I do have a choice: Every morning when I get in the car, buckle my seat belt, and check myself in the rearview mirror, I can become a slave to my anger and let it swallow me up, or I can be curious about it, tune into it, dissect it, and open the door to the truth of what is underneath. Over time, what once felt like a prison transforms into a quiet and safe space for introspection, where I can put myself, and my emotional needs first. I realize quickly that as a mother and lifetime people-pleaser, past attempts at putting myself first have always resulted in deep discomfort as well as a strong tidal wave of guilt. In my car, there is no one to take care of, no one to tell me what to think, what to believe, and what to feel.

After weeks of introspection and soul searching in the ninety minutes of silence each way, I discover that making the decision to explore my anger is only the beginning. My journey has brought me to the edge of a canyon where I am faced with two choices: I can jump into the black void below with no guarantee that anything will catch me, or I can turn around and go back to living a safe, comfortable, and miserable life. Both options terrify me. However, I instinctively know which choice will liberate me.

I've made the decision to jump before, such as moving across the province of Ontario, away from my small hometown and parents' home to start my SLP career. I remember being filled with fear, worry, and self-doubt, thinking, *What if I fail? What if I regret my decision?* I reflect on the fact that I survived that scary leap into the unknown, as I have survived the previous ones. I never once regretted making the jump. The only times I have held regret, however, are the instances when I chose not to jump. And yet, it has been a long time since I last chose to plunge.

The magnitude of this plunge—leaving my marriage—is unlike any previous ones. The thought of going against the grain, the uncertainty awaiting me at the bottom, and the magnitude of responsibility hanging around my neck feels like an albatross paralyzing me with fear. I wish someone would push me. I'm too scared to make the leap on my own. Better yet, I wish someone would swoop in to save me; take me to a faraway land where I can start all over, leaving all my problems behind. I want to live happily ever after, without needing to do the hard work of standing up to my fear.

A little voice that I haven't heard in a long time whispers *sauve-toi*: *save yourself. Save myself?* I'm transported back to my five-year-old self, in my francophone household, singing along to my favorite record by the Quebec singer Nathalie Simard. That spirited, singing girl is barely recognizable as the mute woman I am now. The thought of continuing a life of suppression and inauthenticity scares me more than jumping into the unknown. I also realize that jumping will require a complete letting go: of fear, certainty, stability, and comfort. "Letting go" is not part of my vocabulary. Up until this point, I had built my life around being in complete control.

As I sit in traffic, my uneasiness about surrendering screams for some direction. Desperate, I take a deep inhale. On my exhalation, I realize that I feel a bit lighter, as though the top, thick layer of my anger has dissipated somewhere. I take another deep inhale. In the exhale, more anger is released from my body. Curious, and perplexed, I continue this pattern. Without realizing it, this is my first foray into mindfulness. I have no background knowledge or experience in it. I'm just following what my heart feels is the right thing to do. And it feels good. Encouraged, I make this breathing exercise a part of my daily morning commute routine. With time, the heaviness of anger and darkness gives way to light and brightness, which further opens me up to my intuition.

I'm eventually guided toward the application of other mindfulness techniques, such as gratitude. Focusing on the good in my life—my daughters, my health, my car, and my career—allows me to see the beauty that surrounds me in the present moment. Suddenly, I'm like a child seeing the blue sky for the first time. The intricacies of a snowflake landing on my windshield become a tiny little miracle in the cold Canadian mornings, reminding me that I'm alive.

Soon after the integration of gratitude into my life, I become ever more aware of negative thoughts floating around in my mind: *You never listen. You are crazy for feeling this way. You are cold. You overthink.* These all-too-familiar comments have settled within me as a shameful truth. Over the period of one week, a small voice distinguishes itself from the negative one with a different message. It speaks with the conviction that, despite my faults, I'm actually not a bad person. In fact, I have much love to share. I'm a good listener. I have good friends who enjoy my company. Further, I receive positive feedback about the support I provide as a Speech-Language Pathologist.

Feeling lighter and brighter, over time I open up even further to the sound of my heart's voice as it guides me toward consciously saying these positive messages in short, powerful "I am" statements or affirmations. Statements such as "I am love, I am light, I am a good listener" remind me of the goodness that exists within me. I add affirmations to my morning mindfulness routine and delight in the reality that just a few months earlier I had felt so powerless, but now these statements are empowering me and overwriting the harmful messages lodged in my mind.

Finally, my intuition guides me toward incorporating manifestations and visualizations in my mindfulness routine. As with affirmations, I start my manifestations with "I am" statements, such as "I am financially secure." I giggle as I visualize money coming into my bank account, and bask in the scene I play on repeat in my head: sitting at the bank across a big mahogany desk and meeting the banker's bright eyes as she stamps "approved" on my application for a mortgage for myself. My energetic vibration is elevated when I visualize what it will feel like when the girls and I go to open houses on Sunday mornings and pick out the perfect place, just for us, a house with lots of natural sunlight, love, and laughter bouncing around in the air. I grab on to the belief that I have what it takes to become financially secure enough to pay my bills, take my girls with me to see the world, put food on the table, and give them a good life.

These techniques save me. They distract me from the dark, uncontrollable messes around me and in so doing, they create space. The darkness and heaviness of anger slowly dissipates from my body, making space for love. Time expands. The tight, compartmentalized space in my car expands. The constricted space in my chest slowly dilates, allowing the real me to come through. For the first time in a long while, I can breathe, I can feel, I can be. My new routines let me take back control of my mornings. I feel a sense of purpose and empowerment now as I try to embrace that which feels uncertain and uncomfortable. I can repeatedly close my eyes and bravely leap off.

As a child, I felt invisible. To receive loving attention and praise, I got good grades, dutifully attended church, recited my prayers, and followed rules. In school, I was commended for being a good, quiet, and polite student. Being this way kept me hidden, safe. I was used to conforming and playing small. In grade two, I signed up to sing a song for the class end-of-year celebration. I practiced relentlessly. That morning, my mother curled my hair and I wore my favorite blue dress with a pleated skirt, accessorized with my favorite blue flower necklace. When my teacher called my name, I froze in my seat. My body failed to respond to my brain's message to get up. Fear paralyzed my limbs and vocal cords. I couldn't even respond when my teacher asked if I was okay. Confusion and embarrassment set in. I couldn't jump. Singing in front of my teacher and classmates would show the real me, betraying my quiet role. *Would the real me be liked?* Exposing myself in this way was uncharted territory. It felt raw, vulnerable, scared. So I chose to remain hidden.

I now clearly see that my anger in that car was the build-up of a lifetime of constant self-betrayals, ruled by my need to comply in order to survive. My conformity was a cry for love and acceptance in an emotionally defunct life. It gave me some semblance of intimate connection with others, which I craved deeply. I had originally believed the anger was transforming me into someone I wasn't. However, before the anger reared its ugly head, I was already a stranger to myself because I wasn't living in my truth. I had been so busy ensuring I met all expectations perfectly, lining up my wins like shiny trophies on the shelf for all to see, that I had consistently and repeatedly muted my soul's voice to the point that it was screaming mad and demanding to be heard.

I can see now that a lifetime of repeated conditioning and compliance without questioning made me numb to how I really felt inside. It dissociated me from my intuition and my truth. The few times in my life where I had actually paused to question something that didn't resonate or feel right were either met with dismissal or an authoritative command to squash those thoughts and feelings, giving birth to a practice of constantly doubting myself.

In grade one, my childhood friend Renée drowned in a neighborhood river. Renée's cousin, also in our class, called to tell me the news on a spring Saturday morning. I was making my usual smarties-water concoction in my toy blender for my little sister to drink when my mother announced that someone was on the phone for me. Slightly annoyed at being pulled from my play, I answered the telephone. Annoyance turned to dismay and numbness upon hearing the news. After I hung up the phone, I shared the news with my mother. I don't remember an ensuing conversation at home or at school. Life just continued as though nothing had happened, until one day, our class attended Renée's funeral. I remember the song played at church. I remember finally letting my tears roll down my cheeks. I remember my confusion at seeing the heavy coffin, thinking there was no way my vibrant, cheery friend, the one who always laughed at my stupid jokes, could be in there. By the time we got back to school, it was recess. My friends and I, still raw with emotion from the funeral we just attended, were standing in a circle, crying and openly sharing what we loved most about our friend. The teacher on guard came over and sternly commanded us to stop crying immediately and dry our eyes. I remember watching her in disbelief, knowing inwardly that crying was a natural expression of our sadness. I didn't say anything. I did as I was told. Renée was never mentioned again.

I allowed others to dictate how I should truly feel, what I should believe, as well as the actions I should take. I repeatedly let others dim my light because it was safer to keep myself hidden. I thought so little of myself and was so ungrounded, that it made it easy for others in my life to manipulate me into thinking that the real me wasn't good enough for this world. It made me the perfect victim for gaslighting. It made me the perfect victim for societal, cultural, and religious appropriation. I had naively trusted that the people in my close circle who loved me had my best interest at heart. They knew me best. I should believe their words. I should heed their advice.

In my first year as an SLP, I applied and interviewed for a three-year SLP position in Auckland, New Zealand. I yearned to travel, having felt restricted by my small hometown life, which I had left a few months prior. I reveled in delight at being offered the position. I remember the day I picked up my passport, the picture of my smiling face beaming back at me, my body vibrating with happiness and pleasure. I successfully completed all the required health tests to enter and work in the country. Next up was putting in my resignation and starting to pack. It then occurred to me that in the midst of all this preparation and excitement, I hadn't told my parents the big news. I called my mother, bursting with joy. She reacted in surprise to the news that a job was taking her daughter to the other side of the world for a three-year period. Panicked, she convinced me to do the responsible thing: to stay in Canada for a year and work hard to pay off my student loans. Once debt-free, she explained, I could travel wherever I wanted. My inner voice screamed to keep my original plans. But my sense of responsibility took over. To this day, I still haven't set foot in New Zealand. What I had failed to recognize then, and for many other times afterward, was that only I knew what was best for me. If I had trusted myself, I could have tuned into my intuition and let it guide me.

With a gut-wrenching realization, I had to come to terms with the fact that I, and I alone, had navigated myself to this point. I had controlled this outcome, just as I had controlled every decision I had made up until now. The irony of coming to understand that I had driven myself into a life of powerlessness while actually spending hours with no control, in the car, was not lost on me. All this time, I had been under the illusion that I was in control of my life, when in fact, I was just marching along to do what was expected of me, being a good girl, making something of myself. It took countless hours driving through snow, cold, and achingly slow traffic to wake me up and shake me out of my sleep. When you start owning your rage, change happens.

It was time to level up. I needed to completely unravel myself before my rebirth. Multiple tiny, little deaths of past versions of me had to be mourned. The first "death" was the dissolution of my marriage. The woman in my marriage had served me well for a while. She had served him. However, there was no more space for her to serve either of us anymore. It took time and courage, but I eventually liberated myself from the manipulative clutches of my ex, and it felt so good to be free to explore, diving deeper in search of older versions of myself, still there waiting to be introduced. One by one, they lined up to meet me, exhaling in relief because I was ready to see the truth. There was:

Me, the girl who danced as a means to feel alive.

Me, the girl who screamed to be seen in her writing of stories, songs, and poems.

Me, the little girl who sang her heart out day after day.

Me, the imaginative little girl who enjoyed creating games for herself and her siblings.

Me, the little girl with a curiosity for life who, during a family road trip, casually undressed and let go of her clothing from the back station wagon window to observe other drivers' responses.

Me, the passionate and free toddler who, in the anticipated relief of a cold dip on a hot, summer day, gleefully stripped off her bikini as she waited for the small plastic pool to be filled with water.

So many versions came to meet me, their voices so loud, I couldn't ignore them, so free in self-expression, and creativity, they were all different, and yet so much the same. Familiar and foreign. I was enthralled and I couldn't look away.

What to do now? I wondered. Should I further explore these experiences by making the uncomfortable and uncertain leap into the unknown, or forget them again, go back to my car, and keep driving to and from the shell of a life that had been created by repeatedly abandoning myself? I sometimes chose the safe route because I wasn't ready. I had learned to trust that the part of me that was asking to be explored would resurface at another time when it was safe.

I discovered that a life of truth and presence was sweeter than a life of stagnancy, disconnection, and numbness. And with that dangling out in front of me, I chose to jump—most of the time. The more I jumped, the easier it became to push through the fear, knowing that at the end of discomfort and uncertainty, the liberation of myself and reconnection to my truth would always show up. Every jump allowed me to bid adieu to a fake layer of myself, making space to grow an authentic one that connected to my essence in its place. It wasn't linear, and in each descent, there were obstacles. Sometimes my old patterns reappeared. It hasn't been easy to reclaim my voice. But with every mountain placed before me, I know the climb is worth it. I also know I'll be called to jump when the time is right. Each leap has given me confidence in trusting that despite being bruised and beaten, I will survive. Knowing this makes the decision to plunge into the unknown easier.

My work commute these days is much shorter. Now when I get in the car, I remember how I chose to find an opportunity in the challenge that was my commute, and I smile at how it reconnected me to my truth.

ABOUT THE AUTHOR

Nathalie Cholette is a Speech-Language Pathologist (SLP) with a background in mindfulness, who has dedicated her life to helping children find their voice. She speaks and writes openly about her experiences as a woman who, like many others, started out vibrant, lost in the wonder of her human experience, in love with the freedom of life, and of how, through endless expectations imposed on her from an early age, she lost her soulful voice.

Nathalie considers herself a modern communication specialist, whose professional experience as an SLP, personal experience as a woman, as well as learnings and practice in mindfulness, are expertly blended into her speeches, writing, and teachings.

A proud Francophone, Nathalie hails from Toronto and is a mother of two teenage daughters. She is hungry and passionate about sharing her personal and professional experiences so that other women can reclaim their voice, stand in their own power, as well as become vehicles of positive change in the world.

Deserts to Mountaintops is Nathalie's second anthology project. More information on Nathalie and her first co-authoring project entitled *Honest as a Mother* can be found on her website www.nathaliecholette.com. You can also find Nathalie on Instagram @nathalie_cholette_ and on Facebook @The Art of Letting Go.

JANICE FEARON

The struggle to keep my young son and me from falling into homelessness and abject poverty drove me to continue on this quest for a better life. It was my son's face that I pictured as I moved from address to address, distributing my application envelopes to whomever would take them, my weary feet burning from exhaustion and cold.

THE FLIGHT
OF SURVIVAL

It was a cold Monday morning. The plants had begun to grow again, and new seedlings sprouted as I made my way to the subway station. I took the Q train northbound to Manhattan. A crossbody bag stuffed with one hundred envelopes holding one hundred identical resumes, one hundred cover letters, and one hundred self-return envelopes weighed me down. I had spent the last two weeks at my command station, butt in chair, armed with a steaming cup of tea and the yellow pages. While my son played quietly in the corner with his beloved action figures, I found every address of every medical center, doctor's office, hospital, and lab center within a twenty-mile radius. The struggle to keep my young son and me from falling into homelessness and abject poverty drove me to continue on this quest for a better life. It was my son's face that I pictured as I moved from address to address, distributing my application envelopes to whomever would take them, my weary feet burning from exhaustion and cold. The temperature had dropped, and I could feel spring penetrating my boots.

Thoughts of giving up, getting back on the train, and heading home flashed through my mind. But the truth was, I had no choice but to dismiss them despite the feelings. I reminded myself that spring is when life is born in everything: it's the beginning of new life. So, with every application I handed out, I asked the universe for a new beginning for me and my son.

As I continued walking through the long and lonely blocks that make up Manhattan, I began to cry. I was drowning in my tears; my heart cried out to God for help, and once I regained control of my thoughts and emotions, I just kept thinking: "I've just got to go to the next stop. I've got to get to where I'm going." At one point, I realized with dismay that I was lost. One building looked like the next, and it looked like the other. As I wandered haphazardly through the bustling streets of New York City, I finally stopped to ask for directions. It was not lost on me that I could use the same method of finding my life direction and purpose as I was using to find my way in this moment. Hours passed, and I kept walking. The mantra in my heart became a reverberating theme in my mind. I have to get where I am going. I have to get where I am going. I was down to my last five envelopes.

As I checked the final addresses on my list, I felt a sense of accomplishment. Hope filled me, and I felt like I had won the lottery. I was a victor because I had survived the day's challenge! Yes, I was hungry and exhausted, my throat parched and my body aching, but a thrill filled me as the reality of my accomplishment renewed and sustained me. I had done it! I had finally handed out all one hundred job applications. I had done my part. With a small prayer of thanks to God, my strength was renewed, my hope ignited, and now all I had to do was sit back and wait for someone to contact me. I headed back to Brooklyn just in time to get my son from school; physically drained but mentally buzzing. I just kept telling myself: *I have to get where I'm going.* And then I headed off to my night classes.

I spent most of the time traveling to my classes that night doing the mental math: If I handed out one hundred applications, I should get five inquiries for every twenty; I figured at least one business would be interested. Optimism flooded me, and I was empowered as I visualized what had to be ahead. My darker days of struggle, confusion, and feeling like I didn't belong had to be over. I had simply worked too hard. It was my time to shine.

Days turned into weeks, and I heard nothing. I checked the mail multiple times a day. Every time the light flashed on the answering machine, I rushed over to press play. Nothing. Fear overshadowed me once again; the confidence I had felt as I was dropping off the applications was swiftly disappearing. I didn't know what to do next. I started to panic, but then I reminded myself of the feeling I had had on the freezing spring day a few weeks back, hustling through Manhattan. There has to be *one* company in all of Manhattan that wants me to work; I only need one.

In week eight I got a job offer. It was a low-paying job at a doctor's office, but I took it to build my resume, make connections, and get the job experience I needed to get into the medical field.

It was the first step in getting to where I was meant to go.

I grew up in Jamaica, the third largest island in the Caribbean Sea. I was the fourth born and spent my childhood with my parents and seven siblings. My mother ruled with an iron fist. Due to financial challenges, we often traveled four miles round-trip on foot to high school, unless my mom had extra cash. If I didn't want to walk, I would have to sacrifice my lunch or pocket money to take public transportation. While all of that was tough, the hardest part was that my mom required us to be home thirty minutes after the dismissal of class. It didn't matter to her that we would have to run the two miles home; if we weren't at the house in thirty minutes, there would be a price to pay.

Around the time of my junior year, my mom migrated to the Cayman Islands, taking us kids with her. Shortly after, my dad joined us in hopes of providing a better life for our family. I quickly learned how to take care of the home and my four younger siblings all while still attending high school and ensuring that we never missed a day from school and the Sabbath at church. Looking back, I'm sure that is what prepared and enabled me to keep so many balls up in the air. If one of us developed a cough, we were given a warm cocktail of coffee and rum and expected to "sweat it out," because we weren't allowed to miss school. Even vomiting wasn't enough of an excuse to miss classes. While some may look at this as overly harsh, or abusively rigid, I know my mother was just doing the best she could. What she wanted for us all was an opportunity to escape poverty. And for us girls especially, that meant we couldn't miss one day of our education. Not one.

After completing high school, I spent the next eight years working as a preschool teacher, but by my mid-twenties, I decided to explore America's waters. I had an insatiable belief that there was a bigger world with endless opportunities waiting out there for me. After my son was born, I relocated to the U.S., and boy, was it a strange new world. I was a single mother immigrating from a tropical island, plunked down in the middle of Brooklyn, New York in the month of February. Snow will make you understand how strong you are because being strong (and getting a good coat) is your only option for survival.

Everything was different. The buildings were different, the means of transportation, the weather, the people, the trees, and even the way people dressed. There were days when I was homesick for my homeland. I experienced a longing for familiar surroundings and I missed my family and friends. But as is the case with many things, I learned to adapt.

The train has never been a means of transportation in the Caribbean. Jamaica has no passenger rail services either, but the bauxite companies still use railway lines to transport their materials. The means of transportation for me growing up were always inner-city buses, mini-vans, taxis, and private vehicles. Arriving in America, specifically in the middle of Brooklyn, there were many things that I had to get used to, but the train as the primary means of transportation was a fascination for me.

A couple of months after I arrived, I was walking down Utica Avenue and ran into a childhood friend. My friend and I commiserated over the difficulties of adapting, and he offered a very valuable piece of advice regarding the subway system. He explained that the subway could be tricky, so I had to pay close attention to the stops and ensure that I got off at the right train station, or else I would end up on an unplanned involuntary tour of the city. He recommended I get a map and make sure I understood the difference between northbound and southbound, but above all—and he said this as a means of a mild warning—stay in the middle of the train. He went on to explain that by getting on in the middle, which was the point nearest the conductor, I could ask questions if I was unsure of where to get off. Being in the middle, and being willing to ask questions, was the safest approach to the journey. As we parted, I was bolstered, not only because I had made a connection with someone from home, but also because the Universe was speaking to me, once again, and giving me direction about how to view my life. The central point of connection in my existence has always been a complicated twist of suffering, joy, laughter, and learning. And that middle part, *that* is the great story. In order to tell it, I have had to listen. Ask questions. Humble myself when I haven't known how to get where I was going because in reality, no one does.

As I walked along, working my way toward the subway, I recognized that disappointment, one of the most significant sources of my suffering, was necessary for my growth and development.

Disappointment allowed me to grasp the importance of living a hope-filled life. With every envelope I stuffed, every job I applied for and every door that was slammed in my face over the years, I have gained wisdom and understanding that has led me to a direct path of willingness to endure and move through the unpleasant feelings and emotions of not achieving my goals. Those moments of wandering have allowed me to deepen my faith and trust in God. Until my dying day, I will firmly believe that happiness cannot exist without disappointment. Because disappointment produces perseverance and with that, steadfastness, which is where I find my hope. And, in the end, my hope brings me to abundant joy and laughter.

As time passed, and my career developed, I came to understand that if I was going to get where I was going—the life I was truly meant to live—I would have to first ensure that the destination was aligned with who I was. And who I was, was something I had yet to explore, because I had been busy surviving.

I wrestled with this question as I held my weeping son on the floor of the gritty NYC subway station one afternoon. I was racing toward my second shift. After working all day, I had run home to collect my seven-year-old so I could drop him off at his sitter's, where he would spend the evenings so I could get to my night classes. I had gotten held up and was just two minutes behind schedule. While two minutes seems like nothing nowadays, it was the difference between making the train and subsequently my class, or missing it, and having to wait for the next one, which would dock me points for a tardy arrival. In my haste, I had let go of my son's hand, and as I got closer to the train, I could hear: "Standby for closing doors." I was almost there…and with a sigh of relief, I reached down to grab my son's hand and drag him across the finish line to our next stop. However, as I reached down, all I grasped was air. My heart came into my throat as I frantically looked around, and he was nowhere to be seen. Cold waves of panic washed over me as I turned and fought the throngs of people headed in the same direction as me. Then, as if he had heard the terror reverberating in my heart as his guide back to me, I spotted his tiny body fighting its way toward me through the deep crowd. Tears threatened to spill as I gathered him close to me, and I closed my eyes in relief. I heard the train doors slide shut and realized he was crying too. "Mom, I'm sorry. I know I was slow, and now you are going to be late for school." At that moment, it felt like all 200 bones in my body had broken. I was empty.

My arms, still wrapped around him, the reason I kept showing up, even in the middle of all this pain and disappointment, felt helpless as I held him. "It's ok. It's ok. I will be late, but we will be ok." I repeated this under my breath at first, like a mantra between God and me, but as my heart held on to it because everything else was just so weary, I looked him in the eye and knew—in the deepest part of my knowing—we would indeed be ok.

Sometimes the place we think we need to get to is not the place we need to be. Sometimes we do everything to get to that next appointment, literally and figuratively, and we lose what is most precious to us in the process. We could lose ourselves, our "why," our passion, our health, our relationships. Maybe that place where we *so badly* want to go is not worth losing someone or something, because it's not where we are meant to be at that moment, or ever, for that matter. I was racing to make that train so I could drop my son off and get to class. But where I needed to be in that moment was on that grimy floor, on my knees, crying with my son, extending empathy to him and to myself.

Being a single mom is a struggle. Being an immigrant woman is a struggle. Being Black in America is a struggle. Being a Black, immigrant, single mother in America deems me insufficient to many people. Many would have looked at my situation and said that there were not many places to go from where I was sitting. There were many nights when I would lie awake in worry as my son slept soundly in his bed, and I would wonder the same. What more could I possibly do to keep a roof over our heads and food in our bellies?

Nelson Mandela is quoted to have said many times, "Education is the most powerful weapon you can use to change the world." I wanted so badly to change our world, and I saw no other way of doing it than through education, opening myself up to new opportunities, and using that as a catalyst to get me where I was going. And I knew my mother would be proud. Because it is how I was raised, and probably bred into my DNA, I immediately enrolled in an undergraduate nursing program when I got the job as a medical assistant. I took on weekend babysitting so I could pay someone to pick up my son from school and stay with him until I got home from classes. This way he wouldn't have to rush to catch the train with me. I did all this while working at the doctor's office and attending college full time.

As time passed, I became even hungrier for change in my life and career. I wanted to reach that next level because it was necessary for my son and me. I soon began to make connections on campus and got involved in clubs and organizations. Once again I took that life lesson I had learned so many years before while wandering around, lost in New York City, and started asking questions. It was through this that I got a part-time job on my college campus as an Administrative Assistant to the Director of the Student Academic Advising Center (SAAC). I was given nineteen hours per week of work when I was not in classes. I sat alongside the secretary, helping to perform clerical services such as keeping general files and records, agendas, and important dates, creating fliers and posters, and assisting students with questions and applications.

With every new task I learned, I asked more and more questions. I was from one world and living in another, which quickly began to feel like home. Before I knew it, I blended in with the others. I didn't feel distinctly like the odd one out because I was a single mom, an immigrant, or a woman of color. I felt like I belonged. I loved being in the office and sitting at a desk. I loved how the students would come to me with questions and how I knew just how to help them. And while I loved it, I was now balancing three jobs plus going to school full-time all as a single mother. But with every hour of sleep lost, I knew I was working towards my dreams. I was positioning myself for a brighter future. As I got up in the wee early morning hours of another day, I would visualize what it would be like to live paycheck to paycheck. Most people want to get away from that lifestyle, but because we couldn't get our paychecks to meet, that was my goal. I would watch my son, or the students I served, and it was a truly magical thing, to feel like I had what I needed. I could dig deep, access the grit I needed to help me not to miss classes or work, and be the mom my son needed me to be.

Brighter days were coming. I could see them.

Oftentimes throughout my journey, I would think about my mother, and how she would dispense wisdom cloaked in her opinion as she swept the kitchen floor. "Janice," she would tell me, "if you work hard and long enough, you can achieve anything the universe offers." If you hear something enough, you eventually start to believe it.

Twenty-one years ago, in February of 2001, I came to America with $250.00 in my purse, my three-year-old, and a dream. As of September 2022, I have earned an associate's degree, a bachelor's degree, and two master's degrees. I am currently in the final stage of completing my Ph.D. in Public Policy and Administration with a specialization in Management and Leadership. I am still growing, making connections, and building my career. My son is doing well and is in college now. I cannot be prouder of the young man he is becoming.

There are many things that I still do not understand about America, about life, and the future, but one thing I do know and understand is myself. My trials have strengthened me. My faith has been tested and those tests have produced incredible endurance in me. And endurance gives me the strength to soar to the mountaintop where I will tell the next part of my story.

I live my truth with a purpose that is hard to put into words. I count all my obstacles as life blessings and invitations to be the best version of myself. When I look at myself in the mirror, I see a woman who has overcome a projected life of poverty, instability, and continued disappointments.

Someone once asked me if I ever regret any part of my journey: leaving my home, coming to America, the struggle to survive. Any part, large or small. I took a moment to consider. Regret. I've thought about that word before. As I reflected on the word regret and my life played out before me, I could almost feel the spring coming for my toes, like it did that day while I was pounding the pavement in desperation, begging for a job. It took me having to go through that experience, and the next one, and the next, in order to understand my capacity for survival; to give me the courage to keep moving from the desert to the mountaintop. I've had to advocate for myself, believe in myself when no one else would, and use my voice to sometimes stop the madness in my own head. I've asked countless questions of others, and even more of myself. Sometimes I got the answers I wanted, and a lot of times I didn't. But are there parts of my story I regret? I would say none of it. Because now I know what it feels like to fly.

ABOUT THE AUTHOR

Janice Fearon was born in Jamaica, West Indies, and migrated to the United States as a single mom. Now, Janice works as a Compliance Review Administrator for a state and federal agency where her capability allows her to help plan, organize, contribute, strengthen existing, and create new policies and procedures. Also, she ensures that the agency follows the organization's standards.

Janice is passionate about social change and supporting families and youth within the autistic community to deliver compassionate, individualized services to address adaptive behaviors and skill development for activities of *Daily Living*.

Janice's educational background includes pursuing a Ph.D. in Public Policy and Administration with a concentration in Management and Leadership at Walden University. Janice has earned a Master of Philosophy with a Public Policy and Administration concentration from Walden University and an MBA with a concentration in Management from Long Island University, Brooklyn

Janice has a passion for policy change. She hopes that the implication of her study "Effects of High-Cost Health Insurance on the Uninsured Middle-Class Families of Essex County, New Jersey" will promote affordable health insurance, which could lower death rates and provide better health outcomes. Follow Janice on Instagram @ pinklypassion.

Barb,
Live abundantly!
Sue Muraida

SUE MURAIDA

This chapter contains sensitive material pertaining to child sexual abuse

I take in as much air as my lungs can manage and I scream. From the depths of my soul escapes the primal call for survival and I can't stop it. I don't want to. It is from another world. A world where I am made to be whole, untarnished, loud—a place where I not only experience joy, but I AM joy. A place where I am meant to feel the breeze on my face and explode with spontaneous laughter. A place where I am meant to run freely and make choices and sleep soundly. Even more so, that scream is an escape from years of stifled emotion and trauma. My long-silenced voice is released into the stale, dark air of that warehouse. And for a moment, I am free. And I know this is true freedom because I am willing to lose everything to experience it, even if just for a minute.

BECOMING ME

I take a small sip of air each time we drive into the pale glow of another street light. I don't have the capacity for more. The dark stretches between lights get longer and I take fewer breaths. My chest burns. My heart aches. The roads get smaller and darker and I sit up and look out my window. I move my palms against my thighs. I crave being able to feel something. Anything. It's been months since I have felt anything but fear and disgust. The pounding in my ears drowns out the tires of my uncle's sedan as it rolls into the empty parking lot of a large warehouse. He pulls next to a metal door and cuts the engine. I hold my breath. He takes the keys out of the ignition and the vinyl seat protests as he gets out. I ease my head back against the headrest and swallow.

"Come on, let's go see your car."

His arms spread wide on top of the roof of the car as he thrusts his head through the window. Even a couple of feet away I can feel the burn of his beard on my skin. His pale dress shirt matches the deathly pale of his skin. Crickets chirp. Spearmint hits my nose. His words hang in the air between us as he grinds away. He is patient. Always patient. Always having the upper hand. But something is shifting. Shifting inside me.

My fingernails dig deep into the skin on my thighs as I reach for the door handle. I get out of the car and follow him toward the large tomb of a building. He unlocks the metal door and motions for me to step in front of him into the dark. I hear him flick a switch and a single fluorescent light begins to buzz.

I'm fifteen. Only fifteen. What am I doing alone with an older man in a scary industrial park in L.A.? I shouldn't be here. I should be giggling with my girlfriends about the boy who smiled at me. I should be sitting on my bed writing my persuasive essay. I should be finishing my watercolor painting for art class, but I came here without questioning it. As I always did. I just did what I was told, no matter how it made me feel. From a very young age, I felt belittled by some of those who mattered most to me and I grew up believing my voice held no value. So when my uncle first showed interest by spending time talking with just me at a family gathering, I felt empowered and grown up. I had never been the center of such attention before and I soaked up his predatory words complimenting my body, athleticism, and bright future. I thought I mattered to him in a proud, healthy family member way, but I couldn't have been more wrong. I mattered to him in all the wrong ways.

As my eyes adjust, I see long and dirty shadows wrapping the tools and car parts that litter the floor. As my eyes adjust to the one dim, lonely light, I can make out the dome of the VW Bug to my right. As if to not break the ambiance of the horror film that is my life, he doesn't speak but instead motions with an extended arm for me to go see my gift from him. I can't feel my legs. My heart vibrates. I want to be dead. I don't want to feel afraid anymore. I'm tired of processing how to keep moving, how to keep living. My thoughts exhaust me and I just want to turn them off and sleep.

The air is stale and tastes of grease. Out of the corner of my eye, I can see a wrench lying on the cement near my right foot. The scene in the horror movie turns as my imagination has me grab the wrench, spin, and clock my uncle in the side of the head. I watch in satisfaction as his middle-aged body drops like a deer in a hunter's scope and blood pools near his head. Filled with supernatural strength, I continue to pummel his body with the heavy metal tool, pounding out my pain into every inch of him that has ever rubbed up against mine. I can't stop. His flesh tears apart with each strike and my cheeks hurt from smiling.

I'm pulled from my fantasy when I hear his shoes on the cement floor behind me. As each footfall inches closer, my breathing stops. My lungs burn. I'm lightheaded. The second I feel his breath hit the back of my neck, something very alive inside me breaks wide open. He reaches both of his arms around me and his hands grip my stomach as he pulls me close. Then, as if in slow motion, and for real this time, everything inside me explodes.

My body, mind, and spirit collide in one last effort to save my life; a superpower Marvel has yet to produce. I take in as much air as my lungs can manage and I scream. From the depths of my soul escapes the primal call for survival and I can't stop it. I don't want to. It is from another world. A world where I am made to be whole, untarnished, loud—a place where I not only experience joy, but I AM joy. A place where I am meant to feel the breeze on my face and explode with spontaneous laughter. A place where I am meant to run freely and make choices and sleep soundly. Even more so, that scream is an escape from years of stifled emotion and trauma. My long-silenced voice is released into the stale, dark air of that warehouse. And for a moment,

I am free. And I know this is true freedom because I am willing to lose everything to experience it, even if just for a minute.

My arms flail and I spin to face him, slapping his hands away from my body. The contact with his skin feels like fire. I scream, "Stop touching me! Stop it! Stop it!" My breath is shallow and fast. My hands tingle and my throat constricts. I feel light-headed and bend forward, gripping my head with my hands, willing myself not to pass out. I never take my eyes off of him. I am on high alert.

He jumps back and holds both of his soft hands up in surrender. His dress shirt is wrinkled and partially untucked. Sweat stains soak the fabric under his raised arms. He has stopped chewing his gum and it sits between his teeth. Teeth that have bumped against mine, sitting under the mustache that has scraped my upper lip too many times to count. His defense-filled hands have never known hard work, yet they have touched every inch of me. His muted blue eyes, eyes that have seen all of me, are now wide with fear, and the wrinkles that crawl when he smiles now deepen in the dim light.

I'm empty. I've expelled every molecule of life left in me and my body takes over, inhaling oxygen because it wants me to survive. I smell freedom. I taste victory. I feel agency for the first time in my short life.

"Go ahead, tell my parents! Tell whoever you want! I don't care! I can't do this anymore! I'm done! I'm done! I'm done!" My screams echo in the dark warehouse and then fade to silence.

He gestures for me to follow him out to his car. My fists are balled as my only defense and my breath escapes in short bursts of anger. He doesn't take his eyes off of me. I see his fear and that fuels my courage. I know I've won. I know he will never touch me again. Still, my uncle's silence swallows my bravery whole. He's not saying a word. And his silence lays the groundwork for how the days ahead are going to go.

As I watch the neighborhoods brighten from the passenger seat of his car, I wonder: Can the past year and a half simply be forgotten when we are the only two people who know about it? On the drive back to his condo I decide I'll never say a word about the abuse to anyone. Unless he does. This is it. And it's what I wanted. It's what I want. Silence seems like a small price to pay so that I can now be free.

It's been over forty years since that night in the warehouse. Forty-plus years of struggling to find my voice again. There hasn't been a day that has gone by that I haven't longed to scream again. To shout to the world that I was in pain, and still am now. But the shame of agreeing to my uncle's whims and pleasures all those years ago locked up my voice. Who was I to be upset? I had been old enough to know better. Or so I thought. I now understand that a conflict-ridden relationship with my older brother primed me to land smack dab into the hands of a master predator. I was wooed by my uncle's kind words and showering of gifts and trips. I was blind to his intentions until it was too late. And right when I was starting to connect all the dots, his kindness morphed into terrifying control.

I made a vow of silence to keep my foolish choices hidden, but what I didn't realize was that, without my voice, I would also have no choice. I saw opportunities ahead in my life but I know now that I was looking for a means of escape, not healing.

The silence of my teen years wasn't at all quiet. It was everything but quiet. Out of fear, I chose to hold myself against my own will, deep within myself, and my internal pain was deafening. Daily, I hoped someone would hear me even though I wasn't speaking. I gasped for breath and then held it for too long. I felt faint and was questioned why I was pouting. It hurt. Deep inside. My silence was a self-inflicted bullet that left no exit wound. Layers of scar tissue grew around the silence deep within my soul, holding my voice captive.

I attended school, parties, and family reunions. I graduated, married, and had kids. I found the church instead of faith, and the pain in my heart got worse. As a successful freelance journalist and in church leadership, I was even envied by other moms who wondered how I did it all while also managing to raise four kids. I craved this attention and mistook it for love. I increased the height and thickness of the wall around my heart because I knew deep down my heart wanted more. Needed more. But it was too risky. I had a good life: a beautiful family full of healthy children and a husband who provided for us. It should have felt safe. So, why did my throat often ache as I tucked my children into bed at night? Why was I ashamed of the life I was living? Why couldn't I just breathe?

After exploding in the LA warehouse, I walked away from the abuse, but I also walked away from my true self. I withdrew in shame and the pressure built inside me. Days turned into months and months turned into years. At times the pressure was so great it leaked out and the emotion caught my husband off guard.

He stares down at his plate and I don't move. I hold my breath, a reaction that has become second nature to me. He doesn't often sit still and I'm nervous. The kids have left to go play, their dirty dishes, stray noodles, and sauce spread across the large dinner table. I feel heavy, ashamed, but I've done nothing wrong. We both know we are not happy in this marriage. Neither one of us is fulfilled. I wasn't ready to get married. I tried to explain when he proposed, but I didn't say it right. He couldn't hear it. My family loved him. He kept saying it would be okay.

I look up at him and blurt out, "I'm a good person!"

My words are out of context and in a voice that sounds like a young child. It's a faraway voice. A voice I haven't used in decades. I feel a slight release of pressure in my chest. It feels good to say it. Then the mess of dirty dishes and scraps of food in between us mocks me. My life is a mess. My marriage is a mess. I drag in a shaky breath as shame floods my whole being.

He reacts as an innocent man accused. After thirteen years of marriage, neither one of us has figured out how to share our hearts. Every attempt I make seems to hit his defensive stare right between the eyes and he becomes mute. My hurt wants to get out and land in the arms of compassion. Instead, I feel misunderstood and judged. He shakes his head and turns away. I am too much. Too emotional. He doesn't know me. I don't allow him to get to know me. Resentment adds to the shame and my chest tightens. I feel sick to my stomach and I feel the need to run away.

My words hang in the air over the dinner table for another long minute with no response. I stand up and start clearing the table. He helps. In silence we clean the kitchen, putting everything where it belongs just like we keep putting back the pieces of a marriage that looks presentable to others. My shame builds and I reel myself back in to keep the peace and move on. I've said too much. Again. I leave the kitchen misunderstood and miserable.

My husband wasn't intentionally hurling insults at me every day or making sexual advances against my will. However, if I attempted to share my pain, my true self, I was met with what I perceived as judgment and it shut me down because I didn't feel safe. I would withdraw back deep within myself and let my imposter take over, all for the sake of keeping the peace. I felt on display to an ever-changing audience of new friends and church congregations during seven interstate military moves. We didn't stay in any one place long enough for me to build trust with anyone, to figure out how to sort through my fears. I didn't know how to express what I was experiencing. And so I was silent.

I initially found church instead of faith and it was suffocating. I was presented with an impossible set of expectations that, if I could meet them, I believed would grant me the identity I had always longed for. Instead, I was driven deeper into a routine of people pleasing and overachieving. I became so wrapped in "fake" that I couldn't find myself from within myself anymore. I agreed to volunteer on leadership teams because, well, they asked. For me, saying no was like deadlifting 250 pounds. And, to be completely honest, it felt so damn good to be praised. Praise was also how my uncle drew me into a web of fear, and now that web of fear had grown to include the church.

It seemed like every time I joined a new leadership team we were tasked with writing personal mission statements. The last time I was asked to write a personal mission statement, at yet another new church as part of yet another new leadership team, I laughed out loud. I was embarrassed and self-deprecating as I explained how I could never retain what I wrote. Others laughed and agreed, yet we marched forward with this ineffective task anyway. Everyone began writing, except me.

I felt rebellion building inside me. I did not want to do this again. I was burned out on being asked to do things like this that never seemed to make a difference in my life. So, I decided right then that my mission statement would be funny. My dad is funny. I've always admired his sense of humor and I would like to say I inherited it. It's come in handy when I'm at a loss for words or in an uncomfortable situation. And humor has always been a great way to hide my true self.

The room grew quiet as everyone began to write. The air conditioner hummed. A crumb from a Perkins muffin sat in the center of the table as a witness to our efforts. I clutched my pen, thinking about how to start my funny mission statement. Then it hit me. Let go. What is it church people often say, Let go, let God? Yes! I wrote down Let go. What do you do after you let go? You go out! I was thinking, go out for a long walk to get away from everyone. Better yet, go out and get a drink. Relax a little and forget this whole meeting. I kept tying words together and wrote down "outdo." That was my life. Trying to outdo everyone in an effort to prove myself worthy. Ugh. Too serious.

Within two minutes I had written down a list of short phrases that were tied together by common words. When I got to "come let" I knew "let go" was next. Cool. It was a cycle, just like life. This was funny. Little did I know then that my witty idea would end up saving my life. My mission statement in its entirety:

Let go.

Go out.

Outdo.

Do over.

Overcome.

Come let.

At first, I was just determined to write a statement I could remember and be done with the assignment. However, the very night I created this mission statement I lay in bed and started down the list in my mind.

Let go: If I could, I would let go of a lot of things in my life. Fear was a big one. I was sick and tired of being afraid. Afraid of what people thought about me. Afraid of saying something wrong. Afraid that I would get myself into a situation I couldn't get myself out of. I also desperately wanted to let go of any and all expectations. The expectation of having dinner ready every day at a certain time. The expectation of having sex a certain amount of times a week. The expectation to be a Proverbs 31, biblical-style submissive wife. One after another, the expectations mounted into one giant mess of overwhelm. Was there anything in my life I wanted to hold onto? My children, for sure. My gifts of writing and creativity. My love of adventure and the outdoors. It started to sink in that I could not hold onto what I loved because I was hanging onto all the things I perceived others wanted from me. I was too afraid to let go because I feared their rejection and ridicule. I was being held together by false praise, always on the verge of falling apart.

I wiped tears from my face and glanced at my husband sound asleep next to me. It was time to get honest with myself. I was not ready to get married when I did. I thought back to when he proposed and the discussion we had before I said yes. The discussion was so long that he had to get up off his bent knee to finish it. I was afraid and confused and he worked hard to convince me it would be okay. I said yes and cried every day for the first six months of our marriage. Even then, I worried that my marriage wouldn't last because I wasn't being honest about who I was and what I needed. I couldn't even try to love another in a healthy way when I didn't know how to love myself. I looked back up at the ceiling and moved on to the next part of my simple mission statement.

Go out: When was the last time I was courageous and stepped out of my comfort zone? I couldn't remember. I knew deep down that outside my bubble of people-pleasing was where I would find my true self. And it scared the shit out of me. I knew making a move in the direction of my heart's desires would not sit well with those I was currently living out my daily life with. They were overly conservative in thought and action. I was empathetic and silently cheered on those who expressed their unconventional love and beliefs. During Bible study or at church potlucks, it seemed that not one discussion about women's rights, gay marriage, abortion, immigration, or simple human equity lined up with my beliefs. I didn't utter a word because my unspoken words were dismissed in conversation as unbiblical and irresponsible. I felt trapped on a jury and didn't know how to get off without being hung myself. Stepping out of my comfort zone meant doing it alone. I would need to start over. The very thought of doing so brought a flood of childhood messages from my brother that I was stupid and not worth anyone's time.

My tears, now streaming hotly down my face, were pooling in my ears and I was afraid of waking my husband. I got up, grabbed tissues and a blanket, and moved to the living room couch. The truth was simple; I was embarrassed by the life I was living. It had never felt right, but the people I was in relationships with just kept telling me it was, and so I believed them. The truth that I didn't have the self-esteem to question them and stand up for my own beliefs, cascaded over me, manifesting in a torrent of tears. I made some tea and moved on down the list, my journal overflowing with questions.

Outdo: Am I just getting by? Ummm, yes. That's all I'm doing. If I were to outdo yesterday—basically, do better—I would need to start saying no. Oh, and this was a hard one. No, I don't want to spend another day surrounded by the same people doing the same things. I want to speak up and voice my own thoughts about faith and humanity, desire and love. I wanted nothing more than to outdo every moment of fear-charged apathy to which I let myself succumb.

Now I was getting pissed. My tears had run out and my heart was pounding with the adrenaline that can only come with clarity. I looked around my living room. I didn't fit into the life I was living. I was living this way because I was afraid not to believe the "successful" ones with whom I engaged daily. I was living this way not because it felt right, but because I didn't have the courage to live out what did feel right.

As the minutes ticked away into hours in the middle of the night, I shuddered as I realized I had just done what I had always been afraid to do: I had opened up Pandora's box in my mind. And I knew deep down that closing it back up wasn't going to be an option. I thought about the sun coming up and the responsibilities it would bring with the day: playing my expected roles, caging my authentic self, pretending I was happy. And I just couldn't do it. Not again. Not for one more day. The same primal need to escape that I had experienced in the L.A. warehouse welled up inside of me. Running through this list released that part of myself that I admired. The emptiness inside me was filling up with possibility and I could sense the powerful shape of me taking form. It was intoxicating. I wanted more from myself. So I moved on.

Do over: There is so much I longed to do over. I had no business being married. In those moments of scratching out realizations in my journal, I understood that I didn't yet love myself, which posed the question: How could I love another in a healthy, life-giving way? I wanted to go back in time and shove my uncle against the wall that first time. I wanted to stand up to my brother, fueled by self-love and not fear, and tell him to go fuck himself. I wanted to speak my truths and ideas with conviction and make space for others to speak theirs without judgment. And I knew as much as I wanted it, I couldn't change the past. Maybe I could try a redo, a do-over. I could find grace and forgiveness for my younger self and assure her that I would always stand up for her, from here on out. It was not too late. It was never too late to live authentically.

Adrenaline hit my stomach and my soul broke open like it did in the L.A. warehouse. But, instead of wanting to die, I now wanted to live. A primal need to survive washed over me and at that moment I didn't care what anyone thought anymore. I needed to be me, and it brought a pang of hope.

Overcome: The abuse wasn't my fault. I was set up and traumatized by an adult who had complete knowledge of what he was doing to me. He did not care about me, he cared only about his own needs. That was not my fault. Now I had the opportunity to embrace the broken areas in my heart, heal them, and come out stronger, healthier, and freer because of it. The thought that I had the power to do this scared me. But somehow, it was different from all the other fears that had held my authentic self captive for decades. I would have the power to intentionally be more compassionate to myself. And more than anything, I would be able to overcome the silence.

It was now 2 a.m. and I felt the same way I had when bringing my daughters into the world. The pain was incredible, but I was buoyed by the hope of new life. As endorphins were released into my brain, a huge smile broke across my face. The air was filled with the clarity that I didn't have to live my life in silence anymore. I didn't have to hide my true self any longer. I thought about my daughters again and how I had not labored to bring them into a world where they would learn to be silent by watching my fearful conformity. I wept again, a fresh torrent of tears for them, and for me. I had to do something. I needed to begin speaking from my heart without fear, no matter the cost.

Come let: What would it be like to let people know the real me? My unconventional thoughts and beliefs clearly didn't line up with those of others in my group. Was there anyone who would be able to hear my heart and love me anyway? I circled through this list for what seemed like hours that night. Each thought launched me into another prompt in my mission statement. Each answer satisfied long-held questions of self-worth. I fell asleep, exhausted by questions. But I awoke with so many answers.

I had one friend I knew I could confide in. I would tell Carol everything. We bonded over our exploration of faith. She seemed so sure of the promises the Bible held within its pages for her struggle with chronic illness. I wasn't so sure but was drawn to her assurance. I longed to experience her confidence in an afterlife, a place without abuse, fear, or pain. Together, we wrestled with scripture—our disappointments and expectations—and we always ended our conversations with prayer. I never felt the confidence she exuded, but I always felt accepted and loved, and it kept me coming back for more.

Carol was the one. It was time. I needed to let go of the hold my experiences had over me. For the first time in my life I was motivated to begin making decisions that would benefit me and that would begin a journey of healing, leaving the dead-end road of "fake" behind. From afar, Carol listened to my story of childhood sexual abuse and loved me just as I hoped. Our conversation gave me the courage to tell my husband. And although the conversation with my husband didn't go as well as with Carol, I felt encouraged each time I shared my story with a person I felt I could trust. I let myself entertain wonder and curiosity for the first time since I was a young child. I explored yoga and meditation and found a love for myself in the process. I fell in love with nature and found God there after decades of seeking him where I couldn't find him, in the organized church. I began to dismantle the weak faith I had built on the altar of others' expectations and ideals and searched with defiance for a life-giving foundation of faith. Using meditation, I am continuing to develop my own safe place to communicate with God and reconstruct a faith that is inclusive and empowering.

———————

My divorce is final. The family house has been sold and I have bought one on my own in another state. Love pours into me from my children, soothing my weathered soul. My friend Carol passed away from pancreatic cancer years ago, but she is still there for my questions. I feel the warmth of possibility. My spirit stretches, unfurling from decades of being in bondage to my fear. The air around me is charged with a joy that I'm still sometimes wary of touching for fear it will disappear. It swirls near my heart and occasionally tricks me into vulnerable laughter when I'm not on guard. And it feels so good. I laugh at the fact that I'm laughing.

I set up my camping chair near a group of women. I'm close enough to hear their chatter and laughter, but far enough away so that it is obvious I am here alone. I had to let go of my desire to go to the Peach Festival with someone. My daughters were either busy or out of town and, if I was going to enjoy the beautiful day at the foot of the Grand Mesa in Palisade, Colorado, listening to bands, eating food truck deliciousness, and drinking local beer, I would have to go alone. The thought unnerves me, but here I am, eating my street tacos and drinking a Dirty Hippie dark ale, tapping my foot to the seventies and eighties music I have always enjoyed. And then, one by one, people get up to dance. A few couples, but mostly women of all ages fill the grassy area near the stage. One woman has to be in her seventies. I watch, tapping my foot and eating my tacos. *What would happen if I stepped out and joined them?* A shot of adrenalin hits my stomach, turning my tacos. There is no one to go with me.

As I watch the women spin freely, I consider that I'm also new to town and no one knows me. I've already let go and come alone. What will happen if I go out on that grassy dance floor and dance like hundreds of people aren't watching? I would outdo every dancing endeavor I've ever experienced, which haven't been many. I love music, but I'm not a very good dancer. It doesn't come naturally. I think back on all the times I sat at wedding receptions and didn't dance because I didn't think I was good enough. In a burst of courage fueled by newfound freedom, I set my Dirty Hippie in the drink holder of my camping chair, and, before I can stop myself, I am standing. This is my do-over. This is for all the times I just sat while my soul wanted to dance. With each step toward the stage, I feel like I'm overcoming a lifetime of missed moments of pure joy. I find a place near the edge of the pulsating group, close my eyes, and let go. I dance for the next hour and a half, laughing and meeting those dancing near me. I feel a shift in my soul. It's pure joy. I feel free.

Focusing on my simple mission statement has developed a momentum in my life that grows stronger with every passing month. I am experiencing peace and am growing more courageous with my words and actions. As the world heats up with politics, health concerns, and climate issues, I am faced with living out my beliefs regardless if they are acceptable to others. It is still scary, and at times I feel myself wanting to withdraw so as to not draw attention to myself. But every time I look into the eyes of my children and grandchildren I find the courage to live and love out loud by letting go, going out, outdoing, doing over, overcoming, and letting others in. I am living and loving out loud by simply becoming me.

ABOUT THE AUTHOR

Sue Muraida is a writer, speaker, and pursuer of abundant life. Over the past thirty years, she has worked as a medical photographer, photojournalist, leadership trainer, writer, and teacher. She has written for several publications including the *Casper Journal*, *The Small Group Network*, *Christianity Today*, and The *New York Times*. Sue has published two books, *Change For a Penny* and *The Silent Sound of Darkness* (as Sue Skalicky), and co-authored the anthology *Deserts To Mountaintops: Our Collective Journey To (Re)Claiming Our Voice* (as Sue Muraida). Sue is passionate about teaching and inspiring adults to live each day to its fullest by rewriting the past into the best tomorrows. She is currently the program director for Humanities North Dakota. Follow Sue at www.suemuraida.com IG: @lifeplotline

THE MYSTIC CHICS

"I Find my voice
I Find my truth
I find my freedom"
"I Find Myself" - Mantra (The Mystic Chics - 2020)

For each other, we provided a mirror of truth. Outside of this
sister safety zone, we learned to swallow both sadness and deeper
truths, to not speak up or out, and to present an accepting veneer
in discomfort. However, these early family deaths ushered in more
intense and frequent spiritual experiences for us.

" All we have is now, so be brave and let Love through.
Honor yourself and learn to be true."
"Awaken the Mystery" The Mystic Chics (2020)

HARMONY IN HEALING

As we drove east, en route to Cape Cod, we were headed to the beach, but the destination felt like creation, like possibility. At the resort, the hotel room was full with two queen beds and our suitcases, but we found space to tuck in the keyboard, essential to our songwriting process. Outside, three loungers (of course there were three!) beckoned us to relax and sing freely. On that trip we wrote five songs in two days; one of those songs, "Awaken the Mystery," reverberated in that sweet courtyard-turned-sound-studio. Our personal journeys to-date—our whole selves—were in that song. It became an anthem for the human spiritual journey.

We are The Mystic Chics—modern medicine women who are also family—two sisters (Audrey and Wendy) and their Aunt Mary. Two years ago, given the incredible fear and disconnect generated by world events, we felt compelled to collaborate and provide an empowered, compassionate contrast. We formed a healing business affecting change by healing through substance-free sacred ceremonies, events, courses, and sessions, using energy, sound, movement, and music.

Huge pieces of rose quartz glistened on the garden paths, and as we played and sang in the resort courtyard, passersby paused and smiled, letting us know they felt and received our expression. We didn't yet know what The Mystic Chics would fully be but we were determined to find out. That magical three-day excursion to Cape Cod was the first of many mountaintops for us. We were free from prior parameters and responsibilities: no one asking us to be quiet, to stop singing, or to take care of something. We took time to treat ourselves to a chai latte, to relax our bodies in the pool, and to meditate outside, warmed by the sun. We were united in our common purpose. We had fun in the creative flow, working with whatever showed up. By coming together, the light that is in each of us was amplified.

People have commented how remarkable it is to have three healers from the same family. The truth is that many members of our extended family have spiritual gifts. What we think makes our business collaboration unique is our relationship to each other. The three of us provide one another with the positive aspects of family: understanding, support, encouragement, honesty, and the space to be our authentic selves. In our mystic collaboration, we listen deeply and help others create new versions of themselves. Being a Mystic Chic is a way of living that honors the divine within, leading to a life of mystical synchronicities, awareness and connection, limitless possibilities, and the amazing opportunities the universe is constantly providing. And, the truth is, everyone is a mystical being.

Our union began in earnest several years ago, when the three of us, visiting on Wendy's couch, were discussing healing stories from our individual practices and fantasizing about having a retreat in Sedona, Arizona. The idea dropped in as one of us just put it out there, "Let's form a healing group!" Ideas and excitement punctuated a conversation so full and fast we knew we were on to something.

And yet, each of us had our own path to traverse to get ready for this healing collaboration.

..so don't try to escape, really feel that pain.
It cracks you open, it provides the gain...

Lyrics from "Awaken the Mystery"
The Mystic Chics, 2020

Mary: I was nine when my brother Mickey died in Vietnam, taking the easy laughter in the house right with him. Everyone retreated to a different corner of our home after the soldiers left, and that seemed to be the way of it from then on. No one spoke of Mickey's death. In fact, I learned not to speak of Mickey at all, or share any of my feelings about him, his death, or my grief, especially when my mother was around. One of our family's healthier habits during this time of sorrow was listening to and playing music. We would gather in the living room around my parents' heavy oak cabinet stereo phonograph and play record after record, singing along with the artist, often playing along with one of our guitars, trying to perfect chord changes or strumming patterns.

Shortly after Mickey's death, my brothers and I were playing our new 45 record "Honey" by Bobby Goldsboro. This ballad of death was released in February of 1968, and by the time of my brother's death, three weeks later, the record sold one million copies, making it the fastest selling record in the history of United Artists. Even by modern standards, selling a million copies within a few weeks is a major accomplishment. The sad song, woven around springtime blossoms and the death of a loved one, spoke volumes to all of us, as it was art depicting life—our life at that very moment. It gave us permission to cry, permission that had not been granted in our home in the months since Mickey's death. The orchestral strings modulated and grew in volume, Bobby's voice crooned the lyrics: "Now my life's an empty stage where Honey lived and Honey played, and love grew up..." Those words were timed perfectly to my mother's return home from grocery shopping that day, and walking into the room, she must have felt the depth of emotion emanating from the song as it flowed from the cabinet speakers. Maybe it was that she felt the emotion oozing from all of us, as we sat, teary-eyed, listening to the song. Regardless, with the swiftness and grace of a deer in flight, she darted toward the record player and lifted the needle with an abrupt scratch, catching us all off guard as she spoke in a hushed, low even tone: "Don't ever play that song again in this house."

We didn't play Bobby Goldsboro's song again. Nor did we gather very much as a family in the living room after that. It was too hard, too sad, too uncomfortable, too unpredictable, too everything. As our family drifted apart, we also drifted away from our individual selves and learned to dance around our feelings or the expression of any emotion, avoiding it at all costs. As the months and years went on and the pattern of avoidance and suppression continued, alcohol became a steady companion and coping mechanism in our good old Irish family of eight siblings.

Wendy: I was back in my parents' home after five years on my own. This alone felt like an alternate reality. Many people were sharing their happiness about how good my dad looked, how wonderful it was to see him dancing at Audrey's wedding, what a miracle that the cancer was gone. I listened and smiled, hoping my controlled nod would be enough to hold in the tsunami of what I knew to be true in every cell of my being: he was not going to live another year, maybe not even another six months. I knew better than to disagree and incinerate all that hope, so I kept silent. I was counting the days until Aud returned from her honeymoon. I didn't want to bring her down, but I desperately wanted to know what she was feeling.

Audrey: I was on my honeymoon in the Southwest, looking out the passenger window at beautiful scenery, but instead I was being shown my father's funeral. I saw several details and tried to dismiss them or block them out, but the truth of what was imminent was clear. I knew it would be happening soon, regardless of what the doctors told us. I tried to share what I was experiencing, but was not met with understanding. I was told that I was just worried. I wasn't worried; I was receiving a download of premonitions. Painful, difficult truths that I didn't know what to do with. I knew I would talk to my sister about it when I got back. Wendy would understand.

Our tears fell, sadness pouring out along with relief as we validated the truth we both knew. We felt honored and supported, grateful for the same spiritual affirmation we were each given. It was unthinkably sad and the "knowing" was a heavy weight for us to carry. The weight came partly from a lifetime of dismissal of our gifts: "that's just your imagination, don't be so dramatic," "you're so sensitive," "there's no proof of that," "you don't live in the real world," and more. A constant diet of doubt, fed to us by those we loved, left unseen but deep scars. Others argued against our "knowing." But we knew. The unseen world is always communicating truth, and we had long been listening. Three months later, our forty-nine year-old father died quietly, with friends and family gathered around him, in the living room of the house he had built thirteen years earlier. His blood, sweat, tears, and aspirations were in every piece of that house and when his essence left, pieces of us left with him on that last breath. This, like his younger brother Mickey's death years earlier, was also tragic for the family. Our dad, the first born of this large Casey clan, the junior John, was gone before the senior. It was clear Spirit had been preparing us for his death using visions, but we did not know then what to do with that information. For each other, we provided a mirror of truth. Outside of this sister safety zone, we learned to swallow both sadness and deeper truths, to not speak up or out, and to present an accepting veneer in discomfort. However, these early family deaths ushered in more intense and frequent spiritual experiences for us.

How do we awaken and how do we grow?
How do we become what we already know?
…Oh the mystery, the deep unknown,
Look within yourself, return to home.

Lyrics from "Awaken the Mystery"
The Mystic Chics, 2020

Mary: My journey to sobriety had mystical roots; whispers of truth from the unseen world, intuitively guiding me from fancy wine in a pretty glass to my substance-free authentic self and everything I had been seeking.

A steady wine sipper for twenty-five years, I was a happy hour gal with a daily ceremony I enjoyed. At the end of each day, gathering together my computer, a tall stemmed wine glass, and a bottle of California Chardonnay, I tuned into Hay House Radio, a leading online talk show for spirituality and meditation. This daily dose, accompanied by a glass of liquid relaxation, became a staple in my kitchen at 5:00 each day, as I began making dinner for my family.

It was after my second pour that my interest was particularly piqued, when I heard a show called "Be Your Own Shaman." The host of the show was offering an online meditation course that sounded fun and easy to learn. A lifelong spiritual seeker, I had tried various modes of meditation with little success and had a feeling this course might offer me what I was seeking. I was in search of my true calling and authentic life purpose. I spent most of my time looking outside of myself, even though I was being guided to take a closer look inside. I signed up for the meditation course, received instructions, and before I knew it, I was meditating. It worked! Within two weeks it was as if someone had washed the windows of my life and I could see through the looking glass into me. I now saw my happy hour ceremony for what it truly was: a major obstacle. It stood in the way of all I was searching for: happiness, joy, purpose, clarity, and the ability to be present in the moment.

Eight years ago, the sober curious movement was not as it is now. At that time, I only knew of one person who was alcohol-free. I phoned, telling her I wanted what she had. Without hesitation she said, "I will pick you up and take you to a twelve step meeting that starts at 7:00 p.m. tonight." The meeting was nearby and on the eleventh step. I had no idea what the twelve steps were. Looking it up, I discovered the purpose of the eleventh step was to make contact with God (or the unseen world) through prayer and meditation. *Of course it is*, I thought. The power of meditation: there was a sign to me from the Universe as big as the Universe itself! Ironically, the clarity from my daily practice of meditation magnified my foggy relationship with alcohol.

Spirit brought me full circle with a whisper of truth, and continues to guide me forward in life, with purpose and clarity. Ending that repetitive cycle of alcohol amped up my musical and spiritual gifts. My audio channel opened wide. I enrolled in energy medicine school, began writing my own songs, and in 2018 I opened the doors of my energy medicine and sound healing studio, The Carriage House.

Wendy: I was twenty-seven when my dad died. I was exhausted, frustrated, and angry. Raised to be a people pleaser, albeit unconsciously, anger was not an emotion I readily embraced. Angry women were bitches. Anger led to arguments, hurt feelings, and icy coldness. But everything changed with my dad's death. I felt bereft and lost. I had hightailed it out of my small hometown and created a life for myself in the D.C. metropolitan area, a five-year life that I halted and pulled back from when he got sick. But it was anger that hotly cut through the thick blanket of sadness that threatened to suffocate me and extinguish all joy. This anger lit the fire in me to start exploring all the "whys" I was feeling: *Why him? Why that particular cancer? Why now? Physical health was just one component; what about mental, emotional, and spiritual health?* Humans are holistic beings, so of course one component must affect the others.

I started reading voraciously. Metaphysical books became my lifeline. I would feel anxious if I knew I did not have another book waiting. My dad's physical death was just the beginning of a deeper connection with his soul and a catalyst for me to embark on my own life purpose and start trusting myself. After his death, he sent me messages through songs, license plates, and bumper stickers. These signs were so obvious that for the first time I didn't care what other people's opinions were.

My whole life I had what I termed "knowings." I just "knew" things: when people were truthful or not and why, when someone was upset, when we were going to have a surprise quiz in class (wish I paid more attention to that one), how a movie would end, who was calling. I never really talked about it. If I did share, it was usually met with polite silence, sometimes fear, outright scoffing, or anything in between. For a long time I doubted myself and started an unhealthy cycle of overthinking my emotions instead of trusting them. Silently broadcasting a beam of compassion would have strangers confiding deep, personal secrets and feelings to me. In addition, I would receive comfort, guidance, teachings, messages, and more from vivid sensory dreams that felt more real than actual life. After my dad's death and through all I was reading, I learned these experiences were all about energy, frequency and vibration. Everything finally made sense. Other people's dismissal or doubt of me and what I was sharing didn't have to affect me. Why was I not giving myself credit? Why did I think anyone else had authority over my own experience? I knew what I knew and it was real.

Audrey: I was twenty-three when the hospice nurse pulled my mother, my sister, and me into the kitchen. She calmly and confidently instructed us to tell my dad it was okay to die. Not thinking about what was happening, I just knew what needed to be done. I immediately went into the living room, climbed on his bed, and found the strength to whisper, "It's okay Dad." "I love you so much." One tear traveled slowly down his right cheek. He tried to speak but couldn't. The depth of approaching grief ripped through me with nausea, yet I couldn't stop thinking about that one tear. How was that possible, when he hadn't consumed any liquid or food for days? That single tear validated my courage, my understanding of what he was going through, my loving action.

When my Dad died a few hours later, I was overcome by how beautiful it was to witness his essence go from physical to energetic. As I remarked, "That was so beautiful," family members contradicted me, saying "Stop saying that. How can you say that?" I couldn't help myself. I had feared death, but now witnessed spiritual beauty and grace. Why would they not want to know that? My Dad was no longer in pain. The beauty of that life moment impacted me deeply. It would take years that felt like lifetimes, but I would learn to find the strength to trust and believe in my own experiences of the spirit world, regardless of what others thought and how they treated me, even if it would mean eventually leaving my marriage.

My father's death was the catalyst for my spiritual awakening. In a real way, his death brought me to life. I began reading about Near Death Experiences. I craved knowing what happens in the energy world: the in-between place of being physically dead and yet very energetically alive. It was real: full of love and truth, unlimited and weightless, devoid of suffering, discontent, manipulation, greed, and lies. It was a place with capacity for much more than this human physical density. It became clear that every ending ushers in a new beginning. Reading about the unseen energy world gave me a language for my prior experiences. Even though I didn't know what to call it, I was reading energy fields, discerning truth from lies. I would see apparitions, feel disembodied energy, hear voices. I would walk past someone and just know random facts, like their cat had just died or they had pain in their left shoulder. In college, I began having prophetic dreams. I felt what other people felt. Downloads of information from the energy world would run through me, like I was watching a movie. I had no idea then that my future would be working with energy medicine to help others.

These spiritual gifts amped up after my dad's passing. The night before my first child was born, feeling nervous about childbirth, I awoke to a warm, comforting energy beside me that I recognized as my father. He communicated that everything was going to be just fine, and he was right. My sweet daughter was born hours later, healthy and perfect! For the next thirteen years, I was blessed to be at home raising my three children. In June, 2010, I opened my own energy healing business.

We three, like many, were conditioned to be silent observers. Now, we are using our voices in myriad ways for our work: aligned with channeled messages from Spirit, creating original music and new ways of thinking, toning healing vibrations, sharing our stories, helping others find their voices, opening the directions in ceremony and calling in our ancestors, chanting original mantras, and our favorite: Mystic Chic Chats.

> *I Find my voice*
> *I Find my truth*
> *I find my freedom.*

Lyrics from "I Find Myself - Mantra"
The Mystic Chics, 2020

Mary: I was in my happy place: the downstairs level that I had transformed into a healing studio. I paused to welcome a couple of stragglers hopping on to another group tour. Was it the fourth, the sixth? I had lost track, but it wasn't important. What was important was demonstrating the effects of my hand-held crystal bowl. I love that tool. I love all my healing sound tools. Aspects of my former music teaching career came flooding back, but instead of looking down at upturned little faces, I was looking directly into the eyes of adults who had incredible life stories and were hungry for the information I was sharing. I felt full and confident. I couldn't believe everything we did to bring this event to fruition. Host a public "Sober in the Suburbs" event at my house in two weeks? Sure! Why not? The wry sarcasm was there but mostly outweighed by my enthusiasm.

My dear friend-in-sobriety, Martha, and I are thrilled to see our mutual friend Sam's vision come to life. As someone who is eight years alcohol-free, I am honored to support Sam, owner of Umbrella Dry Drinks, her vision, and the whole concept of embracing more options for sobriety. I knew the first thing I would do is call the Chics. They were on board from the get-go and our three-way magical combination of saying "yes" to whatever opportunity Spirit provides accomplished everything we wanted and more.

Even my springtime plantings were done, far earlier than had it been just me. That is still something that surprises and delights the practical side of me: I might feel like I need much more time for something, but the three of us have an ease and flow and can do much more, more quickly, together than any one of us alone. Through this, I am learning how much I am capable of. And right now, at our collaborative event, I feel a sense of joy and accomplishment.

Wendy: My cheeks hurt from smiling so much. I felt like my feet were barely touching the ground as I traveled from healing studio to The Carriage House tour to the firepit, all the while making connections and talking about my favorite subject: the metaphysical world. What an incredible day this was. We had all hustled to make this happen: run to Staples for posters; plant the impatiens, raise the canopies, set up the equipment, make sure Martha was bringing the snacks. It was a whirlwind from idea to manifestation, but this first "Sober in the Suburbs" event would not be the last. I was excited to have an option for a "grown up" beverage that was not alcoholic. I never enjoyed alcohol. I wanted to; it seemed such an outward symbol of adulthood and sophistication. Finally, in my forties, after literally holding my breath to swallow red wine, I realized how ridiculous it all was and just said, "No, thank you" whenever I was offered anything. Also, it became very apparent that with the energy work I did, absolute clarity was much better for me and my clients. So this event brought a fresh and welcome perspective. Every aspect of planning and taking part in this felt easy, natural, and right. Here it was, an amazing spring day, people strolling the gardens, touring the property, speaking with Martha about her journey and books, enjoying Sam's sophisticated spirit-free sips, and talking with each of us Mystic Chics about all things healing.

I was nervous and sang a wrong lyric when we shared our song of peace, "Be the Change," but no big deal. In the past, my inner critic would have silenced me for the rest of the day for that, but the soul-to-soul connection that I felt from these "strangers" far surpassed any glitch. Plus, I was harmonizing with my peeps, my gals, two people who always have my back. And, as we Chics laughed it off, everyone else took the cue to laugh and have more fun with us. When we talked about making this event successful, we were thinking in terms of numbers and how many would attend. But now that it was here and happening, I knew that it was this special connection that made our event successful whether there were 2 or 200 in attendance.

People were earnest, clear, interested, and respectful. They wanted me to talk with them about my experiences, my "knowing." They had chosen to be here and wanted to hear what we all had to say. I realized with a start that this was the first lull I had felt in three hours! Sam was still serving zero-proof beverages, Martha was chatting and selling raffle tickets, Mary was giving tours of the studio, and Audrey was engaged in conversation. What a fabulous collaboration! This was definitely what we Mystic Chics had in mind during previous brainstorm sessions about ways to spread our messages of healing and self-empowerment and how we could work with and support others, we just didn't know it at the time. Ahhh, thank you, Spirit! A full wave of gratitude tightened my throat. But wait! Where did all the people go? As my gaze swept around, the tightness in my throat grew stronger and squeezed tears to my eyes. There they were. About 20 people, staying past the event time, gathered around the firepit, talking, laughing, sharing their experiences with each other, making plans to attend a future concert, as if they had always known each other, all because, in part, we Chics had honored creative flow and ourselves by forming this group.

Audrey: Speaking all things energy medicine to this new group of eight strangers, I feel their gaze upon me, intent, focused, awaiting more information and full of respect. This is what it means to be nourished. I am in my comfort zone. Love, warmth, and understanding flow from me. I feel these women and men receive all of that; they are receiving me. I hear my own voice: confident, calm, expressive, and passionate. It's my third rotation of bringing people through the energy medicine healing space at The Carriage House. It feels good to be me, enjoying this exchange, fielding their genuine questions. I relax in the energy of their respect. It all feels easy and natural, in contrast to my recent past when I struggled to speak my truth and be who I am.

It is now three years since my divorce. These event attendees are like sponges, soaking in information and energy nonstop. I remember when I was like them, just beginning my healing journey. It makes me smile. My heart bursts with excitement and joy for all that is waiting for them. Walking outside in the bright sunshine, I am struck by crowds of people and their new connections to one another, their smiles, laughter, engaged eyes, and conversations. A quick energetic read of the group revealed tremendous clarity and receptivity.

Is it the sobriety that provides this clarity, I wonder? My body has read alcohol as poison from the first sip I ever took. The reaction was immediate expulsion. Substances carry their own energy and can attract negative sources. Much of energy work is clearing out energies that do not belong to you, and working with energies that substances carry can be challenging. Living a life free from substances provides clarity of mind, energy, and body.

Scoping the crowd, I find Wendy and Mary, as they welcome, educate, and empower the crowd in a high vibrational, warm, genuine way. I see the energy exchange. My heart is at home whenever I am with them. Mystic Sisterhood best describes this unique deep exchange of love I feel for both. Wendy has always been my rock, and

Mary has now added her crystal energy! It washes over me how our first "Sober in the Suburbs" event is an extension of The Mystic Chics and what we offer: safe environment / sacred space, substance - free, unconditional support, music, lively conversation, laughter, wisdom of having been through hard times, respect for all, desire for growth, and integration of spirit. Looking up at the sun, on this gorgeous spring day, I inhale deep appreciation for how far we've come, for all that is in this present moment, and for all that is yet to be.

When we each were in our own desert, we felt like the mountain top would just be getting out of that locale, that mindset, that vicious cycle. But this is how beautiful life can be. We dared to utter, out loud, what we wanted. We wanted to be seen, to be heard, to express, to be healthy, to be respected, to help others, even to help heal the world. And, we wanted to do it together.

Sitting at this mountain top that is The Mystic Chics, we are modern medicine women choosing to live a spiritually centered mystical life. Our climb out of the desert showed us that spiritual guidance is always there for our benefit. When we stop silencing ourselves, stop second-guessing our intuition, the future unfolds better than we can imagine. "Show me how good it can be!"

All we have is now, so be brave and let Love through.
Honor yourself and learn to be true.

"Awaken the Mystery"
The Mystic Chics, 2020

ABOUT THE AUTHORS

The Mystic Chics (Mary Casey Bowers, Wendy Casey, and Audrey Casey Herrick) are modern medicine women affecting change through substance-free sacred ceremonies using energy, sound, movement, and music. They are family—two sisters and an aunt—and currently divide their time between their two studios: The Carriage House energy medicine studio in Alexandria, VA and Awaken with Audrey in Great Barrington, MA. A favorite activity of the Chics is to road trip together with a bag of grapes, Skinny Pop, and Cape Cod potato chips. Their morning routine generally includes an oracle card thought for the day and, when in Virginia, they love warm chai tea and a seasonal scone from Mae's Market.

Mary lives in northern Virginia with her husband Roger and two furbabies: Bella and Casey. She has two grown sons Drake and Michael. A life-long musician, one of her earliest influences was Carly Simon

Wendy lives in the Berkshires of Massachusetts. She has two grown children, Victoria and Jackson. She loves gardening, being outside, and her apple pie won the blue ribbon at the annual town fair.

Audrey lives in the Berkshires of Massachusetts and resides in Florida for part of the winter. She is mother to Hannah, Caitlyn, and Graham, her three grown children. She is a lover of love, cozy blankets, and dark chocolate.

Follow The Mystic Chics on all their social media platforms @themysticchics or visit their website at www. themysticchics.com.

CAMERON CURTIS

Never turn down anything but your coat collar.

While my professional journey has been a long and winding road (with many deserts-to-mountaintop routes I've had to climb), I have come to understand that you can't get anywhere worth going if you aren't willing to take a risk. Small risks give you the courage to take bigger ones, and the fear you feel, if you just refuse to let it take you down, can also be empowering.

THE SOUND OF
RESILIENCE

Of all the advice my grandmother Lois shared, "Never turn down anything but your coat collar" is the truest piece, and it shapes who I am today. Lois Sylvester was a force to be reckoned with. She had amazing legs, I'm talking pinup-worthy. That's a weird thing to say about your grandmother but it's the truth. She could rock a beautiful skirt suit and Stuart Weitzman stilettos or a Talbot's tracksuit and Tretorn tennis shoes. Her short gray hair was always perfectly coiffed. A silver fox. I have memories of sitting on the toilet seat watching her curl her hair into the perfect position. She smelled of a combination of Crabtree & Evelyn rosewater and Nivea hand cream, scents that still bring back a flood of happy childhood memories.

She was a Navy ship captain's wife and wore it well. She and my grandfather married young; he was the love of her life, and she was his. My grandfather died at the age of fifty-five, leaving my grandmother single for the rest of her life. She would never date another man again. After my grandfather's passing, she and her friend Joan traveled the world, putting those great legs and stilettos to good use. They visited China, Russia, Europe—she lived life to the fullest and brought back mementos that I still have today.

My fondest memories are of the holidays we spent together. We would sit and talk for hours. Lois loved a good whiskey sour. Sometimes she gave me sips (when my mom wasn't looking) and sometimes my own to savor. Whatever events were going on in my young life, I knew what her feedback would be. I never got tired of hearing it: "Cami, you know what I always say, never turn down anything but your coat collar."

These words have guided me throughout my life, and not just when I went coat shopping. In fact, they have nothing to do with fashion. I've learned over the years that everything we want in life requires some level of risk. Even something as seemingly benign as choosing eco-conscious toilet paper made from bamboo versus the fluffy, oh-so-soft brand name. How many people have tried the socially responsible version only to realize it's not as comfortable on your hemorrhoids? (For those of you who don't know what I'm talking about, don't worry, your time will come.) Sometimes the risk is worth it because the long-term benefit will pay off. It was her way of telling me to live life to the fullest, take risks, and work hard to do things right.

The first real risk I remember taking was in seventh grade when I decided I wanted to play the piano. My aunt had one and when we would visit, I would sit down at the keys and play for hours. First by ear, and then using beginner books. I loved banging on those keys and it's where my love of music truly began. It was the first time I remember doing something that felt right; my fingers knew what to do. It brought me a certain peace as the music filled my soul. I grew tired of waiting to play on the infrequent visits to my aunt and uncles, so I decided to buy my own. Or locate one so my parents could buy it.

My parents, Dick and Linda, are remarkable people with strong convictions and a powerful work ethic. They always gave me unconditional love and support, and I could go on all day about how they instilled in me all the qualities you want to impart in your children. While my parents were out running errands one afternoon, I decided it was time to take matters into my own hands; I found a piano for sale in the local newspaper and I called and made an appointment for my parents to go see the piano. While they were away, I found a local piano teacher in the yellow pages. They bought the piano and signed me up for lessons. I know how lucky I am to have my parents in my life.

The day they moved the piano into the house was more exciting than any Christmas or birthday. I ran my fingers over the keys and marveled at what I could do. I committed to my piano lessons and then started taking voice lessons, singing solos in a church choir, and taking chorus in high school. In college, I majored in music with a concentration in vocal performance—opera and musical theater. It all started with one small risk, a simple phone call to some strangers about a piano, hoping my parents wouldn't kill me for committing them to an appointment they didn't know I'd made with people they didn't know. But following that little voice inside me made a huge impact on the trajectory of my life.

You may be checking your social media right now to see if I am still an operatic wonder. Let me save you some time: I am not a famous opera singer. I never became one, and I no longer sing except in the shower, car, or for my friends after too many whiskey sours. Even though I have been trained at the highest level to use it, I lost my voice.

Instead of taking the stage by storm as a coloratura soprano, I got married to the love of my life. We left the town where I had started doing professional theater to move to Washington, D.C., and did what most young married couples aim to do: we bought a house.

It became abundantly clear that I was going to have to find a job, like a J.O.B., and one that made real money. It's hard to make real money when you're first starting out as an aspiring performer, so I supplemented. My grandmother's advice came in handy again, and I stayed open to new possibilities and took risks trying a variety of jobs. Each one developed my voice in a different way, guiding me to where I am today.

The first job I found was through a nanny agency. I worked for a family with a parent in a prominent federal position serving under a U.S. President. This was my first foray into being the primary caretaker for someone else's kid. The little boy was two at the time and had two older brothers, one in high school, and the other in college. The mother was in her early fifties, and my charge was a "this is how we save our marriage" baby. My job was to make sure he was clean, fed, napped, and entertained. The mother, a writer herself, was incoherent half the time and the father traveled a lot. I never once met him in person.

I grew to love the little boy. We would spend our days going to the pool at my condo, museums, nearby farms, and FAO Schwarz to play with their train table. It was lonely until I befriended a mother who enjoyed spending time with her child. One day, while we were splashing away in the pool, my charge asked me if I wanted some vodka. I laughed and splashed him and called him silly; then I started finding empty liquor bottles in the couch cushions when I brought him home. I arrived one morning, at the same time I always did, and could hear the mom reading to the little boy. I noticed bloody footprints on the floor leading to the living room and nearly choked on the scene I walked in on— a reminder of the mad scene from the opera *Lucia Di Lammermoor*. I saw the mother wearing a white nightgown covered in fresh blood. She had a gash across her forehead so deep I could see her skull. It was clear she needed medical attention, but because she was intoxicated, she sat down with her son and decided to read to him from one of his story books instead.

I started having trouble sleeping because I would stay up all night, worried about what I might encounter the next day. I decided it was time to move on. I put in my resignation and made sure the father knew that the reason I had quit was that I had concerns for the boy and his safety. I was terrified. It was intimidating, going to a man who worked for the President of the United States, making claims about his wife, and expressing concerns about his son. But I knew it was the right thing to do, and I had to be brave. I felt somewhat validated when my last paycheck bounced, and I realized they had failed to pay my taxes. It wasn't the first time I had been faced with needing to stand up and take control of my situation, but this one really stuck with me. My voice began to grow again.

After too many late nights, I decided that it didn't matter that they were a big shot family; I deserved to be paid and to get some sleep. They needed to be grownups and stick to our agreement. I'm happy to report that they did hear me, and took accountability to fix the issues. That nanny job didn't last longer than six months, but I learned something about speaking up.

Next, I decided to give the preschool teacher gig a whirl. One thing I have known about myself since childhood: I do not like to be dirty and I hate snotty noses. The combination of the two really grosses me out. *Seriously, where does all the snot come from?* I've always thought I was worth thousands (at least that's what I tell my husband!) I was proven correct when I was hired again to be a nanny. The teacher that connected me with the family "in need" (yes, I am using that ironically) was paid in a Louis Vuitton bag for finding me: a white, college-educated, English-speaking nanny. Apparently, I was a rare commodity. The first day I met the "Louis V mom," she was wearing a pair of gorgeous Cole Hahn loafers. I mentioned in passing how much I liked them. Her reply shouldn't have shocked me as much as it did, but it was something to the effect that I would never be able to afford them.

With raised eyebrows and a healthy dose of trepidation, I entered a foyer bigger than the size of my first apartment to meet my tiny bosses. They were two kids under the age of five who had been traumatized when their beloved caretaker had been let go one night and was not allowed to say goodbye to them. When I entered the scene, they were desperate for her and would ask for her every day. It took me weeks to earn their trust, especially the older one. He had a severe speech disorder, and I literally spent hours listening intently to the sounds he was making, watching his body language in order to contextualize what he was trying to express. I became his interpreter. I couldn't know it at the time, but I was acquiring another tool that I would use in my vocal toolbox.

Once again, I was swimming in a pool of dysfunction. Everyone around me was trying not to drown, and I felt like the only life-saver these boys had. I would show up for work in the morning and the mother would lament her exhaustion and head out for a day of shopping. The dad would remind me and the housekeeper that the children should be fed, bathed, and ready for bed before he got home from work at 6:00 p.m. The five-year-old had learning challenges along with his speech disorder, and when his mother turned to me one day and said, in front of him, "He's just so stupid," I knew I was sinking and sinking fast. It was time to go. I gave the mother my notice, and she let me tell the boys myself. I couldn't stand the thought of them feeling abandoned by me too. And then I noticed, my voice grew even louder.

Unexpectedly for me, my next job was working for an orthodontist. (Apparently, my brain sees snot and dirty mouths differently, or maybe it was the addition of gloves and protective eyewear.) I lasted there exactly a year and it was an interesting experience. I've always been a "teeth person," so when I got the opportunity to take and look at mouth x-rays and bend wires that would move teeth, I was in my element. The problem was the orthodontist's office was a microcosm of high school mean girls, and the orthodontist was the all-star football quarterback. These were grown-ass women I witnessed putting soap in other people's milk, and they also made sure I got the most difficult patients. When I showed up to work in the morning, all I was interested in was learning from the orthodontist how to hone my wire-bending skills. I finally realized life was too short to deal with that kind of bullshit and I was too ambitious to stay in a profession where the only way I would get ahead was to go back to dental school. That was a big no thank you.

Next up on this episode of What Do I Want to Be When I Grow Up: I worked at the Phi Beta Kappa Society (PBK), the nation's first and oldest honor society for the liberal arts. Over the span of eight years, I worked my way up from an executive assistant to the director of society affairs. I was finally in my element, and best of all, there were no snotty noses to wipe! This really meant I was a jack of all trades. Everything I did in this job was a risk because I had no idea what I was doing, and I had zero training. Understandably so, as I didn't learn how to work for nonprofits in my music theory classes. Somehow, I managed. Every time a new opportunity would arise, and I felt scared, I would channel my Grandma Lois and I could hear her say, "Cami, never turn down anything but your coat collar!" I would take a deep breath and keep going.

It seemed I had the magic bullet to succeed at this job: the right mix of common sense and asking smart questions at the right time. However, when I discovered the unfortunate fact that the salary difference between me and the next highest paid person was over $100,000, I was spitting mad. I had worked there for almost seven years and felt that my salary was no longer representative of the job I was expected to do. I reached out to a board member and friend, Judith Krug.

Judith was a power player in my network—an incredible woman. She was an American librarian, freedom of speech proponent, and critic of censorship. She was the director of the Office for Intellectual Freedom at the American Library Association beginning in 1967, and in 1969, she joined the Freedom to Read Foundation as its executive director and co-founded Banned Books Week in 1982. Badass doesn't even come close to an accurate description of what this woman did for the world, and for me. She was my mentor, friend, sounding board, champion, and (most importantly) someone I could trust to be brutally honest with me. She gave me a lot of advice, as I would find myself calling her on random Thursday mornings for years, and all of it was good. In some of the most true and life altering words she spoke over me, she avidly supported my right and need to stand up for myself, "because no one else is going to do it for you." After going around and around with her about the massive pay gap I had been made privy to, she encouraged me to do something about it. I finally found the courage to write an official letter of complaint and gave it to my boss, the head of the organization. He read it in front of me. With his raised gray eyebrows and white beard, he peered over his reading glasses like an angry Santa Claus. He responded that my salary was sufficient. "You're making more money than my kids—and they are your age!" I knew at that moment it was time to move on. And my voice grew louder still.

I had hit my stride when it came to planning conferences, so I accepted a position in the meetings department of a large healthcare association. Managing minute details brought me joy, and I was lured by the opportunity to travel and work with smart, creative people. I love working with people who are smart and creative, who doesn't?

Like most things in life, there is often a hitch. Six months into the job, after the novelty wore off, I found myself playing out the scenes from *The Devil Wears Prada*. My boss had grown accustomed to getting all the attention for herself, but I was there too, working hard and using my own personal connections that I had built during the eight prior years.

I found myself working for a real-life Miranda Priestly, minus the Prada. On several occasions, she threatened to fire me in front of vendors I had just met, all while slugging down a cocktail. Talk about uncomfortable. I brushed it off, but I really wanted to scream across the table at her and tell her to fuck off. She constantly second-guessed my judgment when hiring team members who reported to me, although they all worked out and stayed long after we both left. She was incredibly insecure and never liked the respect and attention I received from industry colleagues, my team, or other peers in the organization. Work that started out challenging began to feel more and more boring, as the frustration from her bullshit piled high. Instead of lifting other women up, she used us and stood upon our shoulders, pounding us back into the ground. I would stand back and watch as she left a wake of broken women in her path. On more than one occasion I wondered: *Why do women have to push other women down because of their own insecurities?*

Over three years, the dread crept in slowly day after horrid day. All I could feel was despair. I'm a stress eater, because, you know, "This body doesn't make itself," and I now weighed more than I did when I was pregnant. My marriage to the love of my life was on the rocks; we were fighting all the time. It became almost impossible to get out of bed in the morning because all I would do was lay there and obsess over what was ahead of me. I went to several doctors who diagnosed me with clinical depression, but I didn't believe them. I was in denial because of the stigma surrounding depression at that time. I would try to explain to them that I could still get up and go to work. Didn't people with depression just lay around in dirty sweats and watch the Lifetime channel all day? "I am NOT depressed," I declared.

My declaration was not very convincing as I cried all the way through my appointments. I would leave angry and then just find another doctor who would give me the opinion I wanted to hear: "It could be your hormones. How old are you?" or, "It sounds like you're working with some really tough people—it must be their fault." I refused to let depression be my diagnosis. It wasn't until I found a nurturing female doctor who explained that depression looks different for each person that I accepted it. She was so kind and caring, and I felt like she got it. She really saw me. And so, finally, I agreed to treatment.

Coming to terms with my depression diagnosis was the neon sign I needed to flash in my head: *You're in too deep! Save yourself! Get out of there as fast as you can!* I followed the protocols for leaving the position, and my first stop was my boss' supervisor. She acknowledged the situation, but claimed her hands were tied. I thanked her for her time and moved on to the Senior Director of Human Resources. She was not pleased when I explained that I was in a toxic work environment. I gave her three options: one, she could fix it; two, she could do nothing, at which point I would go to the President and tell him what was happening under his leadership; and three, she could pay me to leave. Her eyes perked up and I could see the wheels turning. I knew at that moment, I was going to have to channel Judith Krug and dig deep—like opera singer deep—to find my voice and be my own champion. This was going to be the most important negotiation of my career, because my marriage and my mental and physical health were on the line. It was the first time in my life I really understood the importance of creating and holding space for myself. It took a minute, but I was really and truly finding my voice again. And I was only getting warmed up.

I was good at negotiation techniques because I had been using them for a large part of my career, but this negotiation was going to save my life. I drew in a deep breath, just like I used to do when I was up on stage getting ready to sing for hundreds of people. The song that came out was a demand for six months' salary and benefits. She stopped cold, slack-jawed in disbelief at my demand. Then she chuckled. She fucking laughed. I took another longer, deeper breath and looked her directly in the eyes, and said simply, "I'm serious." She closed her mouth and rolled her eyes in a way to show me that she didn't have time for my shit. "You can have a month," she said, and went back to her "important work." I took an even bigger breath, the kind you have to take when you are gearing up to sing several measures without breathing, and said simply, "Look, I can stay here, do my job extremely well, and keep enduring this toxic environment. But just know, as a result I will make everyone's life miserable and you will have no grounds to release me." Again, her eyes perked up, flashing with fire now as she perched forward on the front of her chair. Oh, it was on. How dare I threaten her?

Here's the thing. When did we subscribe to the belief that asking for what we want—what we need, hell, what will save our lives—is a threat? Someone had to stand up for me. Who else better to do it than me? The bottom line was that I was a hard worker, a good employee, and I was being treated poorly. I didn't deserve it. No one does. After more negotiation, and continuing to force my voice out into those hard and uncomfortable conversations, I secured five months of full pay and benefits and went on my merry way. Years later, I randomly ran into a supervisor from that time and place in a restaurant, and she actually apologized to me for not listening and responding better to the situation. I felt vindicated. I had won the battle, and the prize was my health and happiness. But as I walked out of the restaurant, head held high with the pride of my perceived validation, this annoying little thought started to worm its way into my mind. *Had I really won the battle or was it just beginning?*

Flaws. I have a few of them, and while I can go on all day about confidence and my ability to move on, I have to acknowledge the fact that I can hold one helluva grudge. It takes a lot for someone to get to that point with me, but once there, you are as good as dead to me. I'll sit and wait patiently for the Universe to correct the injustice (because I know the Universe is always working in *my* favor). However, my preference is always for drama, something really spectacular like the opera *Don Giovanni*, where his downfall is met with fire and brimstone for his wrongs against others. But in true cosmic fashion, it wasn't until sitting down to write out all my wise experiential lessons for this particular chapter that I realized how much power this woman *still* held over me. As I mentally hiked the path from the desert of that toxic situation and relived the moments that were sheer torture with her, my anger was fanned into the realization that I was filled with anger. Pure, unadulterated rage. Rage, because I had been bullied; the truth is, I had been abused. I wanted her to feel the same pain and suffering she had inflicted on me. She had single-handedly destroyed my life for *three years*. Three whole years. Destruction that led me to take prescription drugs just so I could get through my miserable day. And while all that is true, and never will not be true, I also had to come to admit a second truth: I had been holding space for her negative bullshit for *eleven* years. It was actually trauma that I had compartmentalized for over a decade. My trauma.

The mere mention of this woman's name would stir vengeful feelings in me. And I was back there. I would see her at industry events and it was all I could do to hold myself back from literally wanting to punch her in the face, and I'm not a violent person. As she sauntered about the room, all I could think to myself, and I guess to the Universe, was: *Where the fuck was the dramatic karmic activity that I had hoped would plague her for so long?*

Karma acts in mysterious and sometimes less dramatic ways, I realized when I recently found myself at an event with this woman. It wasn't until I was on my flight home that I realized the Universe had corrected the injustice, just not in the dramatic way I had hoped. In the years since I had last seen her I had leveled up. I found myself at the event surrounded by amazing people, bouncing between the different groups, laughing, sharing stories, and reveling in the energy of having a great time. Bobbing around in the pool, with a drink in my hand, I caught sight of her out of the corner of my eye. At first, the same feelings stirred: I was a dog, on guard, hackles raised. My breath started to stall, until all of a sudden, I could see things for what they really were. She was alone. She sat in the corner, an angry scowl pasted on her face. There was no laughter. No belonging. On the flight home, as I reflected on what I witnessed, I looked out the plane window into the limitless view of clouds and atmosphere and realized I had observed similar situations over the last eleven years. My justice was her quiet isolation.

When I arrived home and sat in my own silence, I finally understood that this wasn't about winning. I couldn't forgive her, but as I forced myself to reflect on how alone she looked and how angry she still seemed, I felt a wave of compassion come over me. And then I felt the heat of revelation as I came to understand that I was still giving away so much of my precious time being angry at her. I needed to finally grasp that holding on to all that negativity was keeping me in a prison. I had to release the negativity and turn my prison into a platform; a platform where I could stand and sing a new song.

This time, my song would come from a place of freedom, forgiveness, and a commitment to letting go and moving on. Risks come in all shapes, sizes, and forms. Letting go is risky, but I am finding that it is giving me space to breathe, create, and become the truest version of myself. Reclaiming my true voice wasn't about learning all the right notes or saying the best words. It required me to trust my fear, and quite literally save myself. While my professional journey has been a long and winding road (with many deserts-to-mountaintop routes I've had to climb), I have come to understand that you can't get anywhere worth going if you aren't willing to take a risk. Small risks give you the courage to take bigger ones, and the fear you feel, if you just refuse to let it take you down, can also be empowering. The fear exists for a reason and it will hardly ever steer you wrong. Every decision we make in life is risky (remember the toilet paper). Next time you're faced with a risky decision, stop for a second and consider the possible consequences. Whenever I'm afraid (and God knows, that still happens a lot!), I ask myself the following four questions:

1. Will this decision hurt anyone or anything?
2. Will this decision create financial hardship?
3. What is the consequence of not taking the risk?
4. What does my gut say?

Most decisions are already made in your gut because our gut and brain work in tandem. I always trust my gut, and it has yet to steer me wrong. Listen to your body. The human body is remarkable. It serves as a teacher, a guardian, and a scorekeeper. It teaches us boundaries: when to push and when to pull back. It guards against things that might harm us. Unfortunately, it also keeps score. When your scorecard is filled with toxicity, it will protect itself in various ways. For me, that looked like angry mood swings, depression, and swimming in seas of spaghetti with marinara sauce. For you, it might be constant crying at coffee commercials for no reason thinking, *why can't I be as happy as those motherfuckers with their perfect cup of coffee?!* Depression is a sly mofo and if you aren't taking care of yourself, she will begin to creep back in, and before you know it, you will become a person you don't like.

In music, composers give us rests for a reason: to provide a silent moment to catch your breath and prepare for what's next. It might be an intense run with what seems like a million notes in a short amount of time, or a crescendo that leads to the apex of an aria. I had to think back to my years of training and take a rest. I have to turn down the intensity in my life, so I can hear and nurture my inside voice. Creating a routine that I follow every morning has been crucial for this. It doesn't have to be extensive and it's different for everyone. For me, it looks like snuggling with my dogs while I drink my coffee and try my hardest to meditate. I'm not quite there yet. I'm still a work in progress, and that's okay.

I have learned to never turn down an opportunity to meet someone new and add to my network. I have found the key is to decide what things about me are private and put that on a shelf as I decide what part of my authentic self is open. I never turn down a chance to be honest and say how I am feeling in the moment. Admittedly, sometimes this gets me into trouble, but I usually work it out. Building a network is about giving and receiving. Both parties need to gain something from the connection.

A few years ago, I met this amazing woman at a neighborhood happy hour. She was so smart and cool, and I really wanted to get to know her, so I proposed a get-together the next week. We met at this little wine bar in the neighborhood and had the best time. She excused herself to use the restroom and when she came out of the bathroom, she was smiling as she perched up on the bar stool and took a sip of what is now my favorite orange wine. I took a deep breath, thought about my grandmother, and could almost hear her say, "Cami, go for it!" I think I might have even said out loud, "Here goes nothing, Lois." I looked right at her and decided to be totally honest, "I like you a lot. I would like to be friends with you. Will you be my friend?"

She looked at me with shock and amusement as she took another sip of wine. I braced myself for an uncomfortable rejection. Then she chuckled and said simply: "Sure. I like you too."

The chance of her agreeing to my proposal of friendship was worth the risk of rejection. We are still friends today and she helped me discover my desire to share this story, as well as others. She added something to my life that was missing, and I think I added something to hers too.

Everyone in my well-cultivated network adds value to my life in various ways and I try really hard to do the same for them in return. I've built a large network of professionals and friends that can be relied upon for various occasions. When things take a turn for the worst, the outpouring of inevitable support I receive from this network I have intentionally invested in makes it a lot easier for me to move forward, instead of sitting in the muck of paralyzing trauma. I've essentially made it my business to know everyone. When someone asks me to connect, I remember my mantra (say, or should I say, *sing* it with me now, all together!): "Never turn anything down but your coat collar!" Ah, Lois would be so proud.

Your voice is the only voice you should be listening to. The rest don't matter. (Unless you've got a Grandma Lois or a Judith Krug in your life. I definitely recommend you give them a listen.) But in the end, it is your life, and you get to sing any song you want, any way you want it, any time you want to. You can sing it in the bathroom, in the boardroom, or while you are standing up to the office bitch with a whisky sour in your hand. Use your fear and energy to do what's best for you.

Lead with kindness and trust. Nurture the people you work with and grow the next generation. Be the leader that others aspire to be and not the one that inflicts trauma. A simple mantra that I say to myself is, *don't be an asshole*. It's as simple as that. It takes so much more energy to be a jerk than it does to be kind. Practice self care that works for you and girl, stop beating yourself up if you miss a day. At some point no one will remember us, so live your life in a way that makes you happy. All you have to do is ask yourself for permission, and the answer will always be yes. Take risks without asking permission from others. Experience everything, because there's a whole wide world out there. Meet new and different people and ask them to be your friends (no one is going to say no, I promise!).

I was scared of the dark when I was little. In fact, there was a time when I thought Madame Medusa from the Disney movie *The Rescuers* lived under my bed. Am I the only one who would lay in bed and quietly reassure myself out loud to keep the fear and Madame Medusa away? Isn't it interesting that, before the world tried to steal them away, the sounds of our own voices were what brought us comfort, safety, and enough peace to fall asleep? We should all aspire to get back to that time in our lives. A time when our quiet and soothing inner voice made us feel safe, instead of the negative thoughts of our trauma running through our minds.

I have found that singing my own tune, really learning how to use my voice, is what has given me the strength to get louder, grow stronger, and become more in tune with my own heart. My mountaintop was realizing that I am the most important thing in the world, and no one knows what I need, but me. It's been a long and winding road, but I trust the direction I am headed in, and I am singing every step of the way.

ABOUT THE AUTHOR

Cameron Curtis is a classically trained musician. Was.

Cameron's passion for music, beginning with piano and then vocal performance, began in middle school through college where she graduated with a Bachelor of Arts with a concentration in musical theater and opera. It stops there. She met the love of her life, Scott, got married, moved to Northern Virginia, and bought a house at the age of 23.

She lost her voice.

Cameron's family life has always been solid. Her mother and father gave her unconditional love and support regardless of the path she took. Both encouraged her to be authentic and strong. She had two strong-willed grandmothers who impressed upon her from an early age that you should always take advantage of opportunities, even if they seemed risky. Following that advice, she took a job as an executive assistant for a higher-education not-for-profit. From there she moved her way up the ladder from meeting planning to CEO.

She discovered her true voice.

Cameron is currently the President & CEO of C2 Association Strategies and has more than twenty-two years of not-for-profit management experience. She's led organizations such as the Association for Air Medical Services, MedEvac Foundation International, Society of Interventional Oncology, Association for Clinical and Translational Science, and the Texas Speech-Language Hearing Association. In addition, Cameron provided oversight for meetings and events, domestically and internationally.

Cameron's passion for growing leaders and helping others find their voices shows in her willingness to take advantage of any opportunity that comes her way. Risk is exciting to her, and she lives by the mantra her grandmother taught her, "Never turn down anything but your coat collar." Follow along on her website at www.c2associationstrategies.com or on Instagram and LinkedIn @cunzcurtis and Facebook at C2 Association Strategies.

OLIVIA ASH, ESQ., MS

I could only feel my way through it: the surge of heat rising from my chest, into my face, and out the top of my head. Here it came…the pain culminated with the most intense ringing, a sound so piercing I could see it with my third eye. As rapidly and intensely as it arose, it then dissipated into an exquisite silence. Events like this were happening more often and intensifying with time. I knew something was wrong. The signs of chronic illnesses are often the incessant, monotonous aches of joints and muscles. Sometimes, however, these are overshadowed by periods of sharp, piercing pain. I know such pains well. They are my daily companions, ever-present, awaiting their moments of glory when stress is high, sleep is fleeting, or my faculties are weak.

ADVERSE POSSESSION

Contained Chaos

Hordes of humans laugh gaily in summer's sweltering sun. Oblivious to the sweat dripping from their brows, revelers adjust the sagging cotton clothing clinging awkwardly to their skin. This is a Midwestern summer. Today would be trying for me, so I spent the morning hyping myself up: *You need to do something fun!*

I thought it would be good for me. Having fun hadn't been on my radar for some time because my pain wages war ruthlessly. I'd been engaged in skirmishes and knew what they felt like: breakthrough pain that brought me to my knees. I felt weary from battle and yearned for relief, some semblance of rest from the hypervigilance of scanning the battlefield for another attack of stabbing, burning, tingling, piercing pain. I wanted to spend the day with my mom and three sisters, but the environment would be painful and unpredictable. The piercing cackles, guffaws, shrieks, and shrills, sound layered upon sound into a grating glacier, irritating frayed nerves like fingernails against sandpaper. I wanted to avoid it at all costs. I needed, for the sake of my sanity, to avoid the clamor and the shoulder-bumping of strangers. Instead of the reality—happy people eagerly awaiting their turn to order a deep-fried twinkie—I saw cattle being led to slaughter.

Ugh. The heat, the sweat, the smells. I could feel my stomach turning at the thought as I checked my reflection in the mirror. Would this afternoon of summer revelry just aggravate my pain? The relentless ache in my temples was already belligerent. I did not want to irritate it further. *Yet,* my will retorted, *you must try. You can't hide forever because of pain. It will always be there but you must keep going.*

The smell of elephant ears hits me as I approach the fairgrounds: a sweet combination of aged fat and fluffy dough, doused in powdered sugar, slapped onto paper plates so fragile they can't absorb the grease. Sounds assault me and I ache to run at top speed to the nearest patch of trees, away from it all, and breathe in the silence. Instead, I steeled my senses and gazed up from my feet. The scene before me painted itself in real time: swaths of people migrated like birds, traipsing mindlessly from one venue to the next while sweating profusely. None seemed bothered by this languid stroll, shoulder-to-sweaty-shoulder with strangers, shuffling here to there. As I watched, my stomach churned, my senses ached, my heart raced, and pressure built in my chest. Random movement at varying speeds registered in my periphery as blue-lipped children ran ahead of their parents, waiving cotton candy trails behind them.

Chaotic and languid, the mass of humanity slowly moved. Groups of people, oblivious to everyone, dropped into the flow, causing a ripple effect of trips, halts, and curses. Within each whirlpool, insensible conversations took place. I could see and hear it all at once, the energy of every person directed towards my senses, and my faculties strained at the onslaught. I could discern nothing, yet also pinpoint the slightest high-pitched squeal of a kid, ecstatic from their first roller coaster ride. As we walked, a cacophony of laughter and the low droning of a thousand conversations overwhelmed me. And I cracked.

I heaved the humid August air in and out as quickly as I could, though it felt more like breathing molasses. I was acutely aware of my posture: hands on knees to support my lungs, and how it might have looked to passersby. I struggled to breathe over the steady hum of the food truck's generator. I could not breathe. I could not think. I could only feel my way through it: the surge of heat rising from my chest, into my face, and out the top of my head. Here it came. The pain culminated with intense ringing, a sound so piercing I could see it with my third eye. As rapidly and intensely as it arrived, it dissipated into an exquisite silence.

The echoes of pain throbbed in my right ear as I wept bulbous tears into my hands, snot dripping from my nose. My mom stood by, watching me, frozen in silence. Even through my struggle, I felt the weight of responsibility. She didn't know what to do. Here, crouched behind a state fair food truck near the midway, her six-foot, former Division I athlete daughter was nearly immobile, except for the distinct sound of belabored breaths, combined with halting outbursts of tears. What comfort could she possibly offer in this all-encompassing carnival meltdown?

Oh no. I could sense it approaching: the ever-encroaching blackness and panic-fueled helplessness as one stands on the edge of consciousness. I did not pass out, yet my breaker had been tripped. My anxiety rose. Feelings of failure, frustration, and fear erupted. These emotions always bred shame, shaking my soul, leaving me feeling imperfect and broken beyond repair. I fumbled for an explanation as exasperation reigned, knowing my ability to handle the stress of social situations was weakening. I felt vulnerable, as though I was standing naked in front of a department store mirror with other patrons watching. How could I handle such unpredictability? Exhaustion washed over me, and I resumed the day's frivolity, still aching from yet another attack of piercing pain to my temple. I had no idea what was going on inside of me.

After that day's events, it took nearly a year to receive answers and a diagnosis. With a mixture of sadness and relief, I finally learned the identity of the enemy inside me with the power to turn a family outing into a hostile place.

CHARACTERIZING CHRONIC PAIN

CHOPA. No, it's not a celebratory cry, it's more an outcry from unexpected pain as a stinging blade of electricity rips through your cells, each trembling from the shockwave to your temple. Or perhaps the cry is a low groan: the sad, tired response to the steady burn of arthritis in your tissues. CHOPA is a memorable acronym from my law school days. It's the ingenious creation of my property law professor, Carrie Hagan: a mnemonic device to assist the recall of exhausted first-year students on the doctrine of adverse possession: a means of possessing land for which you don't hold legal title. CHOPA stands for Continuous, Hostile, Open, Possession, and Actual.

The doctrine of adverse possession says that a person who does not legally own land may come to "possess" it by remaining on it continuously, against the will of the land's rightful legal owner. Wrangling this unwelcome trespasser is often futile after the realization that little can be done to remove them. Chronic pain is my adverse possessor; it is trespassing within the landscape of my body and has established permanent roots. My possessor is selfish. Uninvited. Unwelcome. Relentless. And adverse to my wishes.

A Rude Awakening

AUTUMN 1999

I had never felt so compacted and sour with burning anger. I rolled over, staring into the faint light of early morning. The dull throbbing of pain in my shoulder and base of my skull that had become my companion intensified, and I wanted it gone. I had things to do as a freshman in college: study, work, and play a Division I sport. It was my job; I was on scholarship. I had to compete and earn my education, and this pain was preventing me from doing it well.

The pressure mounted on my chest as feelings of failure, shame, and brokenness welled up within me. I began to weep the stinging tears of sadness and grief, often masked as anger. I didn't know what to do. My plans for athletic success were evaporating before my eyes. The pain burned. *Why was this happening?* I swear the sound of pain throbbing through my body was audible. *Couldn't anyone else hear it too?*

By the time I graduated college, however, I had entered a sort of "arrangement" with the adverse possessors. I left campus with a bachelor's degree in exercise science, a metal plate, six screws, and multiple joint surgeries to my credit. I never knew which pain would resurface, and so I kept going. That was the best option.

Answers

MAY 2007

I drove north, my spirit as damp and gray as the skies staring back at me. I was once again searching for answers. I knew something was wrong with my body and its performance; that something was causing my joints to grind, continual aches, headaches, exhaustion, and ceaseless pain. I couldn't figure it out, and this fed the fire of my frustration. I wanted to run, jump, play, and be happy. Balancing my desire for freedom with the realities of managing daily pain from an unknown intruder annoyed me.

"We won't diagnose you with a Chiari Malformation as you're 'on the line,' but it's likely you'll experience some symptoms." The specialist stated this with the nonchalance of a speaker calling out the number at Saturday night bingo.

Great. My cerebellum was slumping into the space reserved for my brainstem, creating pressure and causing pain, intermittent nausea, and dizziness. Not an optimal diagnosis, but it was something to cling to, and it wasn't bad enough to require surgery. That was a win.

A Chiari Malformation is common with my diagnosis: Hypermobile Ehlers-Danlos Syndrome (hEDS), a heritable connective tissue disorder characterized by chronic pain. The collagen within my body was deteriorating like a rubber band forgotten in the junk drawer. A dry, weak rubber band functions poorly, breaking when stretched to its limits: weak collagen fails to properly hold tension in my joints. Therefore, they pop and shift when I try to complete even the most menial tasks. The doctors advised me I could expect a lifetime of ever-weakening body systems because collagen is king. It's a structural protein throughout the body, responsible for strength and integrity. It's meant to be a flexible web that ensures all structures are aligned. I inherited a faulty web, meaning that all my systems were affected. It requires lifetime maintenance and lifestyle adjustments. I would have to work with this diagnosis—it was my only option.

Under the anxious visage of my mom, the specialist remarked that he had never seen the amount of paperwork as I had in my medical record. Yet despite this diagnosis, as I grappled with facing a lifetime of pain management, relief arrived. A spring of hope bubbled within me because I could do something with facts. The unknown is a scary place. We spend our waking hours seeking the fleeting zephyr of control. We plan our days, weeks, months, and lives, all before we have lived them. We need to feel some level of control over life, and especially our bodies. A semblance of autonomy. Having facts about my illness gave me some control over it. Though a specialist also recommended I not bear children and begin taking an antidepressant, peace settled upon me. I was exhausted and saddened by the news, but because I had a diagnosis that I could learn about and work with, my outlook improved.

By that spring, I was twenty-six and had endured eight orthopedic surgeries. I had completed four years of playing a Division I sport where every day consisted of work: practice, strength and conditioning, or competition. The off-season was less grinding. Summers typically played out like this: surgery to stabilize a joint, physical therapy, practice, and then preparation for a new competition season. My body was over it.

I'm a doer. Mom says that as a child, I never stopped. I was curious, full of energy, and "into everything." I want to know how things work. Every personality and strengths test I've completed indicates a strong desire to learn. I choose to use my strength of mind to balance my bodily weakness. I can learn how to manage chronic pain. This means I must learn the pain. I may "do" with less intensity in my forties than in my twenties, but at least I'm trying. And doing. And trying again. And that makes all the difference.

Growing Pains

AUTUMN 2017

The past informs your present but does not predict your future. I wrote this sentiment with a dry-erase marker on my mirror one crisp morning, as I prepared for the exhausting schedule of the day ahead: work, school, and study. I was freshly divorced from a twelve-year marriage and tending my wounded soul. I was teaching adults in the city while wrangling toxicity in my work environment. In the evening, I followed these daily struggles by sitting for hours in colorless classrooms as a third-year law student.

As I looked in the mirror, I applied foundation in an attempt to mask the aches and pains etched on my face, and the toll of emotional loss revealing dark crescents under my eyes. I saw the woman staring back at me and I paused. I sensed hope and resolve in her face. I would make it through this pain, just as I had over the past decade, through surgery after surgery. I felt my strength of will among pain's deep wounds cloaking every cell of my body. My body ached that frosty morning, and so did my weary heart. We mustn't forget the ache of a wounded heart; it, too, may become a source of chronic pain if improperly processed. I reflected on events over the ten years since receiving the connective tissue disorder diagnosis. I was alone. I was in a new house, having parted with my remodeled marital home. And yet I felt a freedom of spirit. My soul craved a safe space, and in this creaky old home, I was building it.

The path before me held potential; it held uncertain endings, but also bloomed opportunities. I had turned a corner in managing chronic pain two years earlier, and because I no longer lived in the emptiness of indecision, I was finally stepping into my life as its director. I had rejected all pain medication. I cautiously befriended what I believed, and began to practice what I intuitively knew to be the healing power of nutrition and movement. I knew my body and heart could recover. From there on out, choosing myself was not a shameful act, but one of immense grace. I accepted myself as a worthy human, a necessary step if I hoped to accomplish all I dreamed.

As I saw Liv in the mirror for what felt like the first time, I knew my trials would serve as a crucible to develop my strength. I knew that my past choices, instead of branding me a failure, would instead be an invaluable well of deep knowledge. Crucibles burn, yet through their heat and pressure, they change their cargo, often purifying it to its essentials. And in such burning change, crucibles are instruments of creation.

The past informs your present but does not predict your future. I often speak this aloud, especially in moments when the familiar fear of failure, frustration, or loss whispers in my mind. The words catapult me forward in the face of chronic pain's clamoring. The phrase reminds me that my joys and tribulations are inherent in human existence. We cannot undo the past, and we cannot predict the future. We can only ever exist in the present. Two decades into managing my pain and life's wins and losses, I am reminded that this simple statement holds the memory of my choices. I approach these memories and ask them to inform my present understanding of today's pain. *How have I grown? How may I grow? How has this pain changed? What can I adjust to best manage it? Could new research benefit my present prognoses? What do I need for my soul? Have I cared for and advocated for myself?*

The words of my mantra are easy to say but hard to live by. Sometimes, I want to scream at the top of my lungs and literally cut out the pain that plagues my head when it's at its angriest. The words "cut out" may seem intense. They are. But so is the pain. I've learned that the more extreme the pain, the more extreme the emotions.

Ceaseless pain and emotion can sow seeds of thought that could ripen into extreme solutions. These thoughts should be weeded without hesitation. Such solutions are suicidal, yet drastic solutions become viable options when symptoms caused by chronic cluster headaches thunder into the body.

By August 2019, I had survived two of the toughest tribulations of my life. The first was receiving the diagnosis of bilateral Semicircular Canal Dehiscence (SCCD) that would require cranial surgery to repair, and the second, taking the bar exam without throwing in the towel or barfing in the bathroom moments before from anxiety and pain. I had studied, cried, read, re-read, recited, and reviewed for weeks. I was absolutely spent. The pressure within my head and neck was akin to a gluttonous tick, and I genuinely feared that it might explode.

After the bar exam, I bee-lined for the market to refuel. I recall lying on the ground on the shaded pathway at a nearby park, listening to nothing but the sound of trees alive in summer. Lying on the ground, wherever I may be, is the quickest remedy to relief.

After two years of fighting for answers from doctors, I also received the diagnosis of chronic cluster headache shortly before taking the bar exam. I had volleyed between medications that caused fatigue, irritability, and pain of their own making. I was offered the option to defer taking the bar, yet I chose to take it anyway because I had put in the work. I reasoned that if I failed, exam practice would be beneficial. I had to keep going. The walls we hit exist to save us from ourselves. Rather than obstacles, they are protectors. They keep us from falling over the edge. I failed the bar on my first attempt. Then I failed it on my second attempt. Exhausted and bewildered, I poured myself into my job. I needed space to be a human before taking the exam when it once again circled around.

Meanwhile, I avoided situations that would trip my trigger. I stopped listening to music and attending concerts, even leaving the symphony mid-program one wintery evening because I could not endure the sounds of giggling children. Their innocent laughter during intermission was a piercing dart to my temple, lodging itself into my brain. That night, tears streaking my makeup, I hiked up the skirt of my cocktail dress as I tore down the stairs. The pain that pierced my temple was now crawling across my face, moving down my neck and into my shoulder. Before I made it to my car, my face went numb.

———————————

Because of the SCCD, I had a literal hole in my skull adjacent to my inner ear. Surgery was required to repair it. Our brains and auditory network are two systems that work together to process all we see and hear. This thin wall of the skull is necessary to properly allow sound to flow as a one-way street. If there's a hole in it, your brain struggles to decipher sounds and becomes overwhelmed by even mundane ones. It also hurts to have a hole in your skull. This hole was likely a factor in my state fair meltdown two years before. My brain's struggle to properly process stimuli underscored my inability to tolerate a child's laugh. I couldn't iron out the wrinkles made by too many simultaneous sounds. And yet, I could hear the grinding of my own joints in my head as if amplified. Though I'd had fifteen surgeries, I never felt as much fear of losing my life—a life I loved—as I did when cranial surgery approached.

———————————

Only after you've endured thirst from desert heat may you savor the life-giving refreshment of mountain spring water. I saw light. My fluttering lids opened and I focused on the cupboards across the room. I recall the image of a quiet, softly lit, peaceful room and felt a similar peace within my soul. I had never felt such relaxation. There I was, alone in the ICU, only two months after COVID-19 burst upon humanity. No family, spouse, or loved one had been there to send me off like a ship to sea as they had rolled me to an icy operating room. No familiar smile to warm my heart upon awakening, or hold my hand in comfort. Yet, I wasn't alone. The nurse warmly greeted me and inquired about my needs. I wanted water. As my eyes struggled to focus and my brain thawed from the effects of anesthesia, a surge of energy grew in my chest. *Ahh! I made it!* Elation emblazoned my mind. The surgeon didn't mistakenly cut brain tissue, rendering me deaf or blind. Yet as swiftly as the energy arrived, however, it dissipated, and sleep overcame me. I leaned in.

The following day I leaped at the offer to stroll around the ICU. I wanted to move, to feel the earth solid beneath my feet. Masked and tethered by my waist to the nurse, like a child to its parent at the park, I completed two laps before I needed to rest. I walked away from that hospital heavier with the addition of a titanium screw in my skull, but lighter in spirit, humbled by the gift of new life. I had an uncertain road ahead, including wound healing, physical therapy, and the mother of all brain tests: my third attempt at the bar exam.

I know within my being that repairing the hole in my skull aided my ability to focus and pass the bar exam. I had rested since surgery and wrangled my cluster headache into submissive manageability, thanks to the serendipitous availability of a new medication. One year after my first attempt, I finally passed the bar, only two months after cranial surgery. Standing in my cozy kitchen, I wept cleansing tears of gratitude and relief.

Twenty-three years since the fire of anger burned in my youthful heart as I wept bitter tears of loss in my dorm room, I now face another foe, one that's been possessing my landscape continuously. Doctors questioned if they caught a glimpse of it in 2007 when I received the hEDS diagnosis. "Let's keep an eye on it," they said. They had hesitated to officially label it a Chiari Malformation.

I look healthy. I care for my body—my landscape, as it were. I tend it imperfectly but consistently. Doctors seem perplexed when they meet me, surprised at alarming diagnoses that don't visually align with my exterior. I work hard and tolerate pain. I "fight through it" and "get the job done." These questionably injurious colloquialisms were drilled into my head by years of athletic competition. I wonder whether the dichotomy between what doctors see and my test results weakens their sense of urgency. I've learned to advocate my case in the face of assumed disbelief.

I struggle with balancing my desire to achieve with the reality of my condition. However, my tendency to press on is waning with time. My body has an expiration date. Yet I still think, *It won't be too bad. I can run, lift weights, or paint my ceiling*…except when I can't. I don't recover well anymore; I must heed the pain's warning. Years of consistent pressure, like water against a dam, have cracked my physical foundations: my vision blurs, my eye twitches, and my face numbs. My sole recurring thought is to relieve the constant, aching pressure with an ice pick to the base of my skull. When pain is an ever-present, unsolicited, "plus one," you learn its personality and habits. And when behaviors change, as they do with people, you know something's up. I think, *Something is wrong; the timing, intensity, and nature of this pain is more intense, more iron-willed. It's drowned out the usual aches and pains and is beating at my door for attention.* It's time I listen.

The cranial surgery in 2020 was successful, but not for long; I once again have a hole in my skull near my inner ear. This is unexpected and likely due to an undiagnosed cause. After conversations with experts, I am doing what I can: compression socks to maintain blood pressure and stave off dizzy spells, genetic testing to confirm my diagnosis, and medication when necessary to reduce the awful pressure pounding the base of my skill. The effect of the medication, often used to treat altitude sickness, is temporary. It helps but creates intense side effects.

One hell of an overwhelming morning, after learning these revelations, I walked into my living room while rubbing my face. I recall the beauty of the day as seen through the golden light cast by tangerine curtains. I burst into tears. *Not again.* I lay on the floor, crying tears of renewed sadness. News of subsequent testing and surgery overwhelmed my floundering efforts to stay emotionally afloat. The dam fully burst and tears rushed through, flooding my cheeks with salty sadness. *Another hurdle,* I wept bitterly. And then, relief arrived and with it a reassessment. *Keep going.*

My future holds further testing to evaluate my spine's cervical anatomy. Once complete, triage begins. An unexpected light in this journey is a physician who leads by action. She advocates on my behalf without asking. I cried tears of relief upon receiving her email. It's uncommon to receive such attuned care in an automaton society. Yet with her support, I am hopeful, and hope is a precious commodity in a world of chronic pain. Questions surface. *Do I repair the hole in my skull? If tests reveal doctors' suspicions, do I undergo surgery?* Answers remain hidden. Until they unfold, I will do what I can with what I have and keep going.

Incessant in its urgency and relentless in its pursuit for acknowledgment: this is chronic pain. It's easy to marinate in the muck of mounting losses. However, in two decades of managing chronic pain, I've learned to more mindfully appreciate the present so I lose less precious life energy. I listen when pain seeks an audience. This permits me to learn its character. By conversing with pain, I have improved my self-care choices, especially for my mind and emotions. Through my experiences, I've grown in wisdom, tempering my inner fire. I am my own best advocate, committed to the cause of fighting pain while speaking my voice. I am responsible for teaching myself about myself. By doing so, I can better represent my wants and needs to my family, friends, and medical professionals who are not living in my body. I've accepted that chronic pain won't stop, but neither will I.

My mom often tells me, "Your Knower knows." Knowledge is power, and the only way out is through. It's that simple. To successfully manage daily chronic pain, I have learned to know what I feel and *feel through it.* I don't recall the exact moment my mind shifted but when it happened, I started living again. I do, however, recall the oppressive feeling of the anvil-heavy weight upon my chest leading up to this shift. As is my modus operandi, my mindset shift occurred through my physical, tactile, kinesthetic senses. The moment is emblazoned in my memory. The moment that switched on the floodlights within my soul and shouted, *Awaken!* That moment, housed within my painful marriage and subsequent divorce, was when I ultimately chose myself. After years of sacrificing my heart's desires on the altar of happily ever after, I knew.

The heavy work of accepting chronic pain and listening to my body could only occur after I chose myself. Choosing myself meant leaving a marriage devoid of true emotional connection and passion. After years of frozen feelings and my disappointed attempts to awaken true affection with my partner, I found myself in a negative self-esteem spiral. I arrived at a crossroads, a bedraggled shell of myself. I was faced with grasping at life or succumbing to sadness. As foreign as it felt to choose myself at that time, my Knower knew it was the necessary step.

With a sense of urgency spawned by my thinning hair and bald patches, I began to apply the wellbeing principles I had learned in graduate school to my behaviors. The doctor's office ordered blood tests: it was adrenal fatigue. My body was literally shutting down from trying to keep it all together without listening, without resting, and without observing myself. I was frantic with physical and emotional pain. I was low on several vitamins and minerals and had gained weight due to my unbalanced hormones and emotional eating. I was avoiding opening Pandora's box with my partner, but there were painful emotional injuries from our relationship that instinct whispered to me needed to be addressed.

Re-energized with focused precision, I leaned on my training as an exercise scientist and health educator. Pain screamed at me for attention; instead of numbing it with cheap medications, I chose to listen. I chose to learn how my body felt each day: how did my joints feel when I did this movement? How did my emotions (and body) respond to familiar relationship patterns? It was a hard journey, but also enlightening. Once again I learned that knowledge is power. Knowledge strengthened my will. Every forward step bred confidence to choose what I inherently knew: that I was worthy of living a life I loved.

Now that I am a wiser woman, I choose to feel the pain when it arrives. And it knocks daily. I listen. I feel. I cry. I rest more often between workouts. I create. I continue researching, learning, and questioning. I appreciate what good exists. This practice is imperfect and difficult, but it did not develop overnight. Only through daily pain, surgeries, and loss did I earn my sea legs to better navigate the swells of chronic pain. I am better equipped and more resilient. I never cease learning about pain's place in the landscape of my body.

Courage is not the absence of fear, it's acting in spite of fear. Resilience is a process of positively adapting to challenging life experiences through mental, emotional, and behavioral adjustments to life's demands. Some days the pain is unbearable. I step away from my desk, lay on the floor, and weep frustrated tears. Then I move along. On other days I am overwhelmed with gratitude as the sun shines warmly on my face. I cry thankful tears. As I watch the clouds color crimson at sunset, my perspective shifts: I am aware. I have a choice. I persist. I can seek care, receive care, and continue forward movement.

There's an amazing clarity that comes with a settled choice. The journey is fraught with indecision and struggle. However, I know pain is my adverse possessor. Climbing an endless path up the mountain exhausts; wading chest-deep in emotions from the parched desert of disappointment weakens. Yet I know that oases exist. I focus on the road ahead and they reveal themselves when least expected.

ABOUT THE AUTHOR

Olivia "Liv" Ash

An artist at heart, teacher by nature, and attorney by profession, Liv believes one of life's greatest gifts is the ability to learn—to grow from within while contributing to life's symphony. Ever learning, Liv holds degrees in Law, Education, and Exercise Science. She's an award-winning published author for her original research in the field of loneliness and law students, seeking to understand why law and other professions struggle with emotional health.

Liv holds Indiana licenses in the fields of Law and Education. She serves as Benefits Compliance Counsel for a national insurance services company where she creates ERISA education content. Liv continues teaching courses in lifestyle wellbeing and curriculum development as Adjunct Faculty in the School of Health and Human Sciences at Indiana University—Indianapolis.

Liv's personal journey in managing chronic pain has brought both humility and an appreciation for life's nuances. She believes wisdom resides within struggles, yet so does learning. Liv seeks her own balance and the beauty within each day by spending time in nature while also celebrating the color and style within the arts. Liv cycles for fitness; paints for balance; and writes both poetry and prose. To express, encourage, and enlighten, Liv founded Liv Balanced, LLC, an evolving creative space where visitors may access wellbeing content, purchase prints of Liv's abstract art, or listen to podcast interviews about managing loneliness.

Learn more about Liv and her creative projects, including the progress of her memoir, at https://www.livbalanced.net/. Contact Liv via Facebook at Liv Balanced, LLC; Instagram @liv_balanced_llc; or email at liv@livbalanced.net.

ILSA MANNING

I was useless, incapable, never smart enough, never well-spoken enough, never brave enough, never strong enough, never forthright enough, always floundering to know who I was, what I was doing, where I was going and what I wanted...

(RE)BIRTH

I was getting old, and old eggs are bad eggs. At least that's what they say and that's how you're treated when you're nearly thirty-six and pregnant: "advanced maternal age." However, I felt I had advanced at nothing, certainly not my age.

By thirty-five it seemed I had failed at everything. Learning French? Failed, despite studying it in high school and college and doing study abroad, and living in France for a year. Career progression? Failed, despite always working hard whatever the role. I was useless, incapable, never smart enough, never well-spoken enough, never brave enough, never strong enough, never forthright enough, always floundering. I didn't know who I was, what I was doing, where I was going, or what I wanted. Except for one thing. One thing I did get right. Love.

It's September in Paris, the start of fall, though the weather is only slightly cooler than when I arrived in the warm, sticky days of August. I'm twenty-two. I'd been working in France as an au pair for about three weeks when we meet. I say France and not Paris because

I live in the *banlieue*—the suburbs. I've failed at my dream of an authentic Parisian life by living in the banlieue. I can't impress people by saying what chic *arrondissement* I live in, and there's a commute whenever I go to town, albeit a quick one. My friends and I debate whose commute is worse since the RER, the commuter train, is often quicker than the Paris Metro with all its stops. Who knows? I often run late, and I often leave early. Either way, on the night we meet I am at the whim of the trains, as usual. On that night, I'm meeting acquaintances who are becoming friends. It turns out the English flock to Paris in their third year of university to study or intern. All alone in a foreign place, I attach myself to a jovial group of these English twenty-somethings, finding solace in our common language and familiar culture.

I finish work about seven thirty in the evening and rush along the dusk-hued sidewalks of my village, doing my best casual speed walk, as a Parisian would never run. I must catch the next train to meet the group at the arranged time; the Metro Bastille stop is difficult for me to get to and if I don't catch the next RER train, I'll be late.

My anxiety has me thinking these new friends will head to the cafés without me. I don't know these people well. What's it to them if the random American is late? In the few weeks I've been in France, I've learned being without family and friends in a foreign country is soul-suckingly lonely. My mental health needs this night out to bond with my peers, form friendships, and help make Paris feel like home.

I breathe a sigh of relief as I catch the punctual RER and easily make the Metro connection, yet the dread of arriving after they've left still swirls like a black mass in my stomach. I will the trains to move quickly. At the Bastille stop, I launch out of the train, classily speed walking through the fluorescent light-bathed Metro tunnels. *Please, oh, please, oh, please, oh, please let the group still be there*, I whisper to the Metro gods.

I exit the station. Honks and exhaust fumes permeate the air as cars circle the roundabout, acting as guards for the Bastille monument. I pause to let my eyes adjust to the busy city scene, and relief washes over me: there they are. I smile. Tonight, I won't be far from home and friendless, just far from home.

There are about ten that make up this sprightly English group. They're mostly girls, but tonight there's someone I haven't met before. Honestly, that isn't too surprising as I've only been to one party with them and it was then that I got a second invitation. As I join the chatter, I glance in his direction. He's still in his work clothes: black trousers and a lavender button-down shirt. Dark haired, dark eyed, tall, and olive toned. As I approach the group, I can sense him and smell his intoxicating Joop cologne. The air is so thick with the rich, heady scent I could cut it with a knife. I can't avoid its magnetic aroma drawing me to him.

I say hello to everyone as we set out, but not to Mr. Joop. Those in the know lead the way. He walks toward the front of the group, helping decide on the first venue: a small, hole-in-the-wall café somewhere not far from the Metro. We cram into the already packed bar and begin scavenging seats in its narrow space. I squish myself onto the bench of a small table we've claimed, others doing the same when my stomach gives a nervous lurch. Mr. Joop is next to me. I turn to say hi and he stands up and moves to another table—without even an acknowledgment. Okay, I see how this is going to go.

But I didn't see; I was wrong. I hadn't failed for once. In the beautifully romantic, magical city that is Paris, we found love. And now, thirteen years later, settled in my mundanely familiar childhood town of Phoenix, Arizona, we pondered having children.

When we'd married—in our late twenties—he had said he wanted children in the next couple of years. That worked fine with my timeline. I was twenty-eight and not ready for kids. In truth, I wasn't sure I even wanted any. He seemed sure he wanted children, and in my mind, two years would be enough time for me to come around to the idea.

Those two years came and went in a blink. He said nothing, I said nothing. Another year passed, and then another until I found myself faced with geriatric eggs and the horrid label of advanced maternal age. Despite his earlier adamance about wanting children, now that the event was upon him, truth be known, he didn't seem up for it. With the pressure of my aging body upon me, it felt time: if we were going to have a family, we needed to get started or decide to never start. I gave birth to a healthy baby girl a month before my thirty-sixth birthday.

Those first two weeks were bliss. It was like the three of us were on an endless exotic vacation. Mr. Joop and I hadn't spent this much time together since Paris, and it was marvelous getting to know our little girl. Amazon delivered diapers, burp cloths, newborn onesies: all the baby paraphernalia we needed, and probably a lot more that we didn't. Family and friends spoiled us with delicious home-cooked meals, baby blankets, clothes, champagne, flowers, and fun hand soaps for the obsessive hand washing now taking place. Life was amazing until it wasn't. Eventually, life became life, and paternity-leave paradise vanished into the baby powder-scented air.

And oh, the crying and wailing, the constant needing and demanding. There was no sleeping, for anyone. Who were these babies that took multiple-hour naps? I was lucky if I got forty minutes. In that forty minutes I needed to do the dishes, wash, dry, fold and put away the laundry, clean the bathrooms, vacuum the house, shower, brush hair, brush teeth, get dressed in something that wasn't pajamas, oh, and take a nap, because, unlike Cinderella, our little pumpkin was up frequently past midnight. I was exhausted and overwhelmed. Any time I took for myself was quickly cut short by a screaming baby.

I was drowning in motherhood and struggling to fully embrace my new role of "Household and Baby Manager." Mr. Joop and I hadn't deeply discussed childcare before her birth, but when three weeks into maternity leave I was laid off, it was a simple decision for me to stay home and be the main caregiver.

In a crazy dichotomy, despite the fatigue and stress of being a new mom, I reveled in it. There were no bonbons; I'm not a lounging-on-the-couch-binging-on-Netflix-or-HGTV kind of girl. But in those moments when there wasn't crying, in those minutes when I wasn't anxious about whether she would sleep, how to get her to sleep, or if I should sleep while she was asleep, I appreciated this precious little girl.

I drank her in. From the soft, milky scent of her head to her huge, penetrating brown eyes right down to her chubby thighs and tiny toes. She was a treasure: something amazing and powerful Mr. Joop and I had created together. My body carried her and bore her, and now it was sustaining her. She and I were irrevocably connected, and it was the most beautiful thing I had ever experienced.

The minutes of the day passed so slowly, but the hours flew by in a mix of joy, wonder, frustration, confusion, anxiety, stress. For me, motherhood had been a challenging yet fulfilling role to slide into. For Mr. Joop, it was more difficult. He was a fish out of water, and without the forty weeks of connection I had had with her, he was at a loss. He was stressed at work and stressed at home. He helped with household tasks and was desperate to take over with baby to give me a break, but she wouldn't have it. Her separation anxiety was too great, and Mr. Joop's patience wasn't enough. There didn't seem to be a place where they could meet in the middle. He was frustrated and angry because he couldn't fathom the mysterious nature of this tiny human. He wanted to understand her needs and wants and easily fulfill them, but he couldn't fix things.

Our home was shrouded in misery. My tendency to look at parenting in shades of grey and his tendency to look at it in black and white caused tension and arguments between us. Our relationship bent under the strain of parenthood, and as I nursed our daughter at countless moments in the night the question that permeated my being was, would we break?

Despite my floundering marriage and difficulty with household and baby management tasks, my mind found space to wander, seeking fulfillment and escape in my pre-motherhood life: fragrance and perfumery.

In the chunk of years between meeting in Paris and having a baby, Mr. Joop and I lived in England for a time. I flitted from au pairing to teaching English as a Second Language to studying for a master's in modern history. Eventually, however, my student loan institution informed me that I had to start paying back some very significant money, tout de suite. I needed a real job that paid well, and fast. I was faced with a choice: return home to Arizona or stay in England. It was a soul-seeking decision for Mr. Joop and me. If I returned home, we'd end our years-long relationship, and if I stayed in England, we'd marry. I stared at him sipping his milky tea while watching the footie, somewhat oblivious to all I was thinking. I contemplated whether we cared about each other enough to make such a formidable decision. There was fearful hesitation on both sides, but yes. We intrinsically knew life was better together than apart and somehow managed to be married and own a house in just over two months.

I still needed a job, so I temped: for a yachting non-profit, for Gartner, for the high street lawyer, for anyone that would have me, really, but I couldn't ever seem to get that coveted full-time role. The reality was that no employer was willing to hire a girl in her late twenties who had no tangible work experience. Frustration and dejectedness sank deep into my being with each rejection. I had a myriad of experiences and was at least a moderately capable person: how could I be failing at this?

Then it happened: my phone rang. I was sitting, uninterested, at a nondescript desk in a large and impersonal office space diligently plugging numbers into a spreadsheet. It was raining again, the outdoor gloom seeping in; the floor was laden with shadows where the harsh fluorescent lights couldn't reach. My fingers mindlessly tapped away while I numbly sat and pondered if I'd ever have a meaningful, challenging role. It was my job agency. A company close by wanted an interview. I was an ideal candidate because they needed someone to work with their French and American locations. For the first time, my inexperience in the workplace didn't matter because my life experiences were perfect. I took a deep, cleansing breath and let the frustration and dejectedness flow out of me. I was ready to begin life in a 'proper' job at a large international corporation.

New jobs bring new experiences, and this role did that and more. It ignited a new passion in me, and, while working at the largest fragrance supplier in the world, I fell in love with the creation of fragrances and perfumes. It's science, but it's art all at the same time. Being in sales and marketing, I was no perfumer, but I took every chance to learn the art. I wanted to train my nose to understand the nuances of fragrance and decipher the intricacies that lay hidden deep within the scents that surround us.

I blossomed and exceeded my role, yet failure chased me anyway. Turns out, being passionate about fragrance, driven, and skilled at the job wasn't enough to conquer near-impossible job progression in a small office. That, coupled with the horrendously expensive English housing market, motivated a need for change. Mr. Joop and I threw caution to the wind, quit our jobs, packed our things, and moved a world away from lush, green England to the arid desert terrain of Phoenix. For the first time in years, I was living somewhere that overflowed with family, close friends, warmth, and an ease to life that exists with abundant sunshine. I should have been filled with joy, but my happiness was overshadowed by the grim fact that I was failing at finding a job.

There were only a handful of beauty and fragrance companies in Phoenix, and all my attempts to work at any of them were ignored. The silence from my online applications, emails, phone calls, and networking was deafening, near defeating. I conjured up the tenacity to keep at it and my persistence paid off. After sixteen months, I landed a job at a subsidiary of one of the largest beauty companies in the world. I transitioned from an international corporation to the tumultuous world of a start-up, whose founder was a beauty industry visionary. And then, three weeks into my maternity leave, this business shuttered its doors and I was laid off.

So, there I was, a twice-laid-off, stay-at-home mom who had worked at two of the largest beauty and fragrance companies in the world, and with one of the world's most iconic beauty founders. I'd worked with global household names and had put together product configurations that sold tens of thousands of dollars in minutes— millions in twenty-four hours. How could my brain not escape to the idea of bringing my own product to market? I had the knowledge, and what's more, I had the network. I contemplated, could I do this? I imagined and obsessed over the possibilities, and it helped. Having this daydream allowed me to escape from the bewilderment of my everyday life. In my imagination, I had an alternative to wondering about sleep issues or googling what I was doing wrong with nursing and diapering, which had to have been impeding baby's development. Was she getting enough stimulation? Was she getting too much? Ugh. My dreams were also a refuge from Mr. Joop's short-temperedness and our inability to communicate due to the haze of sleep deprivation and stress that engulfed us.

It felt like an eternity laboriously toiling through my new life, but in reality, it had only been three short months. During this time, my mental and physical state couldn't manage friendships, which is exactly why my childhood friends Avery and Joan insisted on inviting me to dinner. Going out to an adult meal felt like a mountain to climb, from getting myself ready to preparing everything for the baby in my absence, yet I managed it. My gut told me it was important to disconnect from everything at home and reconnect with myself by way of indulgent food and good friends. Phoenix in February is the ideal mix of sunshine, coolness, and just the right amount of warmth. The golden pink and fiery red hues of that evening's sunset lit up the urban skyline while the heady scent of orange blossoms permeated the air. It was the perfect evening to be with friends.

"Tell us about life with baby then, Ils," Joan demanded. She was a stalwart friend who always got straight to the point.

"Well, it's finite, right? They never stay the same, they're always changing. It's fine and she's great and everything is finite so all this not sleeping and crying all the time will eventually change into something else," I explained matter of factly.

Joan hooted. "Finite! Ilsa, you and your fancy vocabulary!"

"What? But it is finite. It's going to change. I can't think of another word for this situation but finite," I countered, laughing with her and Avery at my elaborate word choice.

"But, seriously, Ils. How are things?" Avery asked knowingly. She and Joan each had older children and were seasoned in motherhood. They were well aware of what I was experiencing. I wanted to hide the truth of my struggles, but it just came flowing out despite my reluctance to share honestly.

"Well, she's not colicky, but close to it. Mr. Joop's having a hard time settling into life with baby, which is in turn causing problems between us, and I'm struggling with the daily tasks of being a household and baby manager. But, it's finite," I said with a shrug, and we all grinned. "What I'm really thinking about is starting my own fine fragrance brand."

"Tell us more!" They encouraged.

The wine was topped up and our dinners were served while I regaled them with my ideas.

"I'm thinking about creating a magical scent. Something that uses exquisite ingredients, smells like nothing on the market, has a bottle that's a piece of art, and that costs one hundred dollars an ounce," I confessed.

"What?!" Joan cawed in disbelief. "What's going to be in this thing?!"

I shrugged. "Unicorns and fairy dust?" I said straight-faced before we all burst out laughing. It felt good to unpack these first months of motherhood with Avery and Joan, knowing our space was safe to share life's ills and ambitions.

I returned to a sleeping house. I was exhausted from the deliciously rich food, crisp wine, and heartfelt conversation. I saw the clean pumping bottles on the counter where I threw my keys and purse. I grumbled, bolstering myself for the task at hand. I grabbed the pump and settled into the whirring of the machine that turned me from the woman who'd been enjoying adult conversation and sauvignon blanc just minutes before to a milking cow. An hour later, nipples red and irritated, I crawled into bed next to slumbering Mr. Joop, who didn't even budge when I pulled the covers from him.

"Wish I could snooze like that," I muttered, staring at the ceiling. Tossing, turning, rolling over: sleep was out of reach as my stomach churned and my head throbbed. The food, the wine, the conversation, the support of friends, everything from that night's dinner slowly swirled within my body and mind. Clenching my eyes to find relief from my aching belly, I couldn't stop replaying the dinner conversation. The word "finite" repeated itself, mixed with laughter, thoughts of my daughter and perfumery, unicorns and fairy dust, and finite, finite, finite…my mind was a tornado of thoughts, a twisting whirlwind of emotions and ideas, converging fast and faster. Finite, baby girl, fairy dust, perfume, unicorns. The thoughts, words, and emotions intensified until they collided in a wondrously miraculous explosion in my heart and mind; my mind's eye was consumed by immeasurable darkness and lit by an infinite number of shimmering stars.

I froze. I forgot my discomfort. My belly didn't ache, and my head wasn't spinning. My eyes were still closed, but I saw it all. Clarity. It's not finite, no. It never was and never has been. It's infinite. The universe, everything in it: infinite. You are infinite. All you can do and all you have done is infinite. This little baby, this little baby that you have: you are not failing her, you are succeeding. You are loving her and feeding her and caring for her and while you see her as perfect… she sees you as perfect. You're looking at everything all wrong. You did not fail and accomplish nothing in being an au pair; you set out to live and work in France, you got a job, packed a bag, and got on an airplane by yourself. That took courage. You succeeded. Everything you've ever set out to do, you've done. You've just never looked at your experiences the right way. You need to flip it all over and see it's not finite, but infinite.

My eyes fluttered open. Goosebumps rushed down the length of my body. My heart beat fast, yet I felt an extreme sense of peace. For the first time, my head was unobscured by self-defeating thoughts. I could see my life for what it was, a massively exciting adventure, not for what I thought it had always been, one gigantic failure. This realization resonated through me, seeping into every cell of my being. I was finally believing in myself, and this self-belief became entwined with confidence, self-assuredness, and love as it coursed through my veins and affixed to my DNA. I recognized this empowering epiphany wasn't for me alone. I needed to share this experience with all women out there. I needed any woman who ever wrestled with self-belief to feel what I was feeling now: powerful, irrepressible, unstoppable.

I had to bottle it. This would be my perfume, my perfume with a purpose. It would use scent to empower women to believe in themselves, see their beauty, and know their strength. Forget the unicorns and fairy dust, the ridiculous price point, and the artistic bottle. The fragrance I was compelled to create didn't need those things, it just needed the magic of this epiphany in a bottle.

My body pulsed with unrelenting eagerness. I had to get this knowledge out of my head and onto paper as quickly as possible. I threw off the covers, but it was too late. The adrenaline had evaporated, and my exhaustion returned. If I got up now and went to the computer, the baby would wake up and I'd write nothing and get no sleep. Resigning to the situation, I drew the covers over me and, somehow, sleep found me.

The early hours before dawn are quiet. The baby's sleeping contentedly after her morning feed, and I've snuck over to the computer. It's dark outside and the overhead light casts a gentle glow on the cluttered desk. The spiritual experience of a few hours before hasn't been some drunken dream or food-induced hallucination, and I haven't forgotten the epiphany with sleep, it's still vibrantly alive within me. Furiously pounding on keys, I record my experience. A living purpose has been born and it couldn't have happened without the birth of my daughter, a birth from a birth. Her unconditional love has shown me that we, and our finite situations, hold infinite possibilities. At that moment, Ilsa Fragrances was born. A birth from birth, from another birth.

Reflecting on my life, I don't know why I never believed in myself nor why I saw my accomplishments as failures. I've no recollection of an event that triggered a crumbling of self-belief or that caused low self-esteem, it's just always how things have been. I know I'm not alone in these struggles. I also know that, despite my vision and the company I've built to spread the message of empowerment to women, my journey is not over. Every day I must remind myself of the things that I've done, that I can do, and that I accomplish. My epiphany that night didn't kill my self-doubt in one go, and creating Ilsa Fragrances didn't grant me perfect self-confidence. However, my epiphany and the experience of starting my own business did give me some much-needed tools.

My epiphanic awakening showed me how wrong I'd been about myself: I'd been an unreliable and untruthful narrator of my own story. My old, faulty narrator had diminished my power and magnificence, but the awakening gave me a new, more truthful perspective on my story. I needed to learn how to look at my experiences for myself, rather than through society's lens. For example, I had always seen the year I spent as an au pair in France as a failure. This was a faulty narrative driven by society's dictate that we go from college to an office role to a career. In the old narrative, because I'd not done this but had skived off to Europe, I had achieved nothing.

When I revisit this part of my story, I visualize shattering society's conventions and restoring reality: the truth is that I had tenaciously sought and found a job in a country on the opposite side of the world. I packed a bag, got on a plane, and moved over 5,000 miles from home. I learned a language, made new friends, survived, and thrived in a culture that was not my own—all by myself. In fact, it had been that year in France that got me my first job in the fragrance industry. The reality was that this time in my life had set me up for success. It was, and always had been, a crucial part of my story.

My awakening transmuted my life, but how could I keep moving forward and hold onto my true narrative when I'd spent most of my life telling myself untruths? I realized that in order to innately know my authentic narrative, I needed to claim it every day, and many, many times a day. I decided to choose a mantra that tapped into the essence of my false narrative, that countered it and kept it from returning:

I believe in myself: I used my capabilities to get a job in a foreign country.

I am strong: I moved across the world all by myself.

I am enough: I do not need to be anything other than myself. I succeed when I am myself. I discovered that any short affirmation that speaks to me and conquers my negative narrator helps me reclaim my voice.

But the mantra wasn't enough to keep me steady; I also need a physical reminder. When I hold a bottle of Infinite No. 1, Ilsa Fragrances' first fine fragrance, in my hands, its weight reminds me that I hold something special inside me, just like the bottle does. I pull the cap off and slowly spritz its rich, warm blend of bright bergamot, creamy sandalwood, and spicy patchouli on one side of my neck, then the other; on one wrist, and then the other. Each spray awakening, igniting, reminding my soul of its power, my body of its strength, and my mind of its capabilities. When I set the cap on and place the bottle on the shelf, I'm ready to take charge of the narrative of my life. Whether it be a fine fragrance, a piece of art, a message written to myself on the bathroom mirror, or even a tattoo, I've found many ways of keeping my self-defeating thoughts at bay and allowing self-belief to shine through.

My story is not unique. I'm not the only resident in the desert of unforgiving self-doubt, thinking I've failed at life. I'm eternally grateful to my daughter for showing me what had always existed inside of me, but that I was never capable of seeing. I am grateful to Mr. Joop for his tenacity, love, and support. Those tumultuous first months with baby were finite and as she, and her little sister, age and grow, so do we, together. With my family's support, I am winning the fight against my negative self-talk, making my way out of the desert, and, indeed, reclaiming my voice and reaching the mountaintop.

ABOUT THE AUTHOR

Ilsa Manning is a mother, founder, fragrance designer, author, and your biggest cheerleader. Born and raised in Phoenix, Arizona she adventured to Europe after graduating with a BA in History from the University of Arizona. She's lived in France, Poland, and England; she's au paired, taught ESL, graduated with an MA in Modern History from Royal Holloway, University of London, and finally found her calling in fragrance while working at the largest fragrance and flavor supplier in the world. Ilsa returned home to Phoenix with a husband in hand and a drive to pursue all things fragrance. After an epiphanic awakening sparked by her new daughter's love for her, Ilsa found self-belief for the first time in her life. Now her mission is to bring this same awakening to all women through her luxury fine fragrance brand Ilsa Fragrances.

You can find her, her empowering fragrances, and positive messages at ilsafragrances.com, on Facebook and Twitter @ilsafragrances, and Instagram @ilsafragrances and @ ilsamanning. She lives in Phoenix, Arizona, with her English husband, two young daughters, and dog that looks suspiciously like a coyote.

ALICE MEEHAN

*I always knew I was living in a "man's world", but it wasn't until
I started this exploration and soul searching that I began to fully
embrace and discover how deeply misunderstood and undervalued
feminine energy is in the workplace. Forgiveness, acceptance,
reflection, empathy, and collaboration are part of what's missing in
our professional lives. Downplaying the value of the nurturer, healer,
compassionate peacemaker in our workplaces creates an uneven,
inequitable world.*

*My hope is that the modern workforce stops viewing the expression
of feminine attributes as weakness, but instead recognizes these
valuable strengths as qualities that create a more balanced,
cooperative, empathetic work environment.*

EMBRACING
THE FEMININE

My husband and I were driving through Old Town Alexandria, on our way to a friend's home for a party. As we maneuvered our way through the familiar streets, I chatted away animatedly, almost nervously. We had not seen these friends in a few years and my anticipation grew, as they were some of my favorite people. As I entered the house, I was hit with a feeling of nostalgia. Everything looked the same, aside from a few minor changes in decor and placement of furniture. Instead of several years, it was as if only a week had passed. Our host poured me a glass of wine and grabbed a beer for my husband. I relaxed on the couch and sighed contentedly. Being together again felt as comfortable as a soft blanket wrapped around me on a cold day. I felt warm, welcome, and content. I was grateful to be back in these people's lives.

Sipping our drinks, we caught up on our families and shared stories, and the topic of a friend's retail store in the area came up. I leaned over the coffee table to grab my glass of wine, smiled, and as I took another sip, I shared my enthusiasm for the space, as I had been to visit it quite a few times.

"It's a really cute store," I chimed in. "I love it."

My husband and the host had just grabbed refills and took their place in front of me as they continued their conversation. I could tell they were guessing about the location of the store, and so I piped in again, a little louder this time, and reiterated that I had been to the shop. I explained exactly where it was located. As if they hadn't heard me, they continued to debate the cross streets and address. I looked over at the others in the room and gave my hand a little wave, to check with them to make sure that I was not invisible.

I set my wine glass back down on the table and scooted to the edge of my seat, and as the leather couch creaked with my weight redistribution, I looked over at both of them and quietly shouted over the five feet that separated us: "Ahem, I know where the shop is because *I have been there.*" I could almost see my husband's brain spinning as he tried to figure out the exact address of said shop. By now, our host had pulled out his phone and was tapping away on the glass screen, searching for the address, which I had already shared. I watched from my seat, shaking my head, pursing my lips and looked on incredulously, as the result of the phone search popped up. They discovered the location and proceeded to say, "Oh yea, that's right!" Spoiler alert: It was the address that I had just given them. *Seriously?*

Like most young women who grew up middle class in the United States during the seventies and eighties, I learned early on that speaking up and showing too much emotion was not seen as a strength, but quite the opposite: these traits were treated as liabilities. We were taught: Don't speak up, don't say too much, don't argue, don't draw attention to yourself, don't be overly emotional, don't cry, don't be too loud. Stay small, stay hidden, don't make waves, don't rock the boat. If you do, you will be seen as out of control, hysterical, crazy, or unbalanced. To this day, I still hear the whispers that society has turned into sentiments in my head.

I often think of my two daughters when these whispers take hold and scratch at the back of my brain. They are completely different, those two. Both are amazing, strong, and fierce young women. It saddens me to know they have to navigate the same societal oppression I have but with a thirty-year time gap in between.

For as long as I can remember I have had access to my emotions on an extremely intense level. Not only mine, but those around me as well. I can feel myself receiving emotions from other people as soon as I enter the same space. I start absorbing their feelings into my own thoughts and energy. This enables me to be more aware of a situation, allowing me to operate from a place that is more caring and attentive. The downside is that it is also overpowering and taxing on my energy. I often tell people when empathy was handed out, everyone got a cup, but I got a gallon. This is my blessing and my curse. Dealing with this intensity of feeling is difficult when those whispers of *sit down, be quiet, don't cry, don't get over-emotional* are on a constant replay in my head.

I remember being around eight years old in the backseat of our family car, my father driving, my mother in the passenger seat. We were weaving through downtown Washington, D.C., as dusk was settling. There were people everywhere, bustling to get to their destinations. I can hear my parents chatting, but I am not really listening. As my head leans against the cold car window, I am fascinated by the people walking in the crosswalks, the street lights bouncing overhead, and the general bustle of the city traffic and noise. *Where did they come from? Where are they going?*

We stopped at a red light and as I looked out to the right of the intersection at the people waiting for the bus, I noticed one man in particular. He caught my attention because he had to have weighed at least 400 pounds. A look of sadness shrouded his entire body. Exhausted, he leaned on his cane as he tried to juggle the packages in his hands. I could feel heat creep up into my face as my chest started to get tight. I was doing my best to keep my tears in and not let anyone in the car see my distress. All my eight-year-old mind could think about was how this man most likely had to endure endless name calling. I could literally feel how hard it must have been for him to be standing there, alone. I instinctively took a few breaths, as discreetly as I could for fear my parents might turn around and ask me what was wrong. I knew if I cried, it would not be received well, so I just tried to make myself as small and quiet as I could and essentially disappear. It was those whispers that came somewhere from the depths of my soul, trying to take care of me: *don't let them see you cry, don't let them know you are sad, don't show any emotion.*

Shortly before I was set to graduate college, my mother and I were sitting at our small, round, kitchen table having lunch of leftover chicken with bread n' butter pickles on the side—it was a favorite of mine. I was excitedly nervous about my future; the prospect of finding a job and going out into the "adult" world was intoxicating. Seeking advice and comfort, as we munched on our pickles, I shared my thoughts with my mother. The conversation took a turn and she said something that triggered me. I don't remember the words, but what I do remember is looking down at my plate as tears started puddling in the bottoms of my eyes. Doing my level best to withhold the plethora of emotions building up inside me, I nearly jumped out of my skin when her hand slammed down on the table and she shouted in my face.

"What? Are you going to cry every time someone says something to you that you don't like? You are not going to be able to do that in the work world, you know!"

My shoulders slumped and I did my best to keep quiet, get small, and finish my lunch like the compliant daughter I had been raised to be. I listened to the whispers that had conditioned me: *We told you, don't speak up, don't cry, don't show too much emotion.* I have come to terms with my mother not accepting my emotional responses. I don't fault her for this. She didn't have the self-awareness and capacity to handle her own emotions, much less those of her child.

My mother's family background encouraged hiding feelings and putting up a happy front. She was not permitted to own her emotions, and, like most other women of her generation, she was the product of a culture where labeling women as emotional or sensitive was a way to discredit them and steal their voices. When this happens generation after generation, eventually it becomes a behavior, and belief inevitably follows that behavior; mother then passes the false belief on to her daughter. But that stops here with me.

Several years ago, I was racing from one meeting to the next. I was the project lead and had prepared all meeting materials and sent them to all the participants with the hope that the meeting would run smoothly and efficiently. I was confident there would be a quick consensus and outcome. As the meeting participants trickled in, we gathered in the dull, beige conference room that barely had enough room for us and the large rectangular table in the middle. I perused my notes and was all set to get started on time.

We were all contemporaries and all female, except for one lead from another team who sat next to me. His bouncing knee and tapping pen distracted me for the entirety of the meeting. The meeting itself was nothing out of the ordinary: we talked through the agenda and proposed solutions. As meetings go, it actually was quite productive. I presented my resolution and received positive feedback and agreement from the group. As we began to fold up our papers and close our laptops in an attempt to leave, the gentleman with the bouncy knees sitting next to me held up his hand as if he was stopping us from crossing a busy street, and said, "Wait, wait, wait."

He could not contain himself as he stood up from his chair, rushed over to the white board, and smirked, all while tapping a marker in the palm of his hand. I sighed, crossed my arms over my chest and resignedly sat back in my seat as he proceeded to chart and repeat almost verbatim what I had just discussed with everyone. I wish I could say I was incredulous and surprised, but I wasn't. As he held court at the white board, I scanned the faces of all the women at the table. They looked bored and weary, and started scrolling or tapping away on their phones. No one had taken their papers back out or re-opened their laptops. You could almost feel everyone internally rolling their eyes, as we all knew we were once again the targets of mansplaining.

When he was done, the room was silent, except for the odd fidget, signaling that it was time to go. The whispers were back. *Stay professional, don't say anything. Don't rock the boat. There is no reason to point out this absurdity. Just be quiet.*

When he was satisfied with his job well done, he strolled over to his seat, sat back down next to me, and against better judgment, I ignored the whispers and leaned over to him. Eyebrows raised to my roots, I murmured, "It's a good thing I like you."

He leaned back in his chair, hand to chest, and gave me a genuinely surprised look. I inhaled, looked at him, and said, "You just mansplained to the entire group what I had already said." I gathered my belongings and stalked off to my next meeting, leaving him in a dust of baffled confusion. I wanted to feel proud for standing up for myself, but the whispers were always there: *Stay quiet, avoid backlash, don't disrupt the meeting, don't get emotional over this. You don't want to be the dramatic, hysterical female in the room.*

At another point in my career, I was working in an organization that had all the trappings of my dream job: a short commute, partial teleworking option, prestige, and a big salary bump. The job was in my area of expertise and it meant working with other teams and collaborating to fix a broken process. I was well-regarded and sought after for support on multiple projects. I loved it, and I was good at it. The first year was stressful, full of meetings trying to deal with the issues and acclimating to the office politics. It was challenging, but I found it fulfilling. I noticed early on that the environment was dysfunctional, but what work environment isn't? I really thought I could make a difference and I believed I was up for the task.

As time went on, I started to notice the toxicity more and more, and I began to soak it in. One particular manager had a volatile and demeaning leadership style. He had many power-plays that he kept in his rotation, but humiliation was his favorite, preferably in front of an audience. As someone who absorbs others' feelings on a deep level, this was disastrous for my well-being.

This manager also loved to schedule an excessive number of meetings. It gave him a sense of control to keep such tight oversight. First, there was the step of scheduling with his assistant. Then, because he would schedule back-to-back meetings, the meetings would inevitably go over time and those who were next on his calendar had to wait in a queue outside his office: the peasants waiting to see their king. These next meeting victims would stand in line, balancing their laptops in their hands as they stood there, surrounded by co-workers wondering who would be the next casualty. The air was heavy with the energy of dread and anxiety as everyone outside his office could hear whoever was currently being berated and degraded.

Another of his favorite power plays was to direct message me and have me scurry up to his office to join a meeting with him and others that was already in progress. No matter where I was or what

I was doing, the expectation was that I would drop everything to go to his office immediately. Each time, I could only hope I was prepared and had the right answers. I would work my way through the traffic jam of laptop-balancing office prey (which only increased my anxiety), before asking the assistant for permission to enter his office. Knocking, I put on my invisible armor. I would send up a prayer that this time would be different and I would be heard and acknowledged.

Once inside, I would sit at a tiny table shoved into a corner of his office. He would lean back in his large office chair with his legs splayed out in front of him, crossed at the ankles. He had his hands behind his head with his elbows flared out with a look of unconcern. With my laptop sitting in front of me, I would type furiously to be sure to capture every word he said, a behavior I started to depend on to ensure I had the backup receipts when he questioned me. During one meeting with him, when he was tearing me and my team apart, I sat up straight, took a breath, looked straight at him and said, "Okay, thanks for the feedback. Now, please tell me something I did well."

He stopped, coffee cup midway to his mouth, staring at me as he wiped dripping hot liquid from his hands onto his pants. Then he asked me to repeat myself. With a deep breath, and quelling the Muppet show that was going on in my head, I exhaled, and said again, "Tell me something I do well." We sat in awkward silence for at least a full minute. He couldn't do it. He could not bring himself to tell me one blessed thing I had done well.

While each of these interactions on its own brought feelings of frustration, hurt, and resentment, individually, they didn't break me. But just like a hoarder who continues to collect papers, garbage, and other things people would throw in the trash, I could not let them go. I was attached to these emotions with the same intensity a hoarder would have. The hoarder's home, over time, becomes so filled with possessions that the place where they are supposed to be the safest, turns into a space that is unhealthy, dangerous, and unusable. Each time I played small and listened to the whispers in the back of my brain that kept me from speaking up, I became the hoarder who was allowing my sacred space to become uninhabitable. The unexpended emotions became hazardous material, building up toxins in my body and soul. I slowly started to lose my authentic self. This loss would eventually and inevitably manifest into chronic illness.

This type of work environment is anxiety producing for even the most desensitized person. For me and my emotional sensitivity, it proved to be overwhelming and damn near killed me. On a daily basis, my chest and throat felt like they were on fire and closing in on me. I was diagnosed with Gastroesophageal Reflux Disease (GERD), brought on by binge eating and stress. On good days, the fire was a slow burn with a constant bitter taste in my mouth and a hoarse voice. On bad days, I would cough, have trouble swallowing, vomit, and eventually lose my voice altogether. It is not lost on me that these ailments manifested in my throat. My physical reactions were a result of my not being able to communicate effectively for fear of being ridiculed and disparaged. Little did I know this was just the start of my health issues.

I kept thinking about my daughters and how I was encouraging them to be strong and outspoken, yet I wasn't being genuine. I continually hid my authentic self and shut down. *What could I possibly do differently? How could I show them the right path, not just talk about it?* The manager became increasingly abusive over the course of the next two years. He was rude, condescending, dismissive, and hateful (especially to others who were not in the room to defend themselves).

He loved to pit people against each other. I was asked repeatedly to provide feedback on other employees' behavior and work. When I would say anything positive, he would prod me to find the negative. He was exhausting and his expectations unattainable. The turnover was nothing like I had ever seen. People resigned regularly. It got to where I could not keep up with the new names and faces, and honestly, I didn't want to. It was getting to be too much of a drain on my emotions to make new connections with co-workers only to see them suffer or leave.

When I walked through the doors of the office each day, I felt like the man in that antacid commercial from the eighties. Uncomfortable, twisted in discomfort, hand holding his chest as he gets out of his bed, seeking medicine for his pain. As he stumbles down the hallway, the hallway continues to get longer and longer and he never reaches the door which leads to his relief. I just kept walking down this hallway of despair, trying to reach an exit doorway that would lead me to a reprieve. The whispers weren't whispers anymore, now they were literal screams lying to me: *Stay quiet, work harder, don't make waves, don't speak up, and everything will be okay.* Again, I looked at my daughters, laughing, carefree, brimming with life, ideas, and truths to share with the world. Is this what I would tell them? I knew the answer. No. I would never tell them to be silent, not now, not ever.

The more I spoke up for myself or defended my team, the more abuse I experienced. "Work smarter, not harder," was his recommendation when I challenged a project scope change or he added yet another new task I now needed to prioritize. "Stop being so dramatic and frenzied. Calm down. Just get it done," he would say. It was insulting and implied that I did not use my expertise and skills wisely. It implied that my work was simple. Working smarter and working harder are not mutually exclusive. I was doing both and it still was not enough. To this day those phrases still trigger me.

I got caught in the loop of thinking that if I just worked harder, (and oh yes smarter!) or if I could just put in a few more hours, or get this one thing done, I could make this work. If I could just show him that I could do it, make him believe that I was worthy, everything would be alright.

No matter how much I tried to ignore the voices, I knew they were there trying to protect me from this persistent, harmful system that held me back. By the third year under this regime, I was self-medicating with food just to get through the day. Binge eating became my go to. I could frequently be found in the checkout line of the grocery store, nearly catatonic after a ten-plus hour workday, my basket filled with chicken tenders and double-stuffed Oreos and sometimes a bottle of sauvignon blanc for good measure. I would know exactly what fare I wanted, and where to find it. My goal was to get out quickly so I could get to my car and start eating my feelings and distress. Once, a woman standing behind me in the checkout line, looked into my basket and knowingly said, "That's my kinda basket."

My face grew hot with shame and embarrassment as I looked over my shoulder and gave her a defeated, "It was a rough day."

My morning rituals began to include stops at the local bakery for a pastry as a means of bribing myself to get to work. As I watched the attendant place my order of a chocolate croissant in the bag, I decided I needed just a little more to keep me going. Throw in the coffee with real cream and maybe a cheese Danish for later and I could face the day. I gained twenty pounds, battled insomnia, and was diagnosed with Meniere's disease which is characterized by bouts of vertigo, nausea, vomiting, loss of hearing, ringing in the ears, headache, loss of balance, and sweating. Oh, joy. Then it was TMJ from all the teeth grinding and clenching of my jaw to stay silent.

Mornings were the toughest. On a good day, I would make it to the bathroom on my office floor to vomit. On a not-so-good day, I had to quietly vomit in the small trash can at my cube. Most mornings, I would lay in my bed waiting for the whirl and hurl ride to subside so I could get in the shower. These were the mornings I allowed shame to pile onto all the symptoms I was experiencing: *Why can't I make this work? Why can't I stop falling apart? What is wrong with me? Why can't I fix this? I am working hard and smart, so what the* hell?

Climbing out of my car each morning, walking through the parking garage, and brushing off the remnants of my morning pastries, it felt like I was entering the Hunger Games. The workplace atmosphere was one of primal self-preservation, and I was starting to take on the personality of someone fighting for their place in the office instead of collaboration, teamwork, and support. If I took someone out first by taking part in the blame game, then it kept me from being in the line of fire. No one was volunteering to be a tribute. I got by on pure survival instincts.

This change in me only added to my shame over not exhibiting the behaviors I wanted to model for my daughters. I wanted to show them they could be their authentic selves, that they could use their voices and they would be heard and accepted. They didn't have to fall prey to or support the dysfunctionality in the world around them. That they could indeed be the change they wanted to see in the world. And then I would think about them being treated the way I was treated and (this paralyzed me the most) the way I treated others. The office behavior was a contagion and I helped spread it via blame and gossip. I was infuriated and humiliated by my own behavior. Continuing to put up with the hostile behavior and taking on those traits was certainly not making anything different. It only made me sicker and more despondent. What would I tell my daughters to do in this situation? I knew exactly what I would tell them to do. *Leave.* No one deserves that treatment. No job is worth losing yourself for.

However strong the desire to break the cycle, part of me felt like leaving would be giving up and giving in. However, I realized that by staying, I was enabling this environment. I also fully embraced that I was not the problem. This was a huge insight for me and gave me courage and strength to take action. I no longer blamed myself for all that was happening to me. It wasn't my fault. I couldn't in good conscience continue to participate in an organizational structure that did not accept strong, outspoken, vulnerable, collaborative, and compassionate women. Work cultures that inspire masculine attributes and dismiss feminine attributes undermine their own success and result in women who become hidden, traumatized, and sick.

As scary as it was to leave the security of a full-time job and find a new one, I knew I had to get out. It was the only way I knew I was truly going to be heard. Words don't always have to be spoken to make a statement, and I reclaimed my voice by using my feet. I resigned and walked away from that poisonous atmosphere. Leaving was a start to my recovery, but there was much more I needed to do. I went searching for answers, solace, and validation, a journey that pulled me into the exploration and acceptance of divine feminine energy.

I always knew I was living in a "man's world," but it wasn't until I started this exploration and soul-searching that I began to fully embrace and discover how profoundly misunderstood and undervalued feminine energy is in the workplace. Forgiveness, acceptance, reflection, empathy, and collaboration are part of what's missing in our professional lives. Downplaying the value of nurturers, healers, and compassionate peacemakers in our workplaces creates an uneven, inequitable world. I hope that the modern workforce stops viewing the expression of feminine attributes as weaknesses, but instead recognizes these valuable strengths as qualities that create a more balanced, cooperative, and empathetic work environment.

This sometimes feels daunting and unattainable. The system, after all, has been in place for thousands of years. I certainly don't have all the answers, but I think the first step is to come out of hiding. We have been conditioned to hide ourselves away, not speak up, not rock the boat, not make waves. By starting to break out of these patterns and embrace our divine femininity, we can start to take back some ground. We have to be brave. We have to unlearn how we have done things in the past. We have to shut down the whispers that reside inside our heads, as much as the ones that float around on the outside. We have to embrace the feminine side and acknowledge the importance and the power that comes when we are in the fullness of true self-expression.

This is difficult, but the alternative is just not acceptable. Doing nothing is not working. I have been in the workforce for over twenty-five years and I have more years ahead of me. This challenge is not going to go away, but I have learned to recognize it and learned I am not the problem. It's the system.

Recently, I faced another employer situation where I had to speak up for myself. I was berated, laughed at, and threatened. Yeah, I spiraled a bit, my chronic illnesses kicked in again, but this time, I was armed with my belief in the divine feminine and with faith in myself. I shut down the whispers and I bounced back faster than ever. My daughters watched this spectacle unfold from the front row, live, and I wouldn't change a damn thing, tears, vertigo, and all. They witnessed it, they uplifted me, and they saw that I did not back down. They are women warriors. And so am I.

ABOUT THE AUTHOR

Alice has been in business management consulting for over twenty-five years. This has brought her great joy and great pain at times. After working in toxic environments and experiencing mistreatment at the hands of male leadership, Alice delved deeper into her spiritual work. She found her true voice through working with the Divine Feminine in cultivating a life of awareness and self-discovery through various practices of spirituality including manifestation, visualization, meditation, moon cycles, and even a little magic. Alice has always felt pulled to women's empowerment. As the mother of two daughters, it is extremely important to her that they are able to live in this world as who they truly are and not be silenced by the patriarchy. Alice wants to share her story, to help other women (especially young women) know they do not have to succumb to a toxic workplace, but can embrace their feminine values and not be afraid to fully use their voice. She hopes her work experience and her spirituality will inspire other women to be their authentic selves and discover their magic. Alice's greatest joys are spending time with her husband and two daughters ("laughing with them is the best thing in the world"), working out, collecting crystals, reading, and sitting on the beach absorbing the sounds and energy of the ocean. Follow Alice on Instagram @alicemm44 and on Linked In at Alice Meehan

ALLY BEHNKE

I was deeply compelled to find a natural and holistic way to get my life back. Surely it was possible to live a life that was not disrupted for an entire week every month while I was menstruating. There is. It was a weak whisper, but still, I felt it. I brushed my arms to shake the energy of disempowerment off me. I felt so little sitting in his office, swallowed up in the big plastic chair, forced into a corner. The whole interaction had felt condescending, as I tried to hold my position, despite being squeezed between the door and his desk. Was this man telling me that the only solution to my endometriosis was synthetic birth control pills? My body's voice had informed me otherwise. Birth control pills may work for some people, but my body was speaking to me through my pain. She was telling me these pills were not my truth.

PAINLESS
CYCLES

Here it comes again. I know this feeling: my chest tightens and my throat starts to close. My nostrils flare and I do my best to keep my upper lip from rising into a snarling grimace. It is the spring of 2017, and I am sitting in the doctor's office. I take a deep breath to ground my body. She is speaking to me and I decide to listen, to feel. I do not listen to the doctor, only to the wisdom of my body.

"No, absolutely not. I am not going on birth control." I shook my head in the direction of the male doctor. "I do not want synthetic hormones in my body. How can this be the only solution?"

He had just run through his birth control sales monologue and responded with a mild threat: "If you don't take birth control, your endometriosis will come back." His tone was appropriately prescriptive. "This is the only way to make sure your endometriosis stays at bay."

I was there for a follow-up visit. One month earlier I had undergone cutting-edge surgery to treat a condition that had plagued me since I became a woman: my endometriosis. I had just completed my first menstrual cycle since the surgery and to my dismay, it was still incredibly painful. Nothing much had changed. I scanned him, the room, and then my body. *Nope.* She said it again. I could hear her, deep down from somewhere inside of me. *No, No, No.* With an exasperated sigh, I begrudgingly thanked him for his time, wished him a good day, and declared my truth. *My body is not interested in hormonal birth control as a solution.*

As I punched at the numbers on the elevator and hurried out to the parking garage to find my car, my brain was spinning. I was deeply compelled to find a natural and holistic way to get my life back. Surely it was possible to live a life that was not disrupted for an entire week every month while I was menstruating. *There is.* It was a weak whisper, but still, I felt it. I brushed my arms to shake the energy of disempowerment off me. I felt so little sitting in his office, swallowed up in the big plastic chair, forced into a corner. The whole interaction had felt condescending, as I tried to hold my position, despite being squeezed between the door and his desk. Was this man telling me that the only solution to my endometriosis was synthetic birth control pills? My body's voice had informed me otherwise. Birth control pills may work for some people, but my body was speaking to me through my pain. She was telling me these pills were not my truth.

As I unlocked my car and climbed in, I felt safe and supported in my familiar space. I could not allow myself to surrender my power once again. I pulled out my garage ticket and waited for the machine to charge me for my time, and with each instruction given to help me leave the garage, I remembered the prescriptive directions forced on me in my late adolescence. I had been prescribed a cocktail of meds by a team of doctors in order to stabilize my moods. I had been put on birth control at the age of sixteen, and I remembered how mentally and physically off the whole experience had felt in my body.

I had spent a good portion of my teenage years walking around like a bloated guinea pig in which different doctors compartmentalized my issues and prescribed a variety of pills for my mood, my skin, and my constant urinary tract infections. Not one doctor ever asked about my diet, which at the time consisted of vending machine food for breakfast and lunch and a nacho supreme with a small Dr Pepper from Taco Bell every night for dinner.

My period pain was always a huge problem for me and the main reason I had avidly avoided nine-to-five jobs most of my adult life. Most employers aren't too keen on having an employee who is going to be unavailable three or four days a month. So I had always sought out jobs with flexible hours, which meant I ended up waiting tables, working as a real estate agent, working for real estate investors, and doing phone sales to avoid having to navigate explaining debilitating period pain with my employers. In my thirties, I had the brilliant idea of working for myself so I could control my own schedule. It was great until I had to attend a meeting, schedule a trip, go to a networking event, or simply be somewhere at a certain time like most normal working people. Instead of making that crucial client meeting or connecting with investors at a social event, I would often end up in the fetal position, curled up on the bathroom floor around a heating pad, disabled by cramps and debilitating brain fog. I did the calculations: I was spending one month of every year of my life dealing with stabbing, body-wide pain that felt like angry gerbils were clawing me apart from the inside out.

As I pulled up to a red light and mentally reviewed my options, I wondered if I was doomed to forever face this insanely painful and disruptive monthly cycle. Was I cursed by the Universe? Was I ever going to be able to have children if I wanted to? Would I ever be able to work a regular job or go on vacation without the fear of it all being ruined by horrendous monthly pain? *Yes.* Again, I heard her voice.

The light turned green and I knew it was time to let go. I felt the weight of years of frustration and disappointment. I heard the echoes of disembodiment that came with all the prescribed painkillers, bosses who shamed me, and nay-sayers who simply made fun of my pain as it came closing in on me. One by one, scenes of bleeding through my skirt at work, running to throw up in a trash can, or canceling important plans at the last minute played out before me like sketches from a pre-pubescent horror show.

Tears streamed down my face in anger as I did my best to stay on the road. With every passing mile, I felt like my body was betraying me. I let out a loud scream. It literally came from the depths of my soul, so deep, deeper than I had ever gone before. I gripped the steering wheel and leaned into it, knuckles white, my whole body gave way to the rage inside of me and I gave that scream everything I had. And then, I surrendered. It had been a long road, but my body was whispering to me one single simple truth: *There is a way to heal.*

Two years before the surrender, I was sitting in an interview at the WeWork Wonder Bread Factory in Washington, D.C. The Bros, as I affectionately called them, had a serious "hustle culture" work ethic. They focused on their goals in business, life, and health and went after them with military discipline. On this day, their backs were to me, and warm rays of afternoon sun stretched across the common area and into the conference room casting long shadows on the floor. Instead of taking their places at the table during meetings, they always made sure everyone in the room knew they were in charge by perching themselves on top of the large table that took up most of the room. It was no different today, and the interview started off with a discussion about the terms of cold calling and locking up deals for them. Raph was a millennial cliche: covered in tattoos and always outfitted in a black t-shirt with his hair swept up into a man bun. He was holding a massage stick in his right hand, playing catch and release with it like a baseball player would with his bat. It was *his company* and he made it obvious that he wasn't interested in my work contributions. I gulped nervously and turned to look at Joe, his business partner, whose energy felt much more empathetic. He had gone to an Ivy League school and looked a bit more refined in his blue blazer. Now that the meeting had started, Joe turned so that his side was facing me and we could at least make eye contact as we talked.

"Why do you want to work with us?"

I made a long verbal list of how much I enjoyed sales, connecting with people, and helping them solve problems. They didn't care. I searched my head for the answer they were looking for and—with a confidence I didn't feel—assured them I would follow their orders, come to the office every day, read all the books they put on their required reading list, and would do my best to meet their Key Performance Indicators. The key to unlocking their interest, however, was agreeing to work for commission only.

I spent the next three months pushing myself into the most ramped up, "go, go, go" mode that I had ever pushed myself in before. I cold called anywhere from five hundred to a thousand people a day on the autodialer, five to six days a week. I read the required books: *The Power of Positive Thinking, The Way of the Superior Man, The 7 Habits of Highly Effective People,* and *Traction,* among others. I did all the things the Bros asked of me, even if it felt a little bit like a cult. After a few months, my bank account reassured me that their methods had traction. I loved practicing my pitch, tone, and scripting for when I got on a call. It got to the point where I could qualify and close a deal in my sleep. "Condition, Motivation, Timeline, Price" was the mantra that echoed in my hardworking mind. I spent days in the rabbit holes of Youtube watching real estate guys cold-calling prospects. It all felt like special training that, combined with the energy of my teammates, meant we were on the brink of something big.

While I continued to grow professionally as I helped build this business with the Bros, I was also becoming deeply indoctrinated into hustle culture. I showed up. I did the grind every day without exception. Without really noticing, I slipped into a very masculine way of being. All the sales, business, and mindset materials I was consuming voraciously were written and produced by men. Their prescribed way of working took over my body, and, without recognizing the two were connected, my body became rigid and my period pain grew worse than it ever had been before. Each month, at the first sign of cramping, I would feel panic swell up over how I was going to hide my perceived weakness from them.

As I lay in bed one night in September 2015, I could see the moon outside my bedroom window. It was full and bright, abundant, luminous, and knowing. I was clinging to a heating pad to ease my physical pain. My mental focus was directed inward and my critical inner voice, which I would later affectionately call "my inner mean girl," was coming through loud and clear in direct contrast to my body's more gentle cadence. I was intimately familiar with both. My body, a quieter more confident voice, always communicated to me in more of a whisper, a full-body knowing. She spoke with grace and ease and always punctuated her messages with gentle love. My inner mean girl—the manifestation of my boss—was always shouting at me. Her tone was grating, jolting, and the color red. She operated out of fear and only had one message: work, work, work.

As my gaze moved from the moon to the trashcan that I had placed next to my bed in case I needed to puke, I was aware that my pain was more than in my abdomen; it traveled all the way up the right side of my body. I had a splitting headache on one side of my head and a throbbing leg, but I was operating in a space of denial about what my body was communicating with me. And right now, I couldn't get up and hustle even if I wanted to. There were times throughout the month where I did want to hustle, and I was good at it. But there were also spans of time where I couldn't.

What I had started to notice, however, was that I did have a natural inclination to want to work during these other times, it's just that the tasks that I could focus on were different. As I reflected from the soft, safe space of my bed, I knew that I could sleep now. In the morning I could focus my energy on things that didn't involve any direct discussion with prospects, leads, or clients. I was in a different mindset when I was bleeding. Instead of feeling outward and extroverted as I did on the days when the hustle excited me, I was analytical, reflective, and intuitive. All strong characteristics to add to my professional skill set, but not things that were necessarily highlighted as strengths in a corporate setting. The whispers started to get excited. I pulled out a pen and my journal and started to write. I told my inner mean girl to be silent so I could listen: *Keep going, you are on the right track.*

After spending months running on adrenaline and coffee, my mind, body, and spirit were completely depleted. My adrenals were shot, and total burnout was imminent. I didn't want to keep working with the Bros, but I was scared to leave. I had all the logical reasons in the world to stay and keep working and grinding, but these reasons were all based in fear. It became very clear after that night that if I was going to save myself, I needed to leave. My body knew what was best for me, and I was starting to hear her.

My obsession with understanding and biohacking my period took over the place and structure that work had always provided for me. I consumed every book, youtube channel, and social media influencer I could find that had anything to say about the woman's body and how to understand what was going on inside me. Over the next few years, the small voice of my body continued to whisper to me. I discovered the author Alisa Vitti and her book *The Woman Code.* Even with all my relentless research, I had never experienced feeling such a level of resonance. It was like I had been lost, wandering out in the desert, and now I had been found. And it overwhelmed me. I understood that I had a twenty-eight-day hormone cycle, but I learned that it was called an infradian rhythm and that my cycle had four energetic seasons: winter (menstruation), spring (follicular), summer (ovulation), and fall (luteal). Once I learned this I noticed ways I could integrate cyclical nutritional support and exercise habits into my daily life and monthly routines. I realized that I still needed to find a medical diagnosis for my period pain as it was getting worse and the quality of my life was becoming more and more negatively impacted.

Even though I took massive action in trying to solve my period pain, I once again found myself up in the middle of the night, unable to sleep. The glowing screen of my laptop reflected back in my bloodshot eyes. I had undergone the surgery for my endometriosis three months earlier and was still in crippling pain with each passing period. Up in the middle of the night and unconsciously channeling all the masculine, yang, "go go go" energy that I could muster, I was searching the internet for guidance on my boom-bust cycles and how I related to myself. I was exhausted. I was half-heartedly listening to my body's voice; however, the voice of my inner mean girl was largely controlling my inner dialogue from a place of fear, and thus, I submitted to a regimented daily routine.

I woke up at 6:00 a.m. for a workout at Solidcore. I followed that with a rigorous work day that was only made possible by drinking a ton of coffee so I could continue the hustle and grind prescribed to me by all the self-help books penned by high-performing men. Still a bit jittery, upon getting home that night, I made a cup of chamomile tea as though I expected it to solve all my problems. I then felt a ping to pull out my notes from that night a few years before when my body was paralyzed by the lifestyle of pain I had succumbed to.

Again, I noticed I was in a similar pattern: super-effective for half of every month, but for the other half I was hitting dizzying levels of burnout and would retreat to my bed with a heating pad and overwhelming brain fog. By tracking my cycle I discovered that the most "efficient" parts of the month were in the ovulation and luteal weeks of my period. Those were the very specific weeks I was able to tap into my superwoman powers and get everything done. Of course, on my week of menstruation, I would completely crash, only to follow with my follicular week where I would experience the aftermath of burnout as I slowly regained my energy. Then I would do it all over again.

Fuck, I sighed into my tea as I was faced with the harsh reality that I was, in fact, a human woman, and my very human woman body actually functioned in monthly cycles. How was any woman supposed to feel good all the time working a nine-to-five job when her body wasn't built to work that way? And then I heard her. It wasn't a shout, it wasn't a whisper, it was an inner knowing that would propel me forward in a way I could never have anticipated. *What would it look like to work in a way that truly supports me and my needs around my cycle?*

The more I connected to that question, the more I cultivated the guides, mentors, communities, and ways of being with myself that felt life-giving and nourishing to my body. I still struggled with my period pain and monthly exhaustion, but, slowly, I realized how critically important the roles of self-care and cycle awareness were for me to show up as my full self more often. I also started working with a coach who helped me explore somatic practices and the radical self-acceptance of my feminine nature. I simultaneously began building up a sisterhood all around me. I sought out women that were a part of the D.C.-based and virtual wellness communities committed to healing themselves. We were figuring out what it would look like to work and build businesses in ways that supported more than just our bank accounts. During this time, I was still wracked with period pain three to four days a month, until a D.C.-based wellness friend gave me a business card for a Mayan Abdominal Therapist at my birthday party and encouraged me to try it out.

As soon as my fingers touched the business card I felt the expansive energy behind it. I was excited to be in touch with the practitioner and reached out to her the next day. We chatted on the phone and I made an appointment to see her during the follicular phase of my next cycle. When I arrived at Kamala's practice, she greeted me warmly and we spoke about my relationship with my pelvic floor and my diet. She had a model of the female pelvic bone structure and showed me how and where women often hold tension in their pelvic space and what to expect. Kamala then set up the room before the massage with copal incense and soft music and I got onto the table on my back. When I was ready, Kamala started the massage just above the pelvic bone of my lower abdomen and worked her way around my belly button in a circular motion. For the second part, I turned over onto my stomach and the massage continued working on the areas of my back that hold my pelvic floor in place. I could feel muscles that I hadn't even known existed, and I finally released and relaxed in that area for the first time in my entire life. I had random memories of old boyfriends and other weird and uncomfortable images come up. As my body released, so did areas of my heart that had been hurt. This was more than just a massage—it was a spiritual experience, connecting my body, in this case, my pelvic floor, to my emotions. *This is how you heal,* my body breathed. *Finally,* she said, and together we sighed and settled into a state of deep relaxation and relief.

It was the weekend after my second massage with Kamala. I was at a tailgating party with one of my friends outside of Nationals Park in Washington, D.C. Soaked from the rainy day, we made our way from the parking lot into the stadium, stopping to purchase Nationals ponchos so we could at least stay a little dry as we watched our home team play. We found our seats and toweled them off, preparing to settle in. As soon as I sat down, I felt something wet begin to puddle in between my legs. I thought I had done a pretty good job of toweling off all the rain, and then it registered. *Dammit. Seriously?*

The wet sensation was indeed blood. My period had started. I immediately began trying to figure out how long it would take me to get out of the stadium, find an Uber in the pouring rain, get to my condo, heat my heating pad, and crawl into bed before the crippling pain would take over my body and ruin the rest of my week. I rushed to the stadium restroom to check the situation and discovered a bright red stain had made its way into my underwear. It was a beautiful bright red, not brown and dull like it usually was. My cramping hadn't started; in fact, I realized, I felt pretty good. A bit raw and sensitive but nowhere near debilitated, and my brain fog hadn't been triggered. Was this happening? Was I actually having a period that didn't make me feel like curling up into the fetal position? I was skeptical. I took a few extra minutes in the bathroom to wait it out, but the pain never came. I put on a pad, washed my hands, checked myself in the mirror, and made my way back to my seat and joined my friend. I made it through the entire baseball game without any cramping or throbbing pain.

Later that night, as I soaked in an Epsom salt bath, I was still reeling from the shock and disbelief that my period had come and I wasn't hanging my head into the toilet bowl. Was the solution a simple massage this whole time? I was almost angry that it had taken me so long to figure this out. After spending a little over half my life suffering from debilitating periods, I had cumulatively lost a little over a year and a month of my life curled up around a heating pad on my bed. Could it be that surrendering to my body's voice, after all this time, had actually been the way?

In the days and years that followed, I poured myself into learning more about female reproductive health and hormone cycles. Just for fun, I Googled "men's hormonal cycle," and I learned that men have a twenty-four-hour hormone cycle, bringing testosterone levels to their highest in the morning and lowest at night. I mulled this over and then felt such an "aha" moment when I read that their hormone cycles are perfectly in sync with the standard nine-to-five workday. Clarity, followed by sacred rage, fueled my desire for answers to so many questions, but mainly I reflected on why this information was not readily available and why it seemed like we were all okay with it. I started to think: *What else is so deeply embedded into my psyche that I blindly accept it?*

I started digging into my definition of success and that is when it hit me: I had been blindly chasing the Bros' version of success. I had accepted it as my own instead of surrendering to my inner voice. What I needed to ask myself was: *What does it feel like for me to embody success?* Not surprisingly, I had all the answers. They were within me the whole time. I've always had everything I have ever needed, I was just too uptight in my body and distracted in my mind to be able to hear my inner guide.

Success, I have come to understand, has seasons and cycles just like nature and my divine femininity. My body doesn't need to run on a twenty-four-hour cycle because I am not a man. Learning about how I am made, leaning into the sensations of what good and right feels like in my body, and being brave enough to accept what my body is telling me has been the key to my reclamation.

It's been a long journey to this mountaintop, and I will always have more mountaintops to climb. The inner knowing and understanding of my feelings that comes from deep listening will never be complete. I am committed to going within, asking myself the difficult questions, and doing what my body asks of me so I can move forward with grace and ease, one painless period cycle at a time.

ABOUT THE AUTHOR

Ally grew up in Northern VA and competed in club gymnastics in her youth. Then in her twenties she spent her time in the art and design worlds of Washington, D.C., and beyond. In her early thirties Ally started real estate investing and developed an entrepreneurial passion for creative problem solving. Throughout her life Ally has always been spiritual, and enjoys soaking up wisdom regarding self-awareness from various modalities and sources. After being seduced by the hustle culture, she found harmony in life by embracing her feminine nature, somatic awareness, and thoughtful self-care practices. She now draws on her life experience to empower other women to listen to the truth of their bodies and take action to create the life of their dreams. She enjoys yoga, rehabbing houses, and spending time with her partner and baby. Stop by and connect with her on all social media platforms @AllyBehnke

GABRIELA BELL

*This chapter contains sensitive content pertaining to domestic violence.

What I couldn't escape were the threats, the vicious games, and the financial abuse. He had taken everything. My life was falling apart, and I knew I was about to become a single mother of four. I was at the mercy of someone I once loved who no longer had a use for us.

FINDING
MY VOICE

The door slammed. Footsteps trudged to the kitchen. The clink of the empty bottle against all the others, followed by the hiss of the next one cracking open, clearly indicated that it could turn out to be another one of those nights. But I was hopeful. Maybe it wouldn't lead to a rage this time? If I just stayed quiet. I hoped tonight wouldn't be the next explosion because, in all honesty, I was so damn tired and worn out. Six months of complicated pregnancy would wear anyone out. Chasing after three young children on top of caring for a baby could do a woman in. I wasn't so lucky that night. The tirade of abuse started:

"Worthless bitch."

"You're nothing but a black cloud in my life."

"I could never afford to divorce you. If it ever comes to that, I will punch out of the military and just disappear."

Dread filled me as I faced the truth once again; there was nowhere left to hide. I knew I should not be married to this man. He did not see me as a partner, let alone an equal. I was simply someone who bore his progeny and took care of everything at home because I was just a mother. Embarrassed, ashamed, and feeling "less than" once again, I'd learned that responding during the rages only made things worse. Staying quiet didn't help much either, but the emotional degradation seemed to end sooner if I retreated into the comfort and busyness of motherhood.

It wasn't the first time that I knew in my heart that I needed to get out, nor was it the first time I didn't have the words or means to untangle myself from being dependent on and secondary to this man. That night's rage took me back to a night nine years prior. We were on a family trip to Ireland for a wedding. I was three months pregnant when I started to bleed. I was left alone to miscarry our first baby by myself in a cold bathtub while he drunkenly celebrated with his family. There was no regard for my needs, my well-being, or my health. I was alone, afraid, and far from home. Somehow, I knew it was better to hide away than disrupt the party. I cried myself to sleep and was sickened when he crawled into bed in the early hours of the morning, drunk, demanding my body meet his needs.

And then, in my second pregnancy, which stuck this time, I found myself in labor and delivery, heart racing, thrilled at the new adventure of motherhood and life as a family of three right before me. But there were no lullabies or sharing of nighttime routines. Once again, I found myself grasping for words I couldn't find when I was berated for his sleep disturbances due to a crying baby.

Postpartum depression hit hard. I would daydream about sleep and visualize myself throwing on a pair of shoes and walking out the door in pursuit of my pre-motherhood life. I so badly wanted to be acknowledged and comforted. I longed to take part in life outside of the home, but now that the baby was here, it wasn't allowed. Absurd contradictions became my life: I was looked down upon for not bringing in an income, and yet, his time was too valuable to watch his own child, so I was forced to give up my professional work.

There were moves, pregnancies, babies (lots of babies), sicknesses, deployments, special needs, career changes, alcohol, abuse, war; it was an awful mix, a messy quagmire of complicated rules and lonely years. It never felt like the right time for me to make a change for my own health, well-being, safety, and security. It never felt like the right time to make myself a priority. As I cleaned up LEGOs, folded another load of laundry, and perused a nearly empty fridge for what to make for dinner, I remembered the woman I used to be: determined and hopeful. But one night turned into months, and the months turned into years, and I'd be slammed, unexpectedly, by a sucker punch of words and threats. They bruised me so deep that they silenced my voice and emptied me out until I literally felt like nothing.

I became a prisoner in my own home. I was a glorified nanny, an indentured servant; kept at home to take care of the children, barefoot and pregnant, tucked away from the things I loved and found interesting. The constant messages of worthlessness I received left no space for my self-esteem. The physical act of being shushed and the public humiliation of never being able to even go to the grocery store alone ground me down from flesh and blood into dust.

Why didn't I leave? Why doesn't any abused woman ever leave? We are evergreen in our hope for reformation. We are peacemakers who unknowingly give up our independence to a person we thought would go to the ends of the earth for us and our partnership because we would for them. I wanted to leave so many times. So many times. But I had very young children and no money of my own. Money, our money, was something that belonged to him because he worked for it and I didn't. And to him, I would always be his nemesis. Unless I got out.

I didn't know what to say, because anything I said was met with hate and anger. To protect my children, I became the buffer. I knew I could take it because that's what mothers do. I knew I would not escape unharmed, but I had to try to protect my children. With every domestic explosion that erupted behind closed doors, my heart sank and my voice faltered. I wished for the calm of better days and the infectious laughter of my children.

As a military spouse, I had given up my career to support my husband and raise our children. Depending on your spouse for safety and security is risky, especially when children are involved. I wasn't near my family and I had no financial resources to call my own. The words "I could never afford to divorce you...I'll just disappear" reverberated in my head. I considered my options. As I lay with my children, trying to get them to fall asleep, all I could see for my future was that of a homeless, unemployed mother of four young children, pounding down every door to find a job, begging for a home, and desperate for security. Every night I would tuck my children into their warm beds and quietly tip-toe to my quiet corner to try to fall asleep and dream of better days. But every night as I drifted off I knew the truth: I was too scared to leave. So, I stayed.

Ever the hopeful one, I prayed that maybe tomorrow or the day after would be the one where he got better. But it never got better. He never got better, and I stayed for so many more years. My biggest failure was not understanding that the timing would never be right. Every time I felt brave enough to try leaving, there was another move on the horizon, a baby due, a baby just born, or a deployment looming over our heads. Instead of figuring out how to make it work, I worked incredibly hard to convince myself that the next life-changing event ahead of us might be the marker that would finally change things for the better. But it never was.

Those surviving in abusive situations understand the fragility and how repetitive time can start to seem. You live for the good times, and figure out the key to bringing more good times is to quickly get quiet and small when the sounds of the empty bottles rattle through the house. Victims of abuse become profoundly efficient at blending in, hoping to avoid the ticking time bomb. We hold on to the false hope of luck but inevitably, the abuse heightens, and all we can think about is things going back to normal once the tension subsides. We think, maybe it won't happen again if I'm lucky. Alcohol and luck are a funny mix because there's no luck at the bottom of a whiskey bottle, two bottles of wine, or a baker's dozen of beers every night. Luck was smart enough to run out the moment he walked through the door in search of a bottle opener. And finally, with a deep level of trepidation, I admitted to myself that it was now or never if I wanted to live.

In 2016, he departed for Europe on military orders. The children and I were to follow a few months later after a home in Italy became available for our family. Unbeknownst to me, he had cleared out our bank accounts and left us penniless. When I confronted him about this, he responded that he needed to be in control of all the money. If the kids or I needed something, it had to go through him. I knew immediately that if I boarded that plane bound for Europe, I was writing my fate in stone. I would never be able to leave, and if I somehow managed to, I'd never be able to return to the United States with my children. As every domestic abuse authority states, the most dangerous time for a victim is when they try to leave. And this was true for me as well: as soon as I told him we weren't coming to Europe under those circumstances, the abuse got worse.

He left for Italy. While he was thousands of miles away I could avoid the physical intimidation, the screaming, the shoving, the walls being hit, and my treasures being destroyed. What I couldn't escape were the threats, the vicious games, and the financial abuse. He had taken everything. My life was falling apart, and I knew I was about to become a single mother of four. I was at the mercy of someone I once loved who no longer had a use for us.

Nobody knew this story. I had never uttered one word. Finally, in an act of desperation, I confided in my best friend. The act of saying it all out loud was the spotlight I needed to see what was glaringly obvious to them. Sometimes you have to borrow someone else's eyes to see what you can't yet.

I was left with four kids, six suitcases, two cats, a parrot, and an old shabby van. I had no home, no beds of our own, and no cash. I was saved by the personal relationships and friendships I had built along the way as a mom, a friend, and a military spouse. With their help, I did everything I could to secure our immediate needs. I went out on a limb and found a house that was within the housing budget that I knew we were entitled to as a military family. I went as far as picking up discarded furniture I found on the side of the road. (Who would have thought that so many people throw entire households out with the Monday morning garbage?) Stick by stick, I crafted a new home for my four children, our pets, and myself. The only people I allowed in were those I trusted.

Sensing the freight train that was coming at me, I frantically started searching for ways to financially support my children. I went back to my first love—the one that never let me down—and started teaching part-time and tutoring on the side. I took a workshop to learn how to boost my resume and enrolled in as many certification classes as I could find in fields beyond teaching. Teaching as a single mom of four would not cut it when it came to feeding my kids and keeping a roof over all our heads.

It wasn't until I was served with divorce papers that viciously accused me of abandoning him and demanded full custody of the children that I felt truly backed into a corner. But it's always darkest before the dawn: his vicious attempt to control me one last time had had the exact opposite effect. It had caused me to find a place within the fringes of the military community that welcomed my voice: a small, yet mighty, military non-profit called Dog Tag, Inc. Finding this group helped me to see a new and hopeful future. This five-month-long fellowship designed for service-disabled veterans, military spouses, and caregivers focused on entrepreneurship and finding a new purpose. Dog Tag allowed me the time and space to find a way out of my predicament, and through that fellowship program, I found confidence, built my professional network, and learned how to craft a plan to launch a small business. But more importantly, it empowered me to find my voice and speak my truth in a way that enabled me to safely support myself and my children.

Two days after I graduated from Dog Tag and was about to launch my new career as a small business owner, my oldest daughter fell deathly ill and my plans for moving forward came to a screeching halt. All the doubts about leaving, right choices, wrong decisions, uncertainties, and fears came tumbling down. I wondered, *How are we going to survive this?* That was the question I had been asking myself for years, but this time, I was sitting in a hospital parking lot on a cold spring morning, willing my daughter to survive. As tears streamed down my cheeks, I pleaded with the Universe for an answer on how I was going to get through this crisis. We had no money and we were very possibly facing homelessness that would send us into a life of poverty that we might never dig ourselves out of. As I watched the dew collect on my car's windshield and I wrapped my coat around me in a struggle to stay warm, all I could say to whoever out there was listening was: *There has to be a way. There has to be a way.* This became my mantra and right there in that parking lot, I found the way.

As a mother of four, a teacher by trade, a woman who grew up in a military family, and a military spouse forced to reinvent herself with every move, I was used to being creative. Life has made me resourceful. I needed to find flexible remote work that fit into my predictably unpredictable life. Before my daughter fell ill, I had taken a side gig as a virtual assistant; I could do the job after my kids went to sleep, before they got up in the morning, while they were at school, and in between helping with homework. While sitting in my car, it suddenly occurred to me that I could possibly work with other small business owners and executives as their part-time virtual assistant. All I needed was a high-speed internet connection, a can-do attitude, and the ability to squeeze in work between all the other demands of my life. And at that moment, while we were all fighting to stay alive in our own ways, Organized Q was officially born.

For nine months, I worked in and outside of hospitals and doctors' offices, waiting in pickup lines for my other children to be released from school, and in between the dreaded phone calls from the lawyer about preparing for our next court date. Organized Q slowly grew, the demand for services increased, and the money started to trickle in. Money doesn't buy happiness but I felt like food on the table and staying out of a homeless shelter sure could, and that motivated me to work harder. Flexible remote work doesn't buy happiness either, but it allowed me to juggle the realities of life while still being able to bring in a paycheck.

Determined not to have my business solely depend on just one person, right before the pandemic hit I hired my first team member. Fortunately for us, as lockdowns and working from home became the norm, our business picked up and we didn't have to convince anyone that remote work could, well, work. It was a slow and steady climb. I kept my focus on gaining new business and opening more doors; we started winning awards and were even recognized for our outstanding work in the community. While I was fighting horrific court battles to keep my children, I was publically rallying for support as a voice for other military spouses and domestic abuse survivors in need of flexible remote work. I found this to be a bit of my new calling as a different purpose began to unfold.

In less than three years, Organized Q went from a company of one to now employing twenty-five individuals: mostly highly qualified and determined women in need of flexible remote work. I'm proud that we just completed our fourth hiring round this year because of the increased demand for Organized Q's services, and we have more than doubled our revenue year after year. Not only have I been able to build my own sustainable professional growth and be the only parent my children really know, but I have also helped dozens of other military spouses and under-employed professionals secure flexible remote work that fits into their complicated lives. I'm a firm believer in lifting as you climb. There's more than enough to go around. I'm very proud of the fact that we are on our way to reaching seven-figure revenues within the next two years, which is a huge milestone for an under-represented, woman-owned, small business, especially one whose founder has been bootstrapping the endeavor since the beginning. It's a far cry from the day that the check for the kids' school milk money bounced because my ex wouldn't approve the expenses.

It has not been easy. I still have days where I hear the echoes of "you'll never amount to anything," or "you're worthless, despicable, and a selfish bitch." Those words haunt me in the middle of the night. There are weeks when I feel the tension in my neck and the weariness in my head, caused by keeping myself constantly on high alert. Even though my ex ended up in court and eventually jail, there will still be battles to fight. And I'm tired—exhausted—from the constant weight of responsibility. I've come a long way since that night I cradled my pregnant belly and lost that innocent one I wanted. And while I have journeyed out of the hellhole of that desert, I can say that the climb to the mountaintop has been exhausting.

Being a single mom is hard. Being a small business owner is hard. Keeping it all together throughout a brutal divorce, the long hospitalization and illness of a child, the other children healing from their own trauma of their lives being turned upside down, COVID, more court cases, and now a recession has taken its toll on me. But still, I'm here. I'm not perfect, but I'm doing my best. Not only for me but for my children. I think it's important to not over-glorify what that mountaintop can look like for some people. I kept myself alive. I kept my children safe. I kept us out of a homeless shelter. We didn't go hungry. And my children have done well in school and are healthy. I created a business that has grown beyond what I ever thought possible. But damn, I'm tired.

The feeling of being alone with nothing to fall back on still keeps me up at night. Worrying that there are no options or that there are too many to choose from is equally overwhelming. I try to keep it simple, show gratitude for what I have, and put one foot in front of the other. And while there's no one else who can do the hard work for us, my experience has been that there are people out there willing to help, lend a hand, share a meal, bring a box of tissues or ruby-red wine, and sit with you until the storm has passed. The hard part is getting over the fear of asking for help and being vulnerable enough so that others can truly understand what's going on.

This journey isn't over. There's always another mountain to climb once you reach the summit. But it's okay to lie down and rest when you get to the top. Take a look around, and then settle in for a long delicious nap. When you wake up, you will see: the view is still the view. It won't go away. And your strength is still within you. Take a long deep stretch, breathe in that fresh mountain air, and congratulate yourself on your survival.

And just keep going.

ABOUT THE AUTHOR

Math teacher turned social impact entrepreneur Gabriela Bell is the founder and CEO of award-winning Organized Q, which provides Virtual Executive Assistant Services to small business owners, executives, and social impact organizations. Organized Q's social impact mission is in providing flexible remote work opportunities to military spouses, veterans, and under-employed professionals.

As a domestic abuse survivor and believer in necessity is the mother of invention, Gabriela is a fierce advocate, speaker, and educator.

As a single mother of four, she has worked tirelessly to build a brighter future for herself, her children, and others in similar shoes. She has been recognized as one of *Forbes* Next 1000 small business owners and is an instructor at NYU's Tandon School of Engineering Veteran Future Labs.

In her free time, Gabriela loves spending time with her four children traveling to new places, sharing great meals, and holding spontaneous dance parties in their tiny kitchen. Gabriela is determined to one day happily live on the beach with the ones she loves while continuing to grow Organized Q and teaching. Gabriela can be followed on LinkedIn at https://www.linkedin.com/in/gabriela-bell and you can learn more about Organized Q at www.organizedQ.com or at @organizedQ on social media channels.

JAMIE SABAT

*I put my finger over the middle of my mouth to quiet him down
with a long, shhhhh. "I think my water broke," I whispered
conspiratorially. In between contractions, I whispered desperate pleas
to Steven not to say anything to the driver. It was so embarrassing.
As I exhaled little puffs of air and tried to hold on to the side of
the car, I heard him say to the driver matter of factly: "Sir, my
wife's water just broke in the back of your car. I will Venmo you for
the damages."*

COMMAND
TO CREATE

I was nervous with anticipation about what was going to happen next. It was a normal night in New York City; well, normal for thirty-seven-year-old me anyway. Ten years prior, I would have spent the night running the streets, and then passed out on the couch only to wake up completely hungover from a week of partying. Now, I spent my evenings parked in a corner of the couch, reading. That is what I had been doing—until my water broke. After spending a really long time in the bathroom, I walked back in the room in an awkward, pregnant-lady sort of way and I made my announcement. I watched Steven as he immediately called an Uber and gathered the rest of the items I needed for a stay in the hospital. I felt many emotions, but mostly nervous, excited, and scared.

By the time the Uber pulled up, I was hunched over my big belly, dragging in deep breaths, then pushing them out. The driver opened the door for me after Steven calmly revealed that I was in labor. Steven was my rock, immovable. He never really got excited or showed too much emotion. The morning I shared that I was pregnant with our child, whom we would name James, he just responded with a quiet, "Good news." As I eased into the back seat of the hired car, I estimated that it would only be a fifteen-minute ride to the hospital at this hour: 3:00 a.m. We began driving from the Upper West to the Upper East Side. *Not too bad.* I continued my mantra: *I'm gonna make it. I'm gonna make it.* This was my first pregnancy and birth. I had no clue what I was doing, and all I kept thinking about were those movie scenes where the mother gives birth in the backseat of a car.

I gasped each time we went over a pothole, gripping the handle for dear life. Suddenly, a gush of warmth filled my pants and began to flood the back seat of the Uber. *What the hell was that? Did I just pee my pants?* I put my hand down to feel around on the seat underneath my bum. There was *something* everywhere. I was confused about what was coming out of me because I thought my water had broken before we left the apartment. I looked down again at my black maternity leggings and realized I was soaking wet, and so was the Uber.

"Are you okay? Are you alright?" Steven asked.

I put my finger over the middle of my mouth to quiet him down with a long, *shhhhh. I think my water broke,* I whispered conspiratorially. In between contractions, I whispered desperate pleas to Steven not to say anything to the driver. It was so embarrassing. As I exhaled little puffs of air and tried to hold on to the side of the car, I heard him say to the driver matter of factly: "Sir, my wife's water just broke in the back of your car. I will Venmo you for the damages."

Just as I finished breathing through my embarrassment, we arrived at Weill Cornell Hospital on 61st Street. My doula was still wrapping up her last client, who had gone into labor hours before me. The thought of having to birth my baby on my own created the perfect storm of anger infused with self-pity. "I wish we had waited until after my water broke to leave for the hospital!" I screamed at Steven as I clutched my stomach. "We are completely off schedule now."

As I watched the minutes tick by on the clock in the cold, sterile hospital room, I flashed back to the night we met Catherine, our doula. Her warmth and energy that night were things I craved mightily now as I visualized my perfect plan: as soon as my water broke she was supposed to walk over to our place and hold my hand. I imagined having her as a guide to birth me, as well as my baby, through the entire process. In my mind, a soft glow of light enveloped us all and it was a spiritual experience for everyone involved.

"I'm planning to have a natural birth. My doula is arriving shortly," I announced to no one in particular. Fear and paranoia began to take over as the life force inside me kept screaming, "You've never done this before. You have no idea what you're doing." As the nurses checked my vitals and hooked me up to various machines, a cold wave of nausea and unworthiness washed over me and settled in my stomach right next to the baby. Instead of questions and kind sentiments of reassurance, I thought I could hear the nurses talking about me behind my back. They could see it, we all could: I didn't know what I was doing.

My life experiences had set me up to feel this way. A black woman deviating from the plan? Not wanting to play by the books when it came to giving birth? That just wasn't done, at least not in my family. Raised in an Episcopalian African-American family, I had been bred to be a rule-follower starting at my own birth. This was reinforced throughout my life, and especially as I walked down the halls of an all-girls prep school in Washington, D.C. We were the real version of the Huxtables, an upper-middle-class African-American family, the kind of family that went to the best universities and socialized with a particular class of people. And the rules for those particular types of people were very clearly outlined.

In between overwhelming contractions, I continued to express what I wanted. It felt like I was stepping into a new personality, a new dogma. I was claiming my religion. But people just kept staring at me like an alien. There was a constant beeping sound taking the place of James' heart. My heartbeat began to sync with his, and yet, I had this awareness that I couldn't quite articulate at the time: Even though I had just told everyone what I wanted, the truth was, I was completely out of control. I was out of control in my body and could not predict what would happen in the coming hours. I kept thinking about the women who had been doing this for thousands of years, and yet, no one could map out exactly how the whole thing was going to end up. Where was the guidebook I had been raised to follow?

The contractions intensified for hours, to the point where my screams were drowning out the sound of James' heart. Finding my religion felt like I was being burned at the stake—and I wanted an escape.

"I want an epidural?" I whispered to anyone listening. It was punctuated with a question mark. Was I asking myself for permission to find some relief from the pain? My nervous system was all out of whack. There was zero trust between me and my body, me and my baby, and me and the universe.

"Are you sure?" I heard, coming from somewhere outside my agony. I nodded in embarrassment. I cradled my head in my hands in abject failure. I had moved so quickly through my resolve. We went from Plan A to Plan B, and everything changed in that moment.

The room was lit up like we were on the surface of the sun. Oxytocin began pumping through my bloodstream and I wasn't in the mood. I was ordered to move from my crouched position on a stool to lying on my side on the cold, metal bed covered in scratchy sheets. I held as still as I could as the needle was placed. The beep, beep, beep that signaled James was okay began to change in pace, and in a matter of seconds, I was moved into another room. The timing was all off. Because I had waited to get the epidural, moving positions and sitting straight up had put pressure on him. More bright lights, and now I was in a room filled with people I didn't recognize. My doula's hand slipped out of mine because only immediate family were allowed, and I started to grow numb in all the right places. I heard more machines beeping, worried whispers, and official people running in and out of the room.

"I'm sorry this isn't going the way you expected," my doctor said as she looked at my chart. The epidural was starting to work alright because I was going numb all over. There was a sense of heaviness in the room. I knew something had gone wrong and fear set in. I didn't have a plan and it felt like the walls were closing in on me.

"Your baby's heart rate is dropping and we must intervene," I heard. Four nurses surrounded my bed as if they were pallbearers about to carry me off to my final resting place. I heard them adjusting my bed frame, cranking and screeching. In my drugged-out state, I thought I was imagining it when they secured me straight-jacket style, right there to the bed, and kept cranking until my head was near the floor and my legs were on display above my head. My stomach gurgled and my dinner started to come up. With my head dangling towards the cold tile floor, James' heart rate started to go up. The doctor smiled with relief. *This is good, this is working,* I thought. All the blood in my body poured into my head and I was overcome with a sense of lightness. The creaking and cranking resumed, and I was brought back to the regular flat coffin position by the pallbearer nurses.

I was ready to meet my son. All the decisions made—wrong or right, bad or good, unworthy or worthy—didn't matter because I was back in the game and ready to fight for both of us. I lifted my arm to signal to Steven. I wanted to tell him I was visualizing Christmas and what it would be like to share those mornings together as a family. I was fighting for our family. But oddly, I couldn't move it. I tried again, a little harder this time, but I couldn't get my dangling arm off the ground. So I screamed. Or I tried to: I opened my mouth to demand to know what the hell was going on, but nothing would come out. Terror-stricken, I realized I was paralyzed. I could not move my body or use my voice. I couldn't breathe. I looked everywhere in panic, pleading with my eyes for help. I couldn't communicate with anyone. I turned my head toward Steven and prayed one simple prayer: *Please be a good father to our son and I promise to always watch over you.*

I relinquished all control. It was a clear moment of reluctant surrender. I settled my gaze on a fire extinguisher at the back of the delivery room even though everything was fuzzy and out of focus in the bright lights. *Is this what passing out feels like? Or maybe, this is what dying feels like.* People began to fade into the background as I felt drummers beating to the rhythm of my death march. Final thoughts raced through my head: *You're a failure. You're already a bad mom. You're going to leave your child abandoned while you just lie here and let go.*

My eyes fluttered back to the fire extinguisher in order to avoid meeting the sets of eyes that were going from my vagina to my face. The doctor grabbed my face and said matter of factly that the only way to save us both was to move forward with a C-section. And at that moment, all of my power left the room. By now my lung capacity was back and I could speak. Physically, I felt strong enough to protest but not one word came out of my mouth. I turned my head to the right to check the machines for my vitals and the nurse began placing a white curtain around my neck that would reach up to the ceiling. The bottom half of my body was no longer within view. Metal tools were dropped onto a tray as nurses sorted through them, and their contact with each other felt like nails on a chalkboard. I felt something move across my abdomen combined with a bit of movement. Suddenly, there was a scream. James was screaming. Tears streamed down my face: *he's alive, he's alive, he's alive.* As the nurses whisked him away and placed him under a warming machine to check him, I puked all over Steven's arm: a fitting ending to an imperfect birth.

As I was wheeled into the "recovery" room, I felt a looming sense of failure and mediocrity wash over me. I felt like I had put my son's life in danger on his first day on planet earth: I almost left him alone to fend for himself. I was able to hold him close to me and nurse him as the doctors monitored both of us. I was thankful for that, but all I could do was cry. The C-section scar was the maternity version of a tattoo that, at least for me, symbolized *loser*. I held on to James for dear life.

We made it through the night with constant feeding and diaper changes. On their usual rounds, the nurses came in to take James for a check-up the following morning. Every time he left I missed him a little.

Twenty minutes later, my doctor entered the room with two nurses. "I heard what happened and I have bad news." I was again blind-sided and looked for a focal point to keep from completely checking out. My heart started pounding in my throat and my c-section incision began to ache. While out for tests, James' heart rate had begun to drop again, and they had been forced to resuscitate him.

What the fuck. I sobbed inconsolably. The doctor came to my side and recentered her voice. She put her hand on my back and explained that it was going to be okay. James would be moved to a special room and kept under a warmer.

"You will be able to visit him," she assured me.

Inadequacy filled the room and my heart. As I wiped the snot from my nose with a pillow, I knew the truth. It was not ever going to be okay. If I couldn't even take care of my baby inside a hospital, how would I care for him outside in the real world? *I'm literally the worst mother alive.*

I stared into space for days. There was paperwork, insurance: one extra day in the hospital. Walking out of the hospital, carrying a diaper bag on one shoulder, my hands were heavy with the emptiness of the car seat. The feeling of the hospital forcing me to leave my child in the care of people who were not a part of him was like being sliced open once more. Nothing about the birth had gone according to plan.

Specialists were brought in, and James was poked and prodded constantly. Tests were administered to check whether his little heart was strong enough to keep us both alive. He needed to pass the heart rate test in order to be discharged. And dutifully, I would be there—the first mother in line in the morning—standing at the ready with my pumped milk in cooler bags, my empty arms aching to hold my son. Grateful and worried, exhausted and wired.

No one told me motherhood was going to feel like groundhog day; up pumping at all hours of the night, then jumping in the shower. Hair dripping, I'd throw on whatever breastfeeding top that wasn't caked in sour milk, and summon an Uber while choking down a piece of toast. All I could think about was getting back to the hospital to get as much time with James as possible. But the groundhog-day existence was a vacation compared to the terror I would succumb to when we finally came back home.

I couldn't put him down. Every time I had the chance, I would get flashes of the fire extinguisher from the delivery room in my mind's eye. I felt my heart pumping and would quake with utter dread that someone was going to take him from me. He went with me for naps, to the bathroom, and we even took showers together: I went so far as to purchase a waterproof snuggy that allowed me to hold him safely around my waist so we could both lather up.

Am I taking this too far? The thought crept in when I would swallow protests when his father wanted to hold him. Looking back, there were so many signs, so many red arrows pointing in the direction of seeking help. Summer came and went. I lived two blocks from Central Park but rarely left the apartment because I was afraid. It was a shocking truth I was afraid to face.

As fall set in, the holidays were a great distraction from the PTSD I was suffering from. We visited my family in D.C. for Christmas, and I quickly decided that what I needed to ease my pain was to be at home with them. I broached the subject with Steven one Saturday morning, as we peeled gum off the stroller wheel after getting off the subway.

"We need to leave New York. It's too hectic and dirty here for children," I reasoned with him.

As he looked for a place to wipe the disgusting gunk off his hands, he seemed to consider it. He was doing a lot of work in the D.C. area anyway and thought it would be a good idea to be close to family as well. I quickly looked at homes with a realtor and found something we liked. We went back to New York, packed our bags, and were in our new family home by Valentine's Day the following year.

Relief, finally. As I unpacked our boxes and created a new home for the three of us, I pictured those Christmas mornings I had held in my mind's eye those many months ago.

I felt relief from a hectic career and a fast-paced city. Relief from the constant fear of losing James and not being able to protect him. I took my time emptying the boxes. I measured precisely and hung the family photos just right. And then I stood back and surveyed the cozy home we had unpacked together and waited for the feelings to come: Contentment. Belonging. Right-ness. But as I fluffed the pillows and tidied the kitchen all I could think was that I felt utterly and totally lost. *Now what?*

Now that I could breathe as I looked in the mirror, washing my hands after changing yet another poopy diaper, I realized my identity was shattered. It wasn't just the grime and city noise of New York that I had left behind for the safety and predictability of D.C. I had also left behind a career in fashion, opportunities to travel the world for runway shows, drinking champagne with influencers, and having something important to say. Now my days were filled with stay-at-home-momming, and it had happened overnight. The transition was jarring.

Most of my days were spent taking care of James and setting up our new home, and time simply…passed. My minutes were filled with laundry and Costco runs with the occasional lunch at the Nordstrom Café with my aunt. I was home with James for about a year (which is something I never thought I would do) when I discovered a French Immersion School that I wanted him to attend. I was elated that he would have socialization, but then the reality of what I was going to do set in. An intense sensation came over my body and I felt a chill precede the racing thoughts once again. *Who do you think you are sending your kid to private school? You're not a good mother to sit around doing nothing all day! What if something bad happens to him because you aren't there watching him all the time?*

I stayed up all night, wracking my brain for answers. I knew that keeping James home would be selfish and unhealthy. I knew that I had grown past the point of extreme fear that his heart would stop if I wasn't with him, as he had grown stronger and into a wobbly toddler filled with so much life. This was his next step. It was clear. No, what scared me the most was that I didn't know what was next for me in my life. It seemed selfish, but I was so fearful of what was next. If he stayed home, I didn't have to worry about what was next, because he was my main responsibility. I could hide behind him. I could keep muddling through motherhood, day in and day out or, I could put him in school and go get a job.

It took a declaration to the Universe, a few coffees and lunches, but finally, I had a job offer. It was entry-level, with a low salary, and the daily tasks were a little mundane. But I was so desperate to get out of leggings and back into high heels, I figured it was worth a shot. The first few weeks were brutal. I was up at the crack of dawn in order to drop James at school on my way into the office. I hadn't driven in over twenty years, since I had spent my adult years living in London, Paris, and New York—cities where a car is a hindrance.

James adjusted well to his classmates and teachers, which was such a relief, but my brain was out of practice and my body wasn't used to sitting at a desk. I had to reorient myself to office culture, rediscovering the rules and how this version of me might comply. There was also the small matter of it being the first time I had worked in an office while I had a baby waiting for me at home. I took time to rest on the weekends and reminded myself that I was doing it for James. He was the most important thing. As I became more confident in the role, I received raises and accolades.

The next thing I knew, I was pregnant once again. I was on a mission every day to care for my son, get to work on time, and hide my belly. Eventually, I revealed that I was pregnant, and the news was received with excitement. My pregnancy was pretty normal. I was hot, tired, and bigger than the last one. My main focus became how to have a natural birth and not a horrific repeat of what I had gone through before. I had made a promise to the Universe and I wasn't going back on that.

In my eighth month of pregnancy, an Instagram story popped up on my mentor Elena Brower's feed. It was about essential oils. I quickly messaged her and asked how they worked. She shared with me how magical the oils were for her and how many mothers had used them to support a natural birth. Next thing I knew, I was reading out the CVC number on my credit card. My first delivery arrived shortly. When I cracked open the first bottle and inhaled, I felt like infinite ancient wisdom from the universe was rushing through my body. I felt so connected.

I quickly researched a birthing protocol using the oils and felt a huge sense of relief at my discovery. My confidence began to soar. I thought, *I have a tool now. I have something to fall back on. I can do this.* All of the necessary oils went into the overnight bag, including a diffuser. When I went into labor, I climbed into the car with confidence and determination that I would see it through. I labored only a short while, as Steven rolled specific oils on my back. We focused on breathing and closing our eyes as I labored in a dark bathroom. I used lavender for relaxation, copaiba to regulate my nervous system, and deep blue to relieve pain. The baby moved down so quickly that my doctor arrived just in the nick of time. And after a few pushes, there she was: Mila, my miracle. As I gathered her to me, I took my power back.

I was so proud of Mila and myself for the birth that took place. I looked down at her, gazing into her clear, wise blue eyes, and I knew she was a powerful being that was going to forever change me. She already had. Somehow, it felt as if we had done it together. I could feel myself let go of the shame, the fear, and the panic that had been my shadow for the last three years. It was the birth experience I had always envisioned, and I had been redeemed. I was able to really enjoy the first few days with her in the hospital. I had the diffuser blasting oils in the background as I sang positive affirmations into her ear. I left the hospital a few days later with my head held high. The nurses clapped for me as I left.

My birthing experiences were so vastly different, and I was now on a mission to tell every expectant mother about what had helped me. Once settled in at home, I took up a post in our king-sized bed where I worked around the clock, nursing Mila and pounding away at my laptop. It was like a channel of direct downloads from the Universe had been opened up when Mila came into my world. Not only had I brought another beautiful human soul into being, but I had a divine sense that I had birthed something else, as well.

Everything felt connected within and without. Things would just happen, like the afternoon a friend set me up with a local yoga studio so I could share what I had experienced. Every week I would set up my oils, and with Mila in a sling, together we would have the most engaging talks about energy work, reiki, nutrition, and self-care.

"I need more energy! I have a newborn and a toddler!" I would joke and then I swiftly signed up for all the sessions as soon as I could. I was ravenous and ready to consume all the Universe was putting in my path. Or more accurately, the path the Universe was putting me on. I was given visions and clarity about how to build my business through various healing modalities. Empowered wellness: that was my direction, that was my path. I came to understand with profound depth that we are the creators of our lives: nothing is happening *to* us; we are always creating it. We need tools to understand why and how we create certain things in our lives so we can release the victim state.

My life was morphing so quickly that it began to put a strain on my marriage. I was traveling a lot for work, speaking all over the country at events and conferences. Home life became on-the-road life. My role at work shifted and I was on a different team; I was even moved to a new location in the office. I started to dress in more feminine colors and materials. But the biggest change was giving up alcohol. I could now energetically feel how it was lowering my vibration. As my metamorphosis drew me more into the "woo" and away from the three-dimensional world, I knew Steven and I had grown apart. We went to counseling, but no amount of journaling could bring us back to the same page. We were very unhappy and we needed a change.

Fear set in on how I would manage a separate household financially. My job provided the supplemental income, with Steven at the head of the table winning all the bread. That old familiar voice of unworthiness that had been with me in the delivery room with James came knocking at the door. *You can't do this on your own. How will you manage it all?* We moved through all the right steps to separate and I managed a schedule for the kids. I relied heavily on my daily meditation practice, journaling every morning, and continued to exercise. Every day, I looked in the mirror and reminded myself that growth is good. If we stayed the same person our whole lives, that would be a lackluster existence. Sometimes we grow together and sometimes we don't; normalizing divorce was key for me, and for my children. Steven and I remained peaceful in front of the kids until I was able to move out.

The move, of course, would match one of the most unsettling times in the past few decades: a global epidemic was impacting the world. My children were being homeschooled and the economy was shaky. *Great timing*, I thought to myself, but I continued to follow my guides. I refused to let fear win and to continue blocking my path as it had always wanted to do before. My energy was beaming with strength and positivity. So much so, that I was attracting clients. As more women came to me for guidance and coaching, I knew I needed to gather the powerful tools I had used for my own personal growth and development. I began to focus on the mind. I took the opportunity to go deeper with astrology, as it was always a tool that I used to figure people out most of my life. I went deep into the science behind it all, and it was profound. I saw how much we as human beings are connected to the planet and impacted by the sun and the moon.

One by one, women would seek me out, and over and over, I saw how I could impact past versions of myself. So many times, there was a feeling of unworthiness or laziness that was holding them back from the life they were meant to live. I knew what that was like. As I listened to these women, I could recall, very quickly, the feelings of powerlessness and shame I too had been paralyzed with in such profound ways. Through birthing James, and understanding my true passion, to getting honest with myself and my ex about the growth that we both were allowed to experience, separately.

I'm sure many mothers would say that their children have become their greatest teachers. Mine have not only been my teachers, but they have become my guides. They hold up a mirror for me so I can see what I am capable of. They have helped me birth a new perspective and purpose. They have ushered in this newest version of myself. The journey has not been easy, but nothing worth having, like bringing a new soul into the world, is. As I stand up on the mountaintop that is my current reality I see that I have been reborn. And the cry that comes with being birthed is now infused with power, restoration, and utter and complete joy.

I am the creator of my life.

I get to decide.

I hold the power.

And that can never die.

ABOUT THE AUTHOR

My own journey of manifesting began with the important decision to live the life I truly desired. What followed was the resolve to let nothing stand in my way of attaining that goal. I accepted myself as my own client and dedicated myself to the practice of manifesting the best life possible. The decision to make the journey and not the destination came not from a life-changing event; rather, it came from a deep awakening that I had not yet reached my highest potential. Only when I changed the path I was on, with the intent of living the life I had always wanted, did I understand that the universe was waiting to show me the answers to life's questions. www.distillandexpress.com @distillandexpress

RACHEL FESKO

*I wasn't just exhausted from lack of sleep as I typed and backspaced,
I was exhausted with my life, deep down in my soul. Every night I
would lie awake thinking: This can't be all I was made for. Running
inside the hamster wheel couldn't possibly be all I was put on this
earth to do. I had shown so much promise in my life. People had
told me I was a world changer and would make a difference, which
I believed to be true, even years later. I sat staring at that screen
remembering the girl I had been eighteen years ago and wondered,
Where did she go? Where did that vivacious, tenacious, ambitious,
"grab life by the balls" girl go? What happened to me?*

FAILURE
ISN'T FINAL

I looked over at the clock for the hundredth time. 10:00 p.m. It was getting late and I had to work the next day. I was dreading how early the kids would be up and how I would need to walk the dog in my old, oversized, snap-up sweatpants to hide my pajama pants. In the next room, I could hear my husband playing his video game, laughing as he chatted with his friends. I sat at my desk, holding back the tears that threatened to fall and unleash all the sadness and frustration I was holding in. I looked back at the computer screen. I had been staring at a blank document for two days, typing and erasing so many opening sentences I couldn't remember what I had even started, written, and rewritten. I was exhausted.

After fifteen years, I had finally decided to fulfill a lifelong dream of obtaining my master's in Communications. My admissions advisor had emailed me three times asking when I was going to finish up my application, but I was stuck and I didn't know how, or even if I was going to move forward. I was scared to death of trying to do grad school with two young kids, a full-time job, and a less-than-supportive spouse. The final step in the application process was to write a "statement of purpose". I had applied to the only graduate school I wanted to attend, and as I sat there listening to the clock tick away the minutes of the night and my life, I couldn't put words to the lifeless feeling I felt in my soul. If I wrote down how I actually felt—well, there was no way the admissions board would let me in. The truth was I was unmoored and directionless in a sea of uncertainty. All I knew was that I couldn't stay where I was if I didn't want to drown. My marriage was falling apart, I was in a new job (again), and had little, if any, social life apart from going to yoga and the gym once a week. I was failing in every area of my life, relationally, professionally, and socially. *How's that for a statement of purpose?* I thought.

I wasn't just exhausted from lack of sleep as I typed and backspaced, I was exhausted with my life, deep down in my soul. Every night I would lie awake thinking: *This can't be all I was made for. Running inside the hamster wheel couldn't possibly be all I was put on this earth to do.* I had shown so much promise in my life. People had told me I was a world changer and would make a difference, which I believed to be true, even years later. I sat staring at that screen remembering the girl I had been eighteen years ago and wondered, *Where did she go? Where did that vivacious, tenacious, ambitious, "grab life by the balls" girl go? What happened to me?*

At age twenty I was a college dropout. My parents had forced me to go to a tiny East Coast satellite Bible college in the backwoods of Virginia, and I hated every second I was there. The religious, overbearing nature of the school, the lack of personal freedom, and the imposed curfew were not what I had in mind for my college years. I wanted an experience: to learn, travel, drink, party, and expand the circle of my understanding to more than just the four walls I had been raised in.

At the age of seventeen, I proudly walked into my parents' bedroom with my plan and announced that I wanted to go to the University of North Carolina, Charlotte, and obtain my MBA while living at home to save on tuition. In her characteristically matter-of-fact way, my mother responded with, "No you're not, you're going to Bible college." Looking back, I had no idea how that one decision defined my entire life. I was never allowed to attend public school, and there was a constant sense that the world was a bad place that we must protect ourselves from. I wanted to live in a world where I could explore and find myself. My parents' mentality kept me from reaching for more and always worried about "what if." *What if what I'm taught doesn't line up with my family's beliefs? What if the classes aren't Bible-based? What if I incur debt? What if I make bad choices? What if I fail?* Because of what I had been conditioned to believe about myself and the world, I obeyed my parents and went to Bible college. After three semesters of living in hell while writing papers about how to avoid it, I couldn't take it anymore, so I dropped out of Bible college and moved in with my aunt.

After dropping out, I would have moved back in with my parents, but while I was in college they had moved my things into storage, moved my sister into my bedroom, and turned her bedroom into their office. I was effectively homeless. I was in complete disbelief and dismayed. *My parents moved me out of my own bedroom? If I had stayed in school, where would I have gone for Christmas or summer break?* I felt completely and utterly rejected. My choice to drop out of Bible college against my mother's wishes effectively exiled me from my family. Even though my decision was right for my soul, I had never felt like more of an outcast. I was wrong in the eyes of the people from whom I still so desperately craved approval.

My aunt and I had always been close, and she was one of the first adults that I trusted outside of my immediate family. She was in her thirties and single, with a successful financial career. She lived in a cute townhome with her two dogs and welcomed me into her second bedroom. I was not a great roommate. My rent was never paid on time, if at all. I left a trail wherever I went and hardly cleaned. Despite that, she taught me about real life in the real world. She taught me things like how to balance my checking account, how much to save on my paycheck, and how to grocery shop. But most importantly, she taught me balance. She showed me that life isn't lived in a vacuum and that sometimes you have to take risks if you want to move your life forward. Even so, after living with her for two years and getting fired from two jobs, I found myself, once more, adrift and searching.

I was visiting my parents one afternoon, when my dad brought me their house phone and said, "Pastor Jack wants to talk to you." Pastor Jack Hayford was a well-respected Pastor in the Foursquare denomination with a huge congregation, and he was my father's mentor. Pastor Jack urged me to go back to Bible college to finish my degree and helped provide a scholarship for me to afford to re-enroll. Rather than going back to the small satellite campus, I decided to attend the main campus in California. Four weeks later I packed my bags, bought a plane ticket, and headed to the West Coast for the January semester.

This time, it was in a school across the country from everything I knew, and it was the best decision I ever made. I entered a world I had only dreamed about and felt at home so quickly it was earth-shattering. California in January is a beautiful thing. The smog clears when it rains, the hills turn green for a few short weeks, and the weather is just perfect enough to have a bonfire on the beach without it being too hot or too cold. When I stepped on campus I fell in with my old high school friend, Jill, who introduced me to her friends. All of a sudden I went from being a nobody in Charlotte to having a circle of like-minded friends overnight. We spent our weekends at

Disneyland and our weekdays studying for A's in psychology. I had finally found the place where I belonged. After so much floundering, life was finally clicking into place.

After months of university bliss, I arrived home in high spirits, but physically not feeling great. I had been battling a sinus infection for months and no amount of over-the-counter medication was helping. My dad noticed how congested I was and, as he passed me another handkerchief, he made an appointment with my primary care physician without my knowledge. My regular doctor was out that day, so I was stuck with Dr. Goodman. At sixty-five, he should have been looking at retirement, but instead, he was still giving old-school physicals to everyone who walked in for a minor ailment. As Dr. Goodman was checking my reflexes and feeling the lymph nodes in my neck, he found a lump on my thyroid. At that moment, my life changed. At the age of twenty-one, I was diagnosed with papillary thyroid cancer. I underwent two surgeries, had two rounds of radiation, and came out of it with a clean bill of health. I was determined to finish my undergrad degree, so after a harrowing summer, I decided to return to school across the country that August and fought cancer while attending my classes. I graduated Summa Cum Laude.

Fifteen years later, sitting at my desk and staring at that empty white page on the computer screen, I pondered the emptiness I felt in my life. I reviewed the highlights and lowlights of the battles I had already fought. *Where did the girl who fought those battles go? How did I lose her? Why was I so supremely unhappy, and how could I get back to who I was before?* I was slowly beginning to see things as they were, coming to terms with unrealized childhood trauma in my past, and the current state of emotional and spiritual abuse I was living with.

Trauma, experienced in my childhood and as an adult, had turned me into a shell of who I was before. While others could see things through a clear pane of glass, my traumatized heart and mind were looking at the world through a kaleidoscope. I tried to see clearly, but could only find hundreds of broken pieces of glass rolling around in a tube. Trauma is like a hammer that pounds a square peg into a round hole, slowly deforming and breaking the peg as it fits a form it was never meant to fill. And all the compressed, broken parts of me were screaming.

What I didn't realize is that my trauma caused me to see the world incorrectly, and created limiting beliefs and cognitive dissonance that I couldn't seem to shake. I knew a different reality existed than the one I had been fed my entire life. I knew the destiny that was before me, but it seemed I could never get there. I knew my truth, but I was constantly being told it was false. This constant conflict within my body created a state of almost constant anxiety with intermittent bouts of depression and symptoms of ADHD. I had a hard time regulating my emotions and regularly dissociated in order to cope. I battled a constant negative self-perception, and had difficulty trusting others or having any truly deep or meaningful connections. I lacked a support system for dealing with my c-PTSD, other than my therapist. My controlled childhood had also made me blind to the warning signs of being in a controlling marriage. Everything seemed normal until it wasn't. Everything seemed fine until the facade cracked and a beam of glorious light came shining through.

As Tony Robbins says, "Change happens when the pain of staying the same is greater than the pain of change." My inner world was in pain, and all I wanted was to be happy, really truly happy, inside and out. My catalyst for change happened in November of 2019, when my best friend forced me to go to a women's conference led by a popular self-help influencer. During the three days we were there I heard numerous speakers tell their stories of hardship, failure, and success. The difference between them and me was that when I failed, I decided it was a life sentence and gave up. These men and women found a way to learn from their failures and keep trying until they found the path they were supposed to follow. Their words began seeping into my soul, and I started hearing my inner child speaking to me again.

I remembered the ideas I had read in the John Maxwell book *Failing Forward* so many years ago, and I started to see hope on the other side of my mistakes. Maxwell said, "The more you do, the more you fail. The more you fail, the more you learn. The more you learn, the better you get." The revelation I came to in the middle of the conference was that if all of these speakers and authors had learned from their failures, forgiven themselves, and used them as fuel for their future, why couldn't I? Furthermore, why were some of the people in my life constantly holding my past over my head rather than helping me move forward? The message that resonated throughout the conference was clear: I have the power to change my life. After three days, it finally sank in. I came home renewed and invigorated. I was ready to change my life, and I had finally realized only I had the power to do it.

One of the first changes I made was to start getting up thirty minutes earlier so I could walk the dog and read a chapter of a self-development book before the rest of the house woke up. I also switched out my sweet tea for water and tried to make time to go to the gym three times a week (as a working mom this normally happened after the kids went to bed). While making these small changes I realized I had let bad habits control my life. I was staying up too late, which caused me to wake up late. I was eating too much processed food and sugar, which affected my mood, energy, and emotional stability. I had let childhood trauma go unchecked, which affected my relationships. Once I realized that my life was my own and happiness was obtainable, I started working towards having a healthier, more productive life.

One of the most drastic changes I made was switching careers. After my photography business fell apart, I became an executive assistant for the CEO of a global hygiene company. The role exposed me to a different lifestyle and showed this poor girl from Indiana how the other half lived. While I valued that experience and the lessons I learned from being in that role, I quickly learned that I was not cut out to be anyone's assistant. Organizing calendars and taking lunch orders only showed me that I wanted to have an assistant of my own. The words I heard from the speakers and authors at the conference continued to resonate in my soul. They had become successful, not *despite* their failures, but because of them. I realized that being an executive assistant was pigeonholing me and was a barrier to my dream of moving up in the company to an executive level, so after getting fired from two different executive assistant roles I decided to take the pay cut and apply for content writing positions.

Another big change I made was diving headfirst into therapy. I had been struggling with depression and anxiety and had been avoiding digging into my life to uproot the trauma for so long that it had now started to creep into and invade every part of my existence. Like kudzu, the vine of trauma was growing over every healthy plant in my life, attaching itself to it, feeding off it, and then expanding over it until all I could see was the pain and dysfunction instead of the garden of growth underneath. I wasn't sleeping well because I was ruminating on destructive thoughts. I was forgetting important deadlines at work because I was so anxious about having a deadline and was afraid my boss would hate me if I completed my tasks incorrectly. I was walking on eggshells at home, which was creating an anxiety-filled atmosphere that trickled down to my children.

As I dove headfirst into doing the hard work within my soul, I found ways to manage my triggers, set boundaries, and find that lost girl inside myself that was driven, ambitious, and focused. It was as if I had walked back in time, found that girl on the side of the road, picked her up, and began carrying her with me again. I became unapologetic about my needs, goals, and boundaries. Unfortunately, this is when my marriage hit its roughest point because the one person I had to set boundaries with the most was my husband. I realized that my home had never been a safe environment, neither growing up nor as an adult, and that, in turn, had prohibited me from becoming the person I knew I was meant to be. I discovered that the person I had denied as my true self and had stuffed away for years was still inside me. Like a caged lion, she was roaring to be let out.

Everything I had learned about psychology during my undergrad years started coming back to me. One of the main things that hit me at my core during this time of rediscovery, was Maslow's Hierarchy of Needs, which basically says that humans have a progression of basic needs that must be met for them to succeed; for children that might mean that being cold, hungry, and tired would make it hard to concentrate in school because their basic needs of food, warmth, and sleep are going unmet. Furthermore, if a child's parents are struggling with resources, or the child is dealing with emotional or physical abuse, it can stunt the child's ability to develop neurologically and form healthy social relationships. This, in turn, impacts the child's self-esteem and ability to become a thriving, functioning adult. This was not only my childhood, it was my adulthood. I had never felt accepted or safe in my own home. I was controlled. I was manipulated. And I had had enough.

Studying Maslow's Hierarchy of Needs helped me connect the dots in my own life. I grew up as the poor pastor's kid in a small town, always wearing hand-me-down clothes, driving the clunker car, and being part of the only family who homeschooled. This made me the odd one out in almost every social situation. Combine that with a controlling religious upbringing, and you've got a recipe for adult survival disaster. I was an anxious, depressed, perfectionist, afraid to try for fear of failure and afraid to succeed in case the positive affirmation I received from others fueled those closest to me to lash out and remind me where my place was. When I clearly saw what I had needed as a child versus what I received, I realized that in each of us there is a desire to find an environment of psychological safety where we can learn, fail, and try again. First at home, then at school, and then at work. Unfortunately, we have been raised in a society where failure is seen as a bad thing and trying is looked down upon. Receiving a failing grade lowers our grade point average, which affects our ability to get into a school that will challenge us. Failure in the workplace means we're written up or fired. Failure at home means a barrage of constant fighting and having to live up to unspoken expectations "or else."

When we grow up in a controlling environment, devoid of choice and freedom, we begin to find security in other people dictating where we should go and what we should do. At the same time, we can internally rebel against the rules because we know we should be forging our own path and differentiating ourselves from others. I realized that the patterns of my past were continuing to dictate my actions to me, rather than having my desires and goals at the forefront of my life, directing and guiding me with my own internal compass.

So, there I sat, in a space of despair of my own making, at 10:00 p.m., trying to finish my application for grad school, desperate for direction. Staring at that blank page titled "Statement of Purpose" on my computer screen, I was suddenly hit by a lightning bolt that turned my despair into determination. At that moment, I was determined to change my life and become that thriving, bold, courageous, ambitious, full-hearted woman again. I didn't know how long it was going to take to get my life back, but I was going to start climbing, knowing eventually I would reach the top of the mountain. When I finally wrote my statement of purpose, I could have opted to fake my way through the document, but instead, I decided on radical honesty. If my current vision and purpose were lacking, I would find it along the way.

Statement of Purpose:

"As a wife and mother, it has been difficult to draft a "Statement of Purpose" that allows a window into my soul during this season. For the last few years, my purpose has been my children, and, as someone who is actively trying to find herself again, it has been difficult to pinpoint exactly what I want to share and tell you why you should grant me admittance. Usually, I am advocating for my children and putting my needs last. However, communication is a long-term passion of mine, and I believe the time is right to pursue a graduate degree.

My professional experience over the last ten years has given me the opportunity to improve my communication skills and realize my desire to see integrated communications in the companies I have worked for. Throughout my various roles—whether I was working for a nonprofit organization, a publicly traded corporation, or a private software company—I found that my passion for the written word has continued to deepen. I have been trusted with writing personal letters for CEOs, crafting newsletters that were to be distributed throughout large companies, and creating white papers that were delivered to thousands of clients. Whatever the context, I believe communication is a skill that must be honed and a talent that must be refined."

I went on to give them my educational background and explain that Purdue's Communications program was the only program I was applying for due to its specific concentrations and applicability to a variety of career options post-graduation. I applied on October 15, 2019, and then attended the self-development conference in November. By December first, I still had not heard anything from Purdue and my anxiety started up: *What if radical honesty was the wrong decision? What if I don't get in? What if they don't like me?* Finally, after four more days of sleeplessness, worrying, and never-ending scenarios that all ended with me as a continuing failure, I received an email stating that I had an important message in my Purdue portal. With shaking hands, I logged out of my computer at work, went down to my car, and called my best friend for support as I logged into the portal on my phone to read the message that would decide my future: "Dear Ms. Fesko, thank you for your application to Purdue's Brian Lamb School of Communication. We are pleased to tell you that you have been accepted to the January 2020 class…" I couldn't read any further and burst into tears. Finally, after years and years of striving, I had validation. External validation, but validation nonetheless. Thus began the first step in finding my footing in this uphill climb back to my core and essence of being.

My days were soon overflowing with books and articles; reading, writing, and responding to discussion questions; crafting final papers, all while juggling full-time work and being a full-time mom. Because I was still a wife with 95% of the household responsibilities falling on my shoulders, I quickly realized that I had to begin making time for completing my degree. I put my YouTube and Instagram channels on hold, politely declined social obligations, and cut my social media time in half. I started saying "no" to everything that didn't serve the purpose of obtaining my degree and doing it with excellence. Setting boundaries and working hard paid off and I received my first "A" with notes and praise from the professor who was not only impressed with my professional experience but also with my ability to communicate. I was ecstatic. *I got an A*! More validation. I was valuable. What I had to say was appreciated. I was making a difference.

Unfortunately, there were still those people around me who told me to "not get a big head," and that I needed to "watch myself." So in an act of resistance, I would remind myself that the person I was told that I should be: the quiet, meek, humble, selfless, wife and mother was the person who felt directionless, unmoored, depressed, and searching. The person I was becoming now was bold, courageous, alive, ambitious, and joyful. I was going against everything I had been taught to believe about myself, and because of that, I finally felt like I was walking the path I was always meant to walk. Despite my fear and misgivings, I continued to push forward.

Two months into working on my degree, the first positive COVID-19 case landed in New York. My entire world would be turned upside down in less than four months. When the world shut down on March 13, 2020, I knew that my marriage wasn't going to make it through lockdown. We were barely surviving as it was. We would work all week with little to no communication and then explode with fights on the weekends. We would go back to work on Monday, emotionally battered and licking our wounds only to repeat the whole cycle. I took solace in escaping to work forty hours a week and then coming home, cuddling my children, and diving head first into my studies after their bedtime.

Six weeks after the lockdown, my husband and I separated. Everything came to a boiling point that became untenable. In that moment of clarity, my life spectacularly broke apart, never to be the same again. I had finally found my voice. The validation I found in stepping out to get my master's and having my writings resonate with my peers and professors had given me just enough confidence to speak up to the one who was least interested in listening. Blazing with courage and backbone, I drew a line in wet concrete that, once solidified, became unbreakable. I was valuable and no one was going to tell me otherwise.

Dutch theologian Henri J.M. Nouwen once said, "Resentment and gratitude cannot coexist, since resentment blocks the perception and experience of life as a gift. My resentment tells me that I don't receive what I deserve. It always manifests itself in envy."

In the days following the separation from my husband, I would take up residence on my couch in a cloud of mixed feelings. I was finally experiencing peace in my house and my soul, but I was in turmoil. I knew I was ripping my family apart and going against every pastor and person in my life who told me one must stay in a marriage "no matter what". At that moment, I had a choice: I could either keep moving forward and listen to my soul's voice, or I could go back and listen to all the voices of my past. I had already made hard decisions— to go back to grad school, to wake up early, to go to therapy, to invest in myself, to change my life—but I knew going back would mean certain death for my soul, and that simply wasn't an option. I had experienced a modicum of freedom and peace, and as I sat there in the corner of my couch, sipping coffee and staring at the wall, I knew I could not let it go now that I knew what it felt like. I had to keep going. I had to keep climbing. I was finally free from the cage and making my life happen one day and one decision at a time. I was scared with every single step I took, but I was moving forward.

Over the next year, I continued to go to the gym, eat in ways that made my body feel its best, drink my water, and get to bed on time. I kept pursuing my master's and I also obtained a second job to keep myself afloat. Splitting custody of the children with my ex gave me time to not only work and study, but to journal, hike, and kayak in the free hours I found myself suddenly having. I started a gratitude and goal journal that helped me articulate the things that brought me joy and keep my perspective as things heated up with the divorce.

As I continued to push forward, I felt myself butting up against those old limiting beliefs of not being good enough and prayed God would send me someone that could help me break through the ceiling I had crashed into. The next day, I received a phone call from a well-known life coach who found my Instagram account and asked if I wanted to join his program. I had a gut feeling this was my answered prayer. I took a leap of faith, handed over my credit card information, and dove in. Three weeks later I had my mental breakthrough. My coach asked me, "Rachel, what is it that you believe about yourself? What is stopping you from getting to the next level?" Through heartbreaking tears, I answered the truth from the depths of my heart: "I don't believe I'm worthy of anything. I don't believe I deserve anything good." After years of humility, undeserving grace, and selflessness being beaten into my soul and spirit, along with a good dose of emotional and spiritual abuse, I honestly believed that I was unworthy of any good thing happening to me. My coach said, "We're going to reverse that today. What do you want your new mantra to be?" After taking a hot second to think about it, I started laughing through my tears because what came to me was simply absurd, "I deserve all of the wonderful things life has to offer." I mean, that couldn't possibly be true, right? But I wanted it to be true, I wanted it to be true in the deepest parts of me. I wanted my failures and mistakes to stop holding me back from running toward the life I dreamed of, but only I could make that happen. And I wanted it so bad. I know it sounds ridiculous, but I wrote that damn mantra on my bathroom mirror, put it on a post-it note on my desk, and kept it on an index card by my bedside. Everywhere I looked, I had my own handwriting reminding me that I deserved to have a good life.

After being in that life coaching program for six weeks, on March 1, 2021, I woke up a new person. Exactly ten months after separating from my husband and a year into my degree, it was as if the fog had cleared from my mind. All of the work I had done in therapy, the line in the concrete, setting boundaries, hiring a life coach, saying my affirmations, practicing gratitude, and keeping up with my day-to-day habits had finally created a tipping point: everything that I had been pouring into the big bucket in my soul had filled it up and was finally spilling over into my heart and life, saturating every fiber of my new self. It felt like my self-love was Teflon that now made me impervious to emotional or spiritual attacks. I was done with my old life and nothing was going to drag me back into it.

After a year, I had finally created an environment of psychological safety, not only for me but for my children. I began thriving at work and started being given more responsibility and direct reports. I began implementing everything I had learned to build a cohesive team. My team has flourished under my belief that we need an environment that is tolerant of failure for us to learn, grow, and succeed. In the areas where my team members fall short, I coach them rather than correct them, and by allowing my team to do their job without micromanaging them, we have raised the level of expectations for the work we're able to produce. There is no room for perfection or walking on eggshells on my team. I ask them what they need and they tell me. There is no fear of failure because we are all working together toward the same goals, and failure is part of the learning process.

In the end, the revelation that has helped me push forward the most is that I cannot hold failure and my future at the same time. If I continue to hold my failures, my hands will always be full of my past rather than reaching forward to grasp my future. Failure is a lesson that we will meet over and over again on life's journey, and it's how we handle those failures that determine how far we will go in life. Are we going to let those failures hold us back? Or do we extract the lesson from them and become determined to do better next time? Do we choose to get up again or do we stay down? Failure was never meant to be final, it's simply a lesson that we choose to draw from along the way, but we must choose. I hope you choose wisely.

ABOUT THE AUTHOR

Rachel is a single working mom and obtained her Masters in Communications and Leadership from Purdue University. Rachel is an experienced writer and speaker, bringing her story of failure and success to audiences everywhere. In a world where perfectionism reigns supreme and social media has created the perfect façade, failures are rarely made public or celebrated.

She's learned that without failure, there isn't growth, and that we need to create safe environments to foster failure where people can fail and try in order to innovate. Her insight helps break down the barriers between our hesitancy to fail vs. our necessity to fail in order to grow and centers around how to build teams that foster creativity and innovation that create an environment where people thrive and love to come to work. You can find her on Instagram: @MsRachelFesko or LinkedIn.

To learn more about
Deserts to Mountaintops,
visit
www.desertstomountaintops.com

Made in the USA
Coppell, TX
26 January 2023

11735684R00249